CLIMATE CHANGE AND

A new agenda for develop

Chris Snyder

Replied to Publisher
Feb 16

Also by Tony Fitzpatrick

Freedom and security
Welfare theory (first edition)
Environmental issues and social welfare (co-editor)
Environment and welfare (co-editor)
After the new social democracy
New theories of welfare
International encyclopaedia of social policy (principal editor)
Applied ethics and social problems
Voyage to Utopias
Understanding the environment and social policy (editor)
Welfare theory (second edition)
International handbook on social policy and the environment (editor)

CLIMATE CHANGE AND POVERTY
A new agenda for developed nations

Tony Fitzpatrick

First published in Great Britain in 2014 by

Policy Press
University of Bristol
6th Floor
Howard House
Queen's Avenue
Clifton
Bristol BS8 1SD
UK
Tel +44 (0)117 331 5020
Fax +44 (0)117 331 5367
e-mail tpp-info@bristol.ac.uk
www.policypress.co.uk

North American office:
Policy Press
c/o The University of Chicago Press
1427 East 60th Street
Chicago, IL 60637, USA
t: +1 773 702 7700
f: +1 773-702-9756
e:sales@press.uchicago.edu
www.press.uchicago.edu

© Policy Press 2014

British Library Cataloguing in Publication Data
A catalogue record for this book is available from the British Library.

Library of Congress Cataloging-in-Publication Data
A catalog record for this book has been requested.

ISBN 978 1 44730 087 8 hardcover
ISBN 978 1 44730 086 1 paperback

Cover design by Andrew Corbett
Front cover: image kindly supplied by www.istock.com
Printed and bound in Great Britain by CPI Group (UK) Ltd, Croydon, CR0 4YY
Policy Press uses environmentally responsible print partners

Poor naked wretches, wheresoe'er you are,
That bide the pelting of this pitiless storm,
How shall your houseless heads and unfed sides,
Your looped and windowed raggedness, defend you
From seasons such as these?

William Shakespeare, King Lear, 1606

I was grieved to see a generous, virtuous race of men, who should be considered as the strength and the ornament of their country, torn from their little habitations, and driven out to meet poverty and hardship among strangers. No longer to earn and enjoy the fruits of their labour, they were now going to toil as hirelings under some rigid Master, to flatter the opulent for a precarious meal, and to leave their children the inheritance of want and slavery.... All the connexions of kindred were now irreparably broken; their neat gardens and well cultivated fields were left to desolation.

Oliver Goldsmith, 'The Revolution in Low Life', 1762

His progress in the improvement and exercise of his mental and corporeal faculties has been irregular and various.... Yet the experience of four thousand years should enlarge our hopes, and diminish our apprehensions: we cannot determine to what height the human species may aspire in their advances towards perfection; but it may safely be presumed, that no people, unless the face of nature is changed, will relapse into their original barbarism.

Edward Gibbon, The History of the Decline and
Fall of the Roman Empire, 1776–88

Contents

List of figures and tables

Figures

Tables

Abbreviations

CO_2	carbon dioxide
ECO	Energy Companies Obligation
EPC	energy performance certificate
EPH	ecological public health
GDP	gross domestic product
GHGs	greenhouse gases
LVT	land value taxation
PCAs	personal carbon allowances
SoP	Statement of Principles

Acknowledgements

I am grateful to those who saw this book while it was getting dressed and were diplomatic enough not to giggle. Although they disagreed with some of my arguments, each was invaluable in assisting me to improve them. I am therefore grateful to Hartley Dean, Ian Gough and Carolyn (Caz) Snell. The referees were also helpful in pointing out how and why an earlier draft needed nipping and tucking. I think William Morris once observed that Thomas Carlyle lacked nothing – except someone who would sit behind him while he was writing and slap him across the back of the head every 15 minutes. My gratitude, as always, goes to Policy Press too.

Introduction

The armed men reach the top of the hill and look down. Beyond a heath lies the river, grey and putrid, and the city it flows through. This is the end of their journey. Here, they would receive justice, or the powers-that-be would cease to be. What had begun as resistance against the latest tax had escalated into an insurrection that threatened to blow the entire social and economic system apart. Many lives had been lost already. The armed men descend to the heath to make camp. The reckoning will begin tomorrow.

On another hill, 24 miles away, another group traces out the waste ground before them. They are armed with spades and hoes. This land is unclaimed and they wish to demonstrate what a community of plain labourers can achieve in a common effort of common ownership. The times are turbulent. Revolutions are erupting everywhere. Yet they know that their simple act of farming will be seen, and responded to, as perhaps the most revolutionary and threatening of all.

Twenty-seven miles from the second group, but just eight from the first, figures armed with torches march through the night, their faces lit by the flames they have already ignited. They must move quickly if they are to disappear again into the darkness before being discovered. Years of frustration have brought them to this. If they cannot own the land on which they are expected to work, perhaps no one should. With nods to one another, torches aloft, they move towards a barn.

These groups never met. They are, in fact, separated across time. The first event happened at Blackheath in 1381. The Peasants' Revolt would be brutally crushed by the boy-King in whom they still had faith and to whom they had come to appeal: Richard II (Dunn, 2002). The second describes the actions of Britain's revolution within a revolution within a revolution. The Diggers occupied St George's Hill in 1649. They would be evicted several months later (Hill, 1991, pp 112-19). The third event happened near Orpington in 1830. The Swing Riots, infamous for the destruction of machinery, started with arson. Those flames would cast the 1830s into a shadow that has never entirely faded, inspiring the architects of the 1834 Poor Law to define as wage-labourers all those who had formally owned the land they worked (Hobsbawm and Rudé, 1969).

They are separated by time but united by much else. Other examples could also have been chosen from the history of Britain's struggles around the first theme of this book: poverty. The 18th century, for instance, was often shattered with food riots that have now been all but forgotten (Stevenson, 1974; 1979, Chapter 5). Many similar events could be cited, going all the way back to the beginnings of recorded history. Livy (1960) observes how disputes over food and land drove the secession of the plebs in 494 BCE. The political system that resulted characterised the Roman Republic for the next 450 years.

The second theme of this book, climate change, also has a longer social history than you might at first appreciate. The 'little ice age' that lasted for half a millennium after 1300 created famines and altered European agriculture (Fagan,

2000). And we, in turn, have transformed the ecosystem. Enclosures[1] created massive hunger which, driving waves of 19th-century emigration, facilitated the land clearances that had a significant effect on carbon dioxide (CO_2) levels in the atmosphere (Fagan, 2000, pp 145-7). And those enclosures were an act both of historical theft (Gonner, 1966) and historical amnesia. You may be a thief, but if you hang on to your booty for long enough, your descendants may be revered as aristocrats, held to deserve their wealth by virtue of God, or blood, or some other inherent quality that everyone else thinks they lack.

Despite the subtitle of this book, therefore, the link between poverty and climate change constitutes a very *old* agenda. And throughout these histories two great forces have warred against one another, sometimes in a battle of ideas, sometimes in direct social confrontation.

Livy (1960, p 147) gave voice to one force in his history of early Rome. Menenius Agrippa addresses the discontented plebs in his fable of The Belly: you complain that we consume resources we do not produce. Yet anyone can farm or hunt. What *we* do cannot be taught. We deserve more because you need us more than we need you. Sixteen centuries later, Shakespeare rendered this speech into poetry.[2] But then Shakespeare did something incredible, something you will not find in Livy's account, something that few, if any, writers had done before him. He gave the poor a political voice:

> ... the leanness that inflicts us, the object of our misery, is as an inventory to particularise their abundance; our sufferance is a gain to them.[3]

Our hunger is not just about empty stomachs. The Patricians keep us destitute because the lower we are, the higher they rise. And the more we consent to this, the more it suits them. Our sufferance is a gain to them.

Centuries before it was given a name, Shakespeare captured and communicated an idea at the heart of modern controversies about the nature of society and political struggles over its future: relative poverty.

Climate change and poverty: an ecosocial agenda

It feels mundane to descend from such lofty heights to the details of today's political and academic debates, but descend we must.

Since poverty has been a feature of societies since societies began, isn't it hyperbole to describe any discussion about poverty as a *new* agenda? What, if anything, does climate change add to the discussion?

Unless we adopt the apocalyptic rhetoric of alarmists and survivalists, climate change is probably more like a slope than the edge of cliff along which we are recklessly dancing. But even if we do face a slope, the gradient is fairly steep, and gets steeper the farther you fall. You do not have to be one of those environmentalists who is always predicting catastrophe 20 years in the future to notice the extent to which the fall has already begun. You are already tumbling down the hill with the summit behind you. And although climate change is truly a global problem, unless we imagine waves of dispossessed ex-millionaires begging for admittance to places such as Namibia or Zambia, we all know who will suffer first and foremost. More than this, unless the fight to mitigate and adapt to climate change is a global effort – uniting rich and poor in a new ecological and social settlement – then it may be futile. A drowning man might take some comfort from the thought that the idiots who sank the ship will soon drown too.

Climate change and poverty are now irrevocably connected, and in ways never encountered before. How, why, to what extent and with what prescriptions for the future is the subject of the book you have before you. But if this is the case, then why not study Namibia, Zambia or dozens of other places experiencing the worst poverty? Why focus on developed nations? Isn't that just more western self-obsession?

Well, first, let's not swallow the bait that says that whatever else developed nations contain, they do not contain poverty. Your wellbeing is in large part related to those with whom you regularly share the social spaces of work, shopping, leisure and all the other activities that constitute everyday life. If your child goes to bed hungry, what comfort is it to learn that millions of children in Africa are even more malnourished? Second, the social development literature is well aware of the implications of climate change (Raworth, 2012). Although aspirations and good intentions sometimes act as a balm for the lack of real, sustained action, this agenda has become firmly established. Finally, unless we mobilise all sectors of the national community, we may fail to tackle climate change adequately. The carbon emissions of the richest 10 per cent of households are three times higher than the poorest 10 per cent (Preston et al, 2013, pp 7-8).[4] Expecting those who typically create the fewest carbon emissions to suffer the greatest consequences is therefore unlikely to produce that mobilisation, here, as much as in Namibia. And if countries like the UK do not act effectively, developing countries will continue to suffer the greatest consequences of all. Helping the world's poorest and engaging with the poverty to be found a few streets away are elements of the same common effort.

Therefore, there *is* a new agenda to be debated, and since developed nations broke the planet, they have the greatest responsibility for gluing the bits back together. This responsibility requires us to recognise the impacts that climate change is having on our poorer neighbours, and to conjoin ecological and social imperatives in a new kind of 'ecosocial' politics.[5]

This book seeks an ecosocial understanding of poverty in developed nations, with particular reference to the UK. It offers a new conceptualisation of the links between climate change and poverty, the extent to which the former exacerbates the latter and the latter has an impact on the former. It presents a theoretical model of causes, symptoms and possible solutions.

For several years now, valuable work has been undertaken across various disciplines. As Lucas (2004, p 112) puts it:

> Problems of environmental injustice afflict many of our most deprived communities and socially excluded groups.... In some cases not only are deprived and excluded communities disproportionately exposed to an environmental risk, they are also disproportionately vulnerable to its effects.

Yet all too often, research projects are separated by terminology, methodology, disciplinary traditions, theoretical grounding and over-specialisation. This book reads across a diversity of literatures, makes them speak to one another and offers a platform for future work. It summarises, analyses and synthesises existing research, data, legislative and policy developments, and other relevant evidence. The key questions it considers are:

- How should we conceptualise and theorise the relationship between climate change and poverty?
- What does an ecosocial understanding of poverty take the causes, symptoms and possible solutions to poverty to be?

Social and natural interdependencies

A new agenda does not necessarily mean we have to reinvent the wheel, however. Increasing attention has been paid to the need to reconcile social and environmental policies since the 1990s (Seymour, 2000, pp 97-110). For instance, the Joseph Rowntree Foundation has run a 'Reconciling Environmental and Social Concerns' programme. (So far as my home discipline – social policy – is concerned, for a panoramic overview see my *Understanding the environment and social policy*, published in 2011.) Gough and Meadowcroft (2011, p 493) summarise the challenge effectively, saying that climate change 'will test the ability of national welfare states to internationalise and recognise collective responsibility for victims elsewhere in the world.' None of this work suggests that we have to radically rewrite existing understandings of poverty, deprivation and social exclusion.

As such, this book adopts a social democratic approach, broadly defined. This means interpreting poverty as caused and shaped largely by the economic system and the property regime within which it is found. For social democrats the problem is capitalism (and particularly an economic liberal version of capitalism) in which profit, competition, inequality and self-interest are allowed to colonise our social relations, economic systems, political processes and moral consciences.[6] Yet social democrats do not recommend a revolutionary upheaval in social and economic relations. We do not have to reinvent the wheel; we just have to repair the damn thing and make it run in a new direction.

Something quite essential has been lacking from social democracy: a comprehensive appreciation of social-natural interdependency. Let me explain what this means.

Environmentalism is concerned with the natural environment, or *the interconnecting web of organisms that exist in a symbiotic relationship of birth, reproduction, death, decay and renewal.* You may not think of yourself as dependent on the tree in your garden or the earthworm burrowing in its soil, but you are. And it is almost certain that by affecting migration rates and natural habitats, humans have accelerated species extinction above its natural rate.

The natural environment would be a source of value and an object of responsibility even in the absence of climate change but, of course, there is no such thing as a non-changing climate.[7] Organisms and climate are interwoven.[8] Three billion years ago (give or take), it was rudimentary organisms that spat oxygen into the atmosphere. And during that time the Earth's climate has experienced many oscillations of warming and cooling. 'Climate variability' is due to processes that would occur anyway in the absence of humans. When we refer to contemporary climate change we are referring more to *the rapid global warming created by human activities pouring greenhouse gases (GHGs), particularly carbon dioxide (CO_2), into the atmosphere and oceans.* In one sense, the term 'climate change' feels like a neutered version of 'global warming'. However, the former term more adequately captures the likelihood that global warming will be experienced in diverse ways across the planet. This book therefore refers largely to climate change.

But the 'interconnecting web' with which environmentalists are concerned has to encompass the ecological *and* the social. Since, obviously, human organisms affect and are affected by the climate, then the means by which humans organise themselves – their civilisation – is woven into that web of interconnections. Most environmentalists are social environmentalists, therefore, understanding that the strands of life are so enmeshed that common distinctions – social/natural, human/ non-human – are just elements along a latticework of dense intersections.

Although elements of it have influenced – and have no doubt been influenced by – mainstream politics, the latter continues to deny the scale of the ecological challenges we face, and to resist the social environmentalist critique. Consider three aspects of that critique.

First, since they are interconnected, the social and the natural are highly inter*dependent* (Victor, 2008, pp 34-7). Social relations mediate our place within, and conceptions of, nature. And if humans were to disappear from the planet tomorrow, the ecosystem would continue to reverberate from the effects of our presence for many centuries. Furthermore, nature is the source and the *sine qua non* of all socioeconomic and cultural resources. This point is obvious to many, for example:

> … society and nature are dialectically related, so that each is a manifestation of the other. Nature is socially produced, and what humans do is natural. (Pepper, 2010, p 34)

Yet all too often nature has been an invisible, taken-for-granted element of social interaction.

Over the centuries, many important thinkers have appreciated that the natural and social are entangled, but it was not until the 1960s that such ideas were disseminated widely (Simms et al, 2006, pp 5-6). The recent, welcome recognition that 'GDP [gross domestic product] growth does not ensure wellbeing' owes much to the environmental movement. Nonetheless, the dependency of our economic systems on GDP growth continues apace, with a consequent, continuing devaluation of natural resources. In contemporary capitalism, the values of acquisition, consumption and competition predominate over those of preservation, equilibrium and renewal. For social environmentalists, by contrast, nature is more than just input on a balance sheet, more than the countryside, 'natural capital' or that fen near the motorway with a rare species of frog. We are the cosmos looking back at itself, nature made self-conscious. Yet in becoming self-conscious, humans strove to liberate themselves from the very ground beneath their feet. We are communal beings who have managed to blind ourselves to the great diversity of communities, across space and time, to which we belong.

Second, proper awareness of this interdependence requires an ontological, moral and sociocultural ethos of limitations, finiteness and mortality that is alien to most mainstream politics. There are only so many resources that nature can supply, and only so much pollution it can absorb. Of course, humans are ingenious at extracting more from less (productivity), and most greens do not advocate that we switch civilisation off before retreating to the wilderness. But given the incredible power and capacities we possess, human activities ought to be driven by a renewed sense of responsibility, one that makes sustainability and humility central. Humans have all too often sought to transcend and deny their mortality by appropriating, subordinating and destroying. An ecological sense of how vulnerable, precious and painfully short life is requires an alternative ethos of the 'three r's': recycling, repairing and renewing; in other words, conservation, stewardship, appreciation and attention to the interests of those (including non-humans) with whom we are interdependent.

Third, this sense of responsibility is best manifested through an associative view of the self where the accent is on *being and relating* rather than merely *having and controlling*. In distinction to the *homo economicus* of contemporary capitalism – where agency is defined in terms of market choice, personal aspiration, hierarchies of status, competitive consumerism and short-term self-interest[9] – the associative self finds its purpose and identity in relational projects with others. To some extent, it resembles the self that inhabits republican and deliberative politics. Its lineage also derives from the socialist emphasis on cooperation and mutualism.

The associative self never occupies a fixed social position *precisely because it is associative*; its identity is reshaped through the ever-changing relations to which it belongs. Its field of action is always dynamic and evolving because social relations are themselves fluid and plastic. This throws light on the weaknesses and strengths of environmental politics. Despite the fact that all humans have an interest in preserving nature, environmentalism has no single constituency, no unifying agent of social change interested in driving forward green reforms (no one occupying the role accorded to the working class by socialists).

But because it does not rely on some 'essentialist' form of collective identity, environmentalism must always reconstruct itself by articulating the universal interests of humanity through the interests of particular communities, including non-human species. The task facing 'selves in association' is therefore intimately political. The negotiation of the universal and the particular is never finished. Take the famous injunction to 'think global, act local'. As we think and act, the composition of the global and local are constantly altered, requiring new thinking, new activities and new interventions. This book therefore emphasises the always-evolving, never-finalised aspects of the ecosocial agenda.

In short, what mainstream politics and contemporary capitalism arguably lack is an adequate appreciation of social-natural interdependencies and the considerable economic, moral, social and political implications of this. Given the extent to which it has dominated many countries over the last four decades, we can lay the blame for much of this at the feet of economic liberalism. However, social democrats have also helped to bring us to where we are – and not only those who embraced the 'new social democracy' of Clinton, Blair/Brown and Obama. The environmental record of social democracies is generally better than that of economic liberal nations but they, too, have failed to drive the real changes that are urgently needed (Bell, 2014; Schaffrin, 2014). The traditional view that social justice requires GDP growth still dominates social democratic thinking, for instance (Fitzpatrick, 2003). This is one reason why I refer to the 'ecosocial' rather than to 'social democracy' *per se*. This book recommends such an urgency, and incorporates it into a reconceptualisation of poverty in an era of rapid and dramatic climate change.

Mapping injustice

An ecosocial understanding of poverty occupies a map that we do not have time to explore in full here. Look at Figure I.1. The top right region can be endlessly populated with concepts and debates. For example:

> Individuals, families and groups in the population can be said to be in poverty when they lack the resources to obtain the types of diet, participate in the activities and have the living conditions and amenities which are customary ... in the societies to which they belong. Their resources are so seriously below those commanded by the average individual or family that they are, in effect, excluded from ordinary living patterns, customs and activities. (Townsend, 1979, p 31; see also p 413)

Indeed, inspired in part by Townsend, this book will often talk of deprivations in relation to not just social but also social-natural resources.

Figure I.1: An ecosocial map

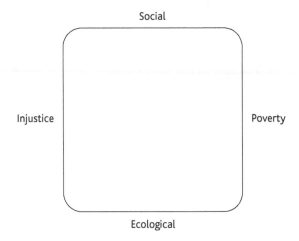

Similarly, we could easily fill the top and bottom left regions. Note that injustice is not the same as inequality. Some inequalities may be perfectly just while some equalities may be unjust. What matters is (1) the nature of the inequality, for example, whether it is characterised by exploitation, oppression or the arbitrary use of power; (2) its source, for example, whether it derives from circumstances over which people have little or no control, such that the distribution of advantages and disadvantages is undeserved; and (3) its consequences, for example, whether the less well-off are significantly disadvantaged in terms of jobs, income, housing and all other elements that people need if their lives are to go well.

As such, Miller (2005, p 5) defined social justice in terms of equal citizenship (civil, political and social rights), a social minimum (to resources that meet essential needs), equal opportunities (so gender, class and ethnicity are irrelevant to a person's life chances) and fair distribution (inequalities should derive only from choice and desert). And Walker (2012, p 1; see also Gardiner, 2011; Bulkeley and Fuller, 2012) is one of many exploring the links between nature and justice in attempting to elaborate 'environmental justice' or what might be called 'ecologically sustainable social justice':[10]

> ... for some people and some social groups the environment is an intrinsic part of living a good life of prosperity, health and well-being, while for others the environment is a source of threat and risk, and access to resources such as energy, water and greenspace is limited or curtailed. (Walker, 2012, p 1)

Populating the bottom right region, however, is much more difficult (Boardman, with Bullock and McLaren, 1999). Dominelli (2012, p 29) has said that,

> Poverty is usually accompanied by the lack of environmental rights, with poor people living in the most degraded environments, in the poorest housing and being disproportionately affected by industrial pollution and natural disasters.

Yet most of the work that has been done in this respect is understandably focused on the developing world. So far as developed countries are concerned, discussions of poverty tend to borrow from the lower left region (see, for example, Seymour, 2000, pp 12-18). Although I make use of Walker's (2012) recent book, it has little to say about poverty *per se*, as a distinct form of injustice.

Defining poverty

The premise of this book is that theories and models occupying the lower right region of Figure I.1 are urgently needed. Fortunately, other regions have sometimes equipped us with the tools we require. Thus Townsend (1979, Chapter 14) incorporates 'environmental deprivation' into his research in terms of outdoor space and facilities, gardens, transport, air quality and play areas for children. In short, this book is rooted in the lower right region of Figure I.1, but roams around wherever necessary.

Injustice and poverty are clearly related, then. By borrowing from the brief overview of injustice and inequality just presented, we could define poverty as (1) an oppressive form of inequality which (2) derives largely from circumstances over which people have little or no control and which (3) significantly disadvantages the least well-off, excluding them from full participation in the activities that characterise their society, so preventing their lives from going as well as they might.[11] Poverty is therefore a form of injustice which is interrelated with, and has an impact on, other forms of injustice. The problem is in deciding where and how to expand on this basic definition.

It has been common to think of justice in materialist terms, as concerning the fair distribution of property, resources and capital. This is tantamount to claiming that 'justice is the fair distribution of material goods through economic systems'. However, this material-distributive approach is limited for two reasons. First, material goods always carry symbolic meaning of some kind. The meaning of wealth and accumulation for early Protestants helped to distinguish them from Catholic traditions and practices (Weber, 1990). Second, economic relationships are saturated with cultural contexts and understandings. A gift in a 'gift economy' has a social significance and value different to a gift in other contexts (Mauss, 2002). In this sense, 'justice is that which members of the same cultural and communal context render towards one another qua membership'. Justice is about procedures (opportunities, openness, mutually respectful representations) as well as specific outcomes.

This friction between material-distributive and cultural-procedural approaches continues.[12] For Nancy Fraser (see Fraser and Honneth, 2003; Fraser, 2008; Olson,

2008), economistic categories and concepts are fundamental for any understanding of cultural injustices. But for Axel Honneth (2007), justice consists primarily of respect for people and recognition of the worth of cultural identities, requiring us to open political institutions to the agents and diverse identities through which communal solidarities are sustained.

Although some prefer one paradigm to the other, few propose that either is entirely sufficient on its own. Material distributions may fail to effect justice unless we also value those to whom the relevant goods are distributed, acknowledging their right to influence the procedures through which distributions are made. Conversely, democratic participation and respectful representations may nevertheless remain thin and insubstantial without the equitable distribution of economic resources.

This distinction surfaces in poverty debates (Bulkeley and Fuller, 2012; Lister, 2013; cf Townsend, 1979, p 249). Who would deny that poverty implies a lack of income, wages, property, jobs, savings and so forth? Yet the poor are also subjected to forms of cultural devaluation, as having nothing to say worth listening to. The vocabulary continually applied to impoverished individuals – from *lumpenproletariat* to scrounger to skiver – is one that dismisses their humanity, misrepresents their social position in terms of some ingrained moral defect and so excludes them from political processes and public debate. Poverty therefore implies both material-distributive *and* cultural-procedural forms of injustice.

This being the case, why pick sides at all? Yet we must tread carefully here. A materialist approach might only lead to a 'mechanical' organisation of resources that does not attend to agents and their identities, that is, *why* people do what they do. But aspects of the culturalist framework are equally unpalatable.

For instance, Lister (2008, pp 111-14) advocates acknowledging the psychological impact of poverty – the stress it produces for those who know how much they are devalued – *without* subscribing to a 'psychologised theory' in which low self-esteem is treated as innate. Psychological effects are created by the poor being 'othered' by the non-poor, she observes. Lister (2004, pp 166-74) therefore wishes the voices of the poor to be incorporated into policy procedures.

Yet this distinction itself presupposes acceptance of the idea of poverty as a lack of material-economic resources. What if you don't accept this? If you reject relative, structural explanations of poverty, and if you allow that those with low self-esteem act accordingly (that is, they lose hope and motivation, succumbing to addictive and self-destructive habits), then presumably we *are* entitled to devise anti-poverty policies that emphasise counselling, behavioural modification and moral-psychological reconditioning. For some, the weight accorded to communal and psychological factors by a culturalist paradigm is a godsend that *does* allow us to 'blame the victim'. To believe that poverty is about malfunctioning families and dangerous neighbourhoods you don't have to believe that low self-esteem is *innate*; merely that it is encultured and socialised in communities that exclude themselves from normal society. Those with an alternative interpretation of agency to Lister's occupy a space in which poverty is attributed to laziness, welfare dependency and deficiency in cultural and communal values. In short, a culturalist emphasis *may* help us to mobilise impoverished individuals, amplifying their voices in the media and political process, but only if the fair distribution of economic resources is already the aim. Without such an aim, an emphasis on cultural values and psychological characteristics risks surrendering ground to those who pathologise poverty.

We should therefore balance the material-distributive and the cultural-procedural, but not collapse them together (see Figure I.2).

Figure I.2: Material and distributive perspectives

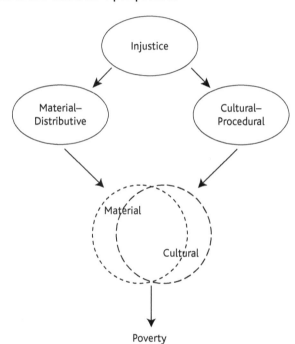

The concept of poverty can make room for fair procedures, participative deliberation and voice, recognition and respect (Walker, 2012, pp 42–51), so long as these are grounded firmly in an emphasis on structural inequalities, inherited dis/advantages, market failures and political-economic strategies. Resources are thus both material (property, income, wealth) and also cultural (the capacity to be heard). Our discussions in the chapters to follow reflect this understanding.

On this basis:

> Poverty is a form of injustice, denoting a relative lack of those resources needed to ensure a minimal standard of living, equal opportunities, mutual social respect and participative inclusion in a society's way of life, and without which it is difficult to flourish, to fulfil one's potential and to achieve or sustain a decent level of wellbeing. Poverty is characterised

> by socioeconomic conditions that empower those who monopolise key resources at the expense of those who do not, such that poor individuals are disrespected by, for instance, being held responsible for social circumstances they did not create and over which they have limited control.

The task of the chapters ahead is to elaborate and build on this definition.

Three points

Several issues are worth highlighting before proceeding.

First, the term 'poverty' sometimes refers to those who experience deprivation. For the sake of convenience, and at the risk of simplification, this book makes reference to 'poor households' and 'poor individuals' as shorthand terms until debates and data require us to say more. But 'poverty' sometimes also denotes wider social conditions and contexts (Tawney, 1964, p 102). The view that such conditions damage not only the poor but the non-poor too – such as the 'spirit level' hypothesis that the wealthy would also benefit from reductions in poverty levels – has re-entered public debates (Wilkinson and Pickett, 2009; Lansley, 2012; Stiglitz, 2012). Poverty impoverishes everyone, to some extent.

Second, this book is not offering a comprehensive theory of poverty. Nor am I trying to operationalise the concept of ecosocial poverty, that is, to offer something that can be immediately translated into the methods of social researchers, although I hope that such an operationalisation will follow in the future.

Third, because this account lacks comprehensiveness, it does not offer an extended discussion of class and capitalism.

We could decide to detach 'poverty' from 'class'. Poverty is associated with a range of identities and vulnerabilities (age, gender, disability, ethnicity and so on), some of which are more class-specific then others. But even in terms of strict economic categories, 'there is no fixed and unchanging group who constitute "the poor"' (Jenkins, 2011, p 237). In Europe and North America there is a substantial turnover in the low-income population, with many experiencing poverty no more than once, and many others moving frequently in and out of the low-income zone from one year to the next. That said, unless we pretend that white-collar professionals are as likely to experience debilitating periods of low income as cleaners and classroom assistants, then it would be ridiculous to detach poverty from class altogether.

Alternatively, then, we might imagine that 'poverty' and 'class' correspond neatly, such that debates about the one give us immediate, clear and unproblematic access to the other. But this only becomes true if your conceptualisations are sufficiently narrow. If poverty is a cultural injustice, then we ought to avoid such narrowness because 'the cultural' is always complex, subjective and messy, requiring 'thick' description of particular contexts.

Therefore, poverty and class each denote a series of overlapping relations, into and out of which a host of economic and cultural dimensions travel. Vulnerable groups, including but not limited to low-income groups in the working class, are those with a higher risk of experiencing poverty more frequently, for longer periods, with greater severity and with more substantial consequences for their long-term prospects across the life course. But that is probably as much as we can say without looking at specific instances.

One implication is that the fight against climate change and the abolition of capitalism are not one and the same (cf Clement, 2010; Foster et al, 2010). No doubt we need to transform our economic structures, and this book is particularly scathing about the economic liberalism that has dominated mainstream western politics for the last four decades. However, I don't pretend to know exactly where this will or should take us. Either a green society has to abolish capitalism in its entirety, or it has to incorporate multiple forms of ownership and diverse economic instruments that can make the 'capitalism versus ...' debate (fill in the blank yourself) a distracting exercise. If green societies must be genuinely associative, deliberative and dynamic (as proposed above), then closing the conversation at the outset against those who defend the greening of capitalism seems like a contradiction. I hope that environmentally sustainable societies will be open, creative and diverse, and I suspect that they need contain more social equality and more *genuine* social ownership than most countries have so far achieved. But, beyond that, since all past attempts to make humanity sing with one voice have been disastrous, I feel uncomfortable with those who insist that they, at last, have found the correct song.

A further note about terminology

Two terms or phrases occur throughout this book: 'ecosocial poverty' and 'an ecosocial understanding of poverty'. They do not quite mean the same thing (see Figure I.3). 'Ecosocial poverty' describes the specific characteristics that pertain within the smaller circle, that is, deprivation and exclusion in relation to what I call 'socionatural resources'. An 'ecosocial understanding of poverty' is the attempt to understand the smaller circle *and* how it relates to the bigger one or, in other words, how deprivation of and exclusion from socionatural resources intersects with traditional notions of poverty as conceptualised and measured in terms of jobs and labour market opportunities, income, benefits and wages, class, education, and so forth. (Bearing in mind what has just been said, that no attempt at comprehensiveness is being made here.) In short, there is the thing that people experience (ecosocial poverty) and the ways in which researchers, activists and others must try to understand the thing.

We might add that if an ecosocial approach is accurate, we can expect the smaller circle to grow larger in the years and decades to come, so that the social policy and ecosocial policy agendas coincide more and more. Many social deprivations are increasingly becoming socionatural deprivations. For instance, food poverty has no doubt always existed, but contemporary food poverty isn't simply about inadequate nourishment or income but also about the pressures on, and the

Figure I.3: Understanding the ecosocial

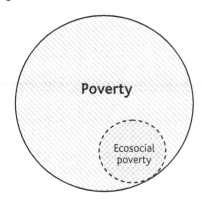

pressures created by, food chains in a world of rapidly increasing population, where developed countries consume a disproportionate amount of the planet's resources.

Synopsis

In short, we need synergies between social policy and environmental policy. A poverty-less society is desirable yet will not endure for long unless global warming is fought. Reducing poverty is an important element of that fight, but it is not a sufficient condition for addressing climate change since some anti-poverty policies are more sustainable than others. Similarly, a green society still characterised by poverty is feasible but surely less sustainable than one that has eradicated poverty, or is at least attempting to do so. As indicated earlier, since climate change is everyone's business, the benefits and burdens of tackling it must be shared fairly and proportionately. Addressing climate change will benefit the poor, but not as much as if we accommodate their particular needs, interests and voices within the political and policy process.

This book tries to facilitate those synergies. It is not an introduction to the climate science (see Eggleton, 2013), or to environmentalism *per se*, and it is not a textbook. So a certain familiarity with both climate science and social science is assumed. The book therefore ranges quite widely across territories that specialists spend decades exploring and defending against those – like myself – who fly through at whistle-stop speeds. The 21st century needs its specialists. Yet because the problems we confront transcend boundaries –intellectual and geographical – we also have to cross them if we are to address those problems effectively. In short, the 21st century needs greater interdisciplinarity, not less. The following topics were chosen accordingly. Chapters One to Four constitute the more theoretical and conceptual parts of the discussion, while Chapters Six to Ten are more empirical, offering summaries, analyses and synthesises of existing research and data.

Chapter One critiques the 'capabilities approach' since this has become such a key point of reference in debates about poverty and (for some) humanity's place within and obligations towards the natural world. Although not wanting to reject the capabilities approach, I do argue that it has some limitations, especially regarding the basis for its claims and its tendency to reify wealth and capital. Chapter Two therefore pursues a resources-based approach, exploring concepts such as natural assets and intrinsic value. It explores the links between socioeconomic and natural resources, introducing key principles enabling us to understand the characteristics of socionatural resources. Since all resources exist across space and through time, Chapter Three examines the former, proposing that within contemporary capitalism social spaces are highly fragmented and antagonistic. An ecosocial politics enjoins more solidaristic spaces, for which new understandings and distributions of socionatural resources are required. Chapter Four then performs a similar exercise regarding time, making the case that a re-socialisation of time is needed to overcome the dislocations and short-termism to which market-dominated societies are prone.

Chapter Five offers a summary of Chapters One to Four, and extracts the key principles and categories that Chapters Six to Ten then apply to discussions of poverty in the context of the key socionatural resources: energy, food, land, air and water. In each case we investigate the causes, symptoms and possible solutions to 'ecosocial poverty'.

Chapter Six asks how we can protect the incomes of the poorest and ensure that all people can access sufficient household energy, while achieving reductions in carbon emissions. It concentrates on debates in and around the subject of fuel poverty. Chapter Seven explores food poverty, the dominance of corporations and supermarkets within the food chain and the ecological destructiveness of modern habits and practices. It critiques what some key authors term the 'ecological public health' approach. Land is such a vast subject that it is split into several sub-themes. Chapter Eight reviews debates concerning housing and urban densities, looking at how the recent decline in social housing and the rise of urban sprawl – with all of its attendant ecological impacts – have been driven by under-regulated housing markets. It seeks an understanding of such developments in terms of rent-seeking, positional competition and positional externalities. Chapter Nine applies that framework to three more land-related subjects: transport, flooding and waste facilities. For instance, against a background of welfare state retrenchment, it understands the rise in transport poverty as both cause and consequence of housing markets and low urban densities. Chapter Ten concentrates on air pollutants in relation to health, carbon emissions and deprivation, before discussing the nature and relevance of water poverty.

My thesis throughout these later chapters is simple: the ecologically excessive, careless and destructive use of key socionatural resources is closely connected to the social deprivations that characterise that usage for millions of those on low incomes. The overuse and misuse of socionatural resources are intimately linked. In essence, this is what constitutes an ecosocial understanding of poverty.

Notes

[1] This is the transformation of what had been common land into private estates, initially made through communal agreement (Hoskins, 2013, pp 141-2). Goldsmith gives an account of its consequences for rural households in an epigraph to this book (p v).

[2] *Coriolanus*, Act 1, Scene 1, 95-154.

[3] *Coriolanus*, Act 1, Scene 1, 18-21.

[4] Please note that I am aware that 'carbon' and 'carbon dioxide' (CO_2) are not the same. However, I use 'carbon emissions' as shorthand for the latter and refer to greenhouse gases (GHGs) when referring to methane, water vapour and CO_2.

[5] 'Ecosocial politics' is a social environmentalism that is allied to (but not quite the same thing as) a social democratic environmentalism (see below).

[6] I refer throughout to 'economic liberalism' rather than 'neoliberalism'. There are many forms of liberalism: some are old, some new, some good, some bad. The term 'neoliberalism' risks collapsing them all together. Both terms, however, denote a paradoxical combination of free markets and corporate dominance – paradoxical for two reasons. First, because tending to serve a corporate agenda, these 'free' markets are more free for some than for others; and second, because the capitalist state regulates whatever and whoever it needs to in order to secure that agenda.

[7] One of the reasons – apart from greed, of course (Oreskes and Conway, 2011) – why the climate change agenda is still resisted by many is because if God created the world then surely it must have reflected His perfection. To posit changes to the world is tantamount to saying that it wasn't perfect originally. And if it wasn't perfect originally, then perhaps God isn't perfect. Perhaps God doesn't exist. That reasoning may also explain much of the resistance encountered by Lyell when studying geological development, by Darwin when promoting biological evolution, and by Wegener when theorising continental drift.

[8] The climate includes the atmosphere, hydrosphere, land surface, biosphere and cryosphere.

[9] An ethos centred on the ego where we are constantly flattered into self-importance by companies hungry for our money, desires, energy, debt and time: a you-topia.

[10] Some hate this association. For Scruton (2013; see also Gray, 2007, pp 200-3), our instincts spread out from a love of home and family to encompass a country and its culture. By appealing to such motivations (the need to preserve what one loves from destruction), environmentalism and conservatism can converge. It is because it has been dominated by leftist wishful fantasies that environmentalism has failed. The counterargument is that without some appeal to abstract and universal principles, we have no yardstick against which to assess our provincial habits and no protection against the occasional descent of those habits into prejudice, small-mindedness and violence against anything perceived to be strange, new or other. 'Home' and 'country' are constructs – albeit powerful ones – and we should not hesitate to ask whether what people value is indeed worth valuing.

[11] Social exclusion is therefore incorporated within (3). It is possible to experience social exclusion without being in poverty – a wealthy pensioner may lack mobility, family and other social connections, but not the oppressive relations of (1) or the adverse circumstances of (2). It is also the case that some people on low incomes will experience less social exclusion than others. Within this book, however, we treat poverty and social exclusion as similar manifestations of injustice, such that one regularly accompanies the other.

[12] I am content with a twofold distinction. If we had more time we could disentangle the terms further, for example, the material-procedural and the cultural-distributive. Schlosberg (2007), for instance, regards 'recognition' as distinct to 'proceduralism'. For the purposes of this book, however, I am wary of slicing concepts too thinly.

RETHINKING POVERTY:
CONCEPTS AND PRINCIPLES

ONE

Capabilities

The capabilities approach is arguably the most influential, recent innovation in debates about justice and poverty. Does it offer a convincing basis for an ecosocial understanding of poverty? This chapter explores three subjects – philosophy, social policy and environmentalism – in response to that question. My view is that for all its virtues, the capabilities approach contains serious flaws. First, it is not clear that it offers a secure enough grounding for ecosocial principles; and second, it has been too dismissive of the material-distributive paradigm (with specific reference to resources such as income and wealth), with all the attendant dangers we warned against in the Introduction earlier. That said, since the capabilities approach represents a broad church of opinion, offering a variety of perspectives on and responses to the 'distributive paradigm', neither should we reject it entirely. To this end, I adapt the concept of a meta-capability that will lead us into the discussion of resources that follows, in Chapter Two.

Philosophy

Outline

The central claim of the capabilities approach is that there is no straightforward metric of justice and wellbeing (Nussbaum, 2006, 2011; Sen, 2009; Anderson, 2010, pp 87-95). Those who focus on an 'equality of welfare' or an 'equality of resources' are being insufficiently comprehensive. The basic argument is this.

We can know approximately what it means to be well and to fare well. All humans (indeed, all living creatures) require adequate levels of nourishment, shelter, health, communal interaction, and so forth. But the capabilities required to realise these basic 'functionings' are highly diverse. Capabilities must imply some notion of substantive freedoms and opportunities, but what these mean will vary from context to context. The capabilities that you need in order to achieve a decent life will not be entirely identical to those in other geographical places and historical eras.

The originators of the capabilities approach part company at this point. Sen (2009, pp 231-47; see also Levine and Rizvi, 2005) believes that the best we can do is mark out a 'space of capabilities' that equips people with the freedoms they need to live their lives as best they can. By contrast, Nussbaum (2006, pp 392-401) offers a list of capabilities that she holds to be universally applicable:

- live a life of normal length;
- possess bodily health and integrity;

- cultivate and express imagination and thought;
- form emotional attachments;
- form and pursue a conception of the good and engage in critical reflection about one's life;
- interact and be respected by others;
- relate to the natural environment and other species;
- play and enjoy;
- have some control over one's political and material circumstances.

Peoples and communities must be empowered to shape and control the social, political, cultural and economic institutions that translate these abstractions into concrete social realities. Therefore, both Sen and Nussbaum reject any attempt to be over-prescriptive and top-down.

The implications of the capabilities approach are wide-ranging and profound. For instance, recent research has shown that affluence does not necessarily translate into wellbeing (Offer, 2006). You may have a higher income this year, but you are not necessarily better off in other, non-monetary terms than you were last year. Such findings chime with the view of the capabilities approach that the characteristics of wellbeing are highly diverse (Massey, 2005). As such, income is only one of a range of relevant indicators. The value of £1,000 to a person with a disability will not be equivalent to its value for a non-disabled person, since the former will typically have to spend more of that £1,000 on basic living costs (Burchardt, 2004, pp 739-44; Terzi, 2010). We therefore need not a single metric but a much wider range of indicators that take into account the many factors – the personal and social endowments – that enable a life to go well or badly. Since the 1990s, the United Nations Development Programme (UNDP) has published an annual 'human development' report that gives figures for literacy, participation in education, gender and racial equality, life expectancy, and so forth.

Yet the implications of this go beyond the methodologies of economists and statisticians; they are also political. For example, the Left has often seen the redistribution of income and wealth as essential to improving social justice. But for the capabilities approach, income and wealth merely *enable* people to do certain things; whether people are *actually* able to do them depends on a host of other factors, as in the example of the £1,000 above. Just distributions are only one facet of *social* justice.

For those interested in understanding and alleviating poverty, the implications are therefore both methodological and political (Grusky and Kanbur, 2005). The capabilities approach agrees – and is in many respects related to – the emphasis on social exclusion that emerged in Europe in the 1980s. It is not enough to offer a snapshot of poverty since poverty is complex and dynamic. It helps to have a poverty line that everyone can understand, yet it is also wise to develop a range of poverty thresholds and indicators that try to capture the multifaceted characteristics of what poverty and exclusion really mean. The politics of reducing poverty, and the social policies needed to make this happen, are much more complex than we used to think. For instance, unlike generations of Marxists, we cannot imagine that poverty is caused merely by capitalists extracting surplus value from workers through wage exploitation. Workplace relations and contracts may be important but they, by themselves, do not explain why women are typically poorer than men and black people typically poorer than white people. Instead, we need to conceive of a 'poverty of capabilities' that encompasses both absolute definitions and relative ones (Burchardt, 2008; see also Townsend, 1993). Poverty is what Sen (2009, pp 254-60) calls 'capability deprivation'. Ultimately, what poor people are deprived of is the right to live lives of dignity, freedom and respect in which they possess the opportunities to fulfil their potential.

So how should we assess the capabilities approach? How much of it should influence an ecosocial understanding of poverty? There are two critiques I wish to offer here (cf Brighouse and Robeyns, 2010).

First critique

While the capabilities approach is a stimulating 'broad church' of perspectives, this can also make it seem fuzzy and indistinct. 'Sen's capabilities have never been operationalised satisfactorily', says Bradshaw (2011, p 94). In particular, although it refers to something as fundamental as 'beings and doings', we may worry about the foundations on which the approach is meant to rely.

This, after all, is something that Nussbaum and Sen also appear to worry about. For Nussbaum (2011, pp 70-6), Sen is both too diverse and not diverse enough. She views him as not being diverse enough because, for Sen, freedom is *the* overarching social good. But, according to Nussbaum, not everything that we should define as good can be included under the heading of 'freedom'. Some freedoms are more important than others and some freedoms conflict with others. We have to prioritise freedoms, she argues, and therefore need additional principles and concepts if we are to do so effectively. A simple appeal to 'freedom' cannot provide a sufficient framework when what that framework has to do is adjudicate between competing freedoms. Nussbaum acknowledges Sen's commitment to democratic deliberation, but argues that this then risks being *too diverse* since conversations must be shaped and directed by formal mechanisms (political institutions, constitutions, legal procedures) if they are to be efficacious. If we allow majority opinion too much power, there is a danger that the capabilities of unpopular minorities may be undermined. Finally, Nussbaum (2011, p 76) argues in favour of political liberalism and against using 'the idea of capability as a comprehensive theory of the value or quality of life.'

We consider Sen's response shortly. For now, it is important to appreciate that while at first glance the disagreement between Nussbaum and Sen appears fairly trivial, should we develop a list of capabilities or not? The difference is actually quite substantial because it goes to the heart of what, for decades now, has been a central problem for philosophies and politics of justice.

To what extent is justice a universal principle? Anti-universalists have contended that universalist accounts are too insensitive to social constructions, cultural traditions, contextual meanings and local understandings of how and why people interrelate (Flyvbjerg, 2001) – Kantianism is often the exemplar here (Fitzpatrick, 2008a, Chapter 3). Universalists have replied that without some shared, common denominator, there is no basis for human rights, social progress and communication across cultural-national contexts (Habermas, 2005, pp 104-08, 260-6). Much of the sound and fury that characterised these debates in the 1960s-1980s has abated, with many theorists content to accommodate a spectrum of alternative ways of balancing the universal and the particular. This also seems true of the capabilities approach. The approach, however, risks offering a paradoxical embrace of both excessive universalism *and* excessive particularism.

For this, essentially, is the accusation which Nussbaum and Sen *both level against one another!*

Nussbaum's critique runs as follows. Sen prefers an account of the good that is so comprehensive that it risks eclipsing other, distinct understandings of the good (such as 'care'). But as well as being too universalist, Sen is also too much of a particularist. Without a cross-contextual set of liberal institutions there is no guarantee that freedom will prevail. Although 'freedom' can accommodate diverse models of social and political interaction – in short, there are many different ways of 'living reasonably' – for liberals like Nussbaum there must come a point when a community ceases to be free and therefore ceases to be just. Sen does not specify what that point is, and so does not consider what happens when freedom is undermined by those who either reject freedom outright or who subvert it while *claiming* to support it. In short, Sen gives too much prominence to freedom *and* to the capacity of communities to respect and institutionalise those freedoms. He is both too universalist and too particularist. To avoid the possibility of the capabilities approach becoming all things to all communities, Nussbaum offers a list designed to anchor cross-cultural debates about desirable social reforms.

Yet Sen throws a similar accusation back at Nussbaum. For Sen (2006, pp 49-50, 92-3), it is liberalism that is too universalist, leaving liberals deaf to their specific western accent, overestimating their record as champions of tolerance, democracy and progress, while underestimating the extent to which the values of freedom have been advanced by non-western and non-liberal traditions. Western liberalism has enabled the west to claim ownership of, and therefore expropriate, ideals and values that are actually global in origin. We should therefore enter into a dialogue with a multiplicity of global voices rather than reaching prematurely for a transcendentalist universalism that offers closed, limited models of public reasoning. Sen (2009, pp 388-415) advocates 'open impartiality' which rejects parochial assumptions. So, in accepting Rawls' (1999) view that we should seek an overlapping consensus of reasonable doctrines, Nussbaum risks allowing a prescriptive and elitist western liberalism to set the terms of a debate that should be genuinely global.

Therefore, according to Sen, it is Nussbaum's list of capabilities which is too particularist. It does not offer a sound basis for making cross-contextual judgements because the content and the boundaries of human capabilities should always be open to question, contestation and revision by communities. Even a skeletal list of capabilities risks closing down legitimate debate. In short, liberalism needs to de-westernise itself through a truly global, pluralist ethic rather than a static universal one. Thus it is Nussbaum who risks an excessive particularism, closing the door on a genuine cross-cultural discourse. For Sen, suspicious of those with lists of 'dos and don'ts', the capabilities approach should merely offer a tool for ranking different sets. The capabilities approach tell us,

- If you want x, y and z, then do 1
- If you want y, z and x, then do 2
- If you want z, x and y, then do 3

and leaves communities to make decisions about which of these to prefer.

In short, the dispute between Sen and Nussbaum is actually considerable since it concerns fundamental disagreement about the extent to which justice is universal, about the nature of liberalism and so about the role of liberalism in trying to promote justice.

Now perhaps I am overstating the problem here. It may well be that further thinking and discussion will resolve the disagreement between Sen and Nussbaum. (They each acknowledge this possibility.) Or, even if this does not happen, perhaps it does not matter. Maybe the capabilities approach is simply a wide field of debate that usefully directs us away from simplified accounts of justice.

Perhaps. Yet it may also be that the capabilities approach introduces indeterminacy into debates about justice and, by extension, the injustices of poverty. If both Sen and Nussbaum have a point in their criticism of the other, it may be that each has identified something about the capabilities approach that makes it insufficiently grounded: vague, generic, slippery, indefinite, indistinct and overextended in both scope and ambition. This is not to reject the capabilities approach necessarily, but it may be better to regard it is an adjunct to existing politics rather than something which is radically distinct (see also Daniels, 2010). This takes me to my second critique.

Second critique

Capabilities theorists demonstrate varying degrees of scepticism towards the idea that the just distribution of material and economic resources is a central component of social justice (see Fitzpatrick, 2008b). To a large extent this involves rejection of Rawls' emphasis on primary goods, especially the prominence he gives to income and wealth. Rawls, they insist, concentrates too much on what people possess and not enough on what people can substantively achieve. For instance,

> Sen and I both argue that Rawls's theory would be better able to give an account of the relevant social equalities and inequalities if the list of primary goods were formulated as a list of capabilities rather than as a list of things. (Nussbaum, 2006, pp 50-1)

> A woman may be as well off as her husband in terms of income and wealth, and yet unable to function well in the workplace, because of burdens of caregiving at home. (Nussbaum, 2006, p 53)

Sen proposes that we should pretty much reject Rawls; Nussbaum argues that we can and should adapt parts of the Rawlsian system (cf Iversen, 2003). The sentiment of the second quote recurs often in the capabilities literature and, in response to it, Pogge (2010, pp 20-1) observes that those who focus on resources do not overlook intrafamily distributions; they merely conceptualise them differently.

But it is the first quote that captures something quite common in the capabilities literature, that is, reference to income and wealth as static 'things'. As such, some argue that it is better to relocate income and wealth so that they occupy a more marginal place within a wider formulation of capabilities:

> If people were fully able to realize their capacities as human beings, the matter of riches and poverty measured in terms if commodities and incomes would become secondary. (Levine and Rizvi, 2005, p 47; see also Levine, 2004)

Thus, the allegation is that because income and wealth are a 'means to an end', and not the end itself, we should not fetishise economic resources, material objects and goods into something more important than the humans who either possess or lack them (Nussbaum, 2003, pp 50-1, 53; 2011, pp 41, 57-8).

Are the capabilities theorists on to something here? Should we displace income and wealth from the central position they have long occupied within a politics of justice? Two arguments suggest that we do not have to be so drastic.

First, Pogge (2010, p 21) proposes that resources-based and capabilities-based accounts both concur about the importance of relational holdings:

> ...the value of any level of income depends in part on what incomes other participants enjoy and that, partly for this reason, an institutional order may be unjust because the incomes it makes available to some are too low relative to the incomes it makes available to others ... the relative size of incomes should be incorporated into an appropriate resource metric.

Similarly, those committed to the capabilities approach might accept that capabilities are bound up with the relational holdings regarding income and wealth. In opposition to Levine and Rizvi, it could then be claimed that people would only be fully able to realise their capacities once the basic structure of society (and therefore the just distribution of riches, commodities and incomes) has been established.

This critique is more positive than a second possible response, one made by a capabilities advocate. Bourguignon (2005, p 77) proposes that systems of redistribution and social insurance 'aimed at reducing inequality or "relative" income poverty' are not enough to eradicate social and economic hindrances. Instead, the 'income poverty paradigm' should give way to a focus on endowments, or the multiple assets, attributes and opportunities that characterise individuals in their social environments. However, since endowment redistribution is not easy, equalising the distribution of income and wealth *is* an approximate way of ensuring that assets and endowments are distributed more equitably. Bourguignon (2005) therefore suggests that the poverty paradigm be extended and made complementary with the endowment paradigm (cf Fitzpatrick, 2011a).

Although it still begrudges income, wealth and the poverty paradigm as a 'second-best' approach, Bourguignon's suggestion at least establishes some clear water between those (such as Levine and Rizvi) who are quite dismissive of the paradigm of income poverty, material resources and distributive justice.

If there is a risk of fetishising income and wealth (of allowing them to occupy the place that should be reserved for human attributes), there is also a risk of reifying them (of making them appear less human than they really are). This is arguably the mistake that those who characterise income and wealth as 'things' make (for a longer analysis see Fitzpatrick, 2008b). Sen et al cite no evidence that Rawls objectified income and wealth. But, whether he thought in such terms or not, capabilities theorists then risk adopting this caricature as their own. Income and wealth become fixed in their arguments either as objects (notes, coins or numbers in an account) or as a rigid tool of statisticians and economists. Yet income and wealth are not 'things', as Pogge observes – they are social relations, symbols of, and weapons deployed within, structured systems of social class power that shape not only external endowments (opportunities and liberties) but also our internal sense of worth in relation to others.

It is the displacement of income and wealth (my second critique) that perhaps feeds the indeterminacy of the capabilities approach (my first critique). In the decades since Sen gave his 1980 Tanner Lectures, 'capital' and 'class' have, if anything, become more important than they were during the heyday of state welfare in the 1950s and 1960s, when Rawls and other resourcists were developing their ideas. Free market capitalism has become virulent and class inequalities have generally deepened. Yet 'capitalism' and 'class' are rarely to be found in the indexes of the key texts of the capabilities approach.

Perhaps they just haven't got around to it yet. Hick (2012, p 304) observes that, 'a capability assessment should provide information for such a critique to be constructed.' Hick repeatedly distinguishes means (resources) from ends (capabilities), saying that the latter has priority over the former (2012, p 301, cf p 304). But capitalism is not only about outcomes; it is a system in which ends (unjust inequalities) are reproduced systematically according to the inequalities of power conferred by the ownership of key resources. In separating ends from means and then downgrading (and perhaps even dismissing) the latter, Hick himself demonstrates the emptiness of the 'haven't got around to it yet' excuse.

This obviously leaves hanging some big questions over how we should continue to theorise class and capital,[1] yet the capabilities approach seems curiously reluctant to engage with that debate at all, even though simple invocations of human rights and dignity sound directionless without at least broad answers to them (Feldman and Gellert, 2006). For instance, Nussbaum (2006, pp 315-24) criticises multinationals for exploiting their workers, but it is not clear how far she imagines reforms of the socioeconomic *system* must go for this to be rectified – as opposed to merely encouraging multinationals to be 'nicer'. We can all advocate a rise in wages for the low paid, but without a firm grounding in a materialist reading of economic distributions (for example, one that identifies wages as subservient to profits, shares and short-term market values), such a demand risks taking on the quality of a cry for humanitarian charity rather than a demand for justice and real empowerment.

Therefore, while we should be grateful to it for offering a complex, diversified understanding of wellbeing, it is far from obvious that the capabilities approach should dislodge more traditional thinking (Kelly, 2010, p 78), as some of its most enthusiastic adherents claim.

Social policy

Where do these critiques take us? To what extent should social policy commentators embrace the capabilities approach?

Some deny that it has much to offer. Dean (2009, 2010, pp 85-9) has expressed scepticism towards what he calls the approach's abstract liberal individualism for three reasons.

First, although the approach enjoins public deliberation as a means of exercising and guaranteeing our freedoms, democratic deliberation requires attention to 'social conflicts and hidden forms of oppression' that a concern with freedom *per se* may be incapable of recognising and repairing. Second, although the capabilities approach speaks the language of interdependency and interconnection, it still works with a notion of the self as 'abstract bearer of capabilities'. The 'space of capabilities' is one of disconnection (of selves coming together) rather than substantive connection (in which they already *are* together). Finally, the capabilities approach is silent on the impediments to freedom created by capitalist markets, for example, the extent to which capitalist wage labour alienates us from our social humanity. Indeed, its liberal individualism may make it unable to offer a proper critique of market capitalism. Dean's conclusion seems to be that while the capabilities approach can enrich our understanding of substantive freedoms – and of the social reforms needed to deliver them – it rests on a 'thin' conception of the self which fails to embody a sufficient 'critical autonomy' to prevailing ways of thinking, acting, being and relating.

The third of these criticisms corresponds, at least in part, to the point made at the end of the last section. Whether we should accept Dean's other critiques depends on fundamental social and moral philosophical issues. There is no coherent, one-size-fits-all school of liberal individualism. Some identify choice with 'consumer choice in a free market' while others believe that agents are always social agents whose beliefs and practices are interconnected and whose cultural communities help to configure who they are. The former is committed to a Robinson Crusoe version of the self that obscures oppressions by treating them as 'natural'. But is this true of all forms of liberalism and individualism? At its best, liberalism represents a diverse philosophical tradition that can offer a perspective on these issues that is reasonable, capable of improvement and broadly consistent with at least some aspects of the more solidaristic outlook that Dean prefers. If we abandon the liberal tradition, then we surrender it to those who would identify liberalism with what is just one of its elements, that is, 'negative' free market liberalism and right-wing libertarianism. So far as justice is concerned, neither liberal nor solidaristic politics are served by pitting the one in opposition to the other.

Other commentators have indicated that social policy has much to learn from the capabilities approach.

Wolff and de-Shalit (2007, pp 36-73; see also Burchardt, 2008) argue that a just society is one that gives priority to the least advantaged, that is, those who experience and become trapped within a 'cluster' of disadvantages. To be disadvantaged is to lack 'genuine opportunities for secure functionings', they say. Someone is disadvantaged when their functionings become insecure involuntarily, or when they can only secure some functionings by making others insecure 'in a way that other people do not have to do'. What matters is an individual's level of functioning *and* their prospect of sustaining that level. Such disadvantages are likely to be corrosive in that one will often create or intensify others. For instance, a lack of access to social networks may affect access to job opportunities, reducing that person's income and so having knock-on effects on health. The job of government should be to 'de-cluster' those disadvantages so that it gradually becomes harder for us to identify who the least advantaged are. The corrosive interaction of disadvantages needs to be challenged through pluralist, multidimensional social policies, since it is unlikely that just one redistributive method will suffice.

Poverty should therefore be understood as a corrosive disadvantage: '... what primarily matters is not how much money or resources one has, but what one is able to do and be' (Wolff and de-Shalit, 2007, p 147). This is because what matters is not just lack of money but also anxieties about money and the possibility that *taking steps to increase income can make things worse through exposure to risk*. Thus, *adding money is not always the way to rectify the corrosive disadvantage of lacking it*. This is most likely to occur when people have little sense of the future being better than the present, when they are pessimistic about their future prospects and so more likely to fritter away any gains that come their way. In short, although money is important, giving Rawlsian priority to the worst-off will not, by itself, erode the distance between the bottom and the top. Addressing disadvantage instead implies policies which:

- develop internal resources (personal enhancement effected through education and training)
- improve external resources (cash compensation where people are given money, as well as targeted resource enhancement through in-kind goods and services)
- reorganise social structures (improving people's status by changing social environments and the rules through which institutions operate). (Wolff and de-Shalit, 2007, pp 173-4)

The potential problem with this argument, however, resembles one we have already encountered. While Wolff and de-Shalit acknowledge the importance of income and wealth, this falls short of a critique of *capital*.[2] Their position probably dovetails with some notion of asset-based welfare, since long-term security is crucial to the 'de-clustering' of disadvantages. However, the links between asset-based welfare and their policy recommendations are not made clear, and they offer no critique of capitalism. To what extent, for instance, would the reduction of disadvantage genuinely alter the stratifications of social classes? Furthermore, money is purchasing power where the purchasing power of one person is relative to, and indirectly shaped by, the purchasing power of others. The power one has to do and to be is closely dependent on the power others have to do and to be. A lack of money is equivalent to a lack of power to shape one's destiny. Without this realisation, like Sen and Nussbaum, Wolff and de-Shalit risk treating 'income and wealth' into a reified, thing-like, technocratic category. Giving people more money may not ensure that corrosive disadvantage is rectified, but a material-distributive politics is concerned not with raising wage levels or benefit levels for the sake of it, but with redistributions of the socioeconomic power which capital confers. For instance, sometimes the distribution of money will itself drive forward the distribution of socioeconomic power. This is the case when generous pension provision strengthens the bargaining hand of organised labour.

In short, enabling people to control principal socioeconomic resources *is* crucial to rectifying disadvantage; this means shifting key resources from private into public hands (not equivalent to state ownership, please note), and equalising access to and control of those resources so that what an individual lacks relative to others is reduced.

As we saw earlier, then, even sophisticated versions of the capabilities approach risk conceptualising money as a statistical abstraction, ignoring the role played by socioeconomic resources such as capital. Injustice in the distribution of income and wealth does not account for everything, and the capabilities approach remains important by drawing attention to this fact. Yet, in a capitalist society, economic resources and capital account for much. The anxieties about long-term security that help to corrode capabilities are less likely when one commands or has access to the requisite resources. Money is not a 'thing'; it is that which shapes, enforces and helps to distribute power across the social field.

Environmentalism

Let us turn finally to our third topic. How might the capabilities approach relate to debates about climate change and environmentalism?

Schlosberg (2007, pp 29-37; see also Agyeman, 2013, pp 38-40) makes capabilities central to his theory of environmental justice. He does so for the now familiar reason that, while it remains important, the distribution of economic goods alone cannot ensure that those to whom those goods are distributed are valued (recognition), nor that such goods will enable individuals and communities to flourish (capabilities). Justice depends not just on receiving goods, but also on the freedom and opportunity of agents and communities to shape their social meaning and the institutional processes through which they are distributed. But although we may recognise their value, can non-humans be the agents of *procedural* justice? Schlosberg insists they can, but only over time, as an alternative ecological ethic is developed.

Schlosberg (2007, pp 142-58) performs a particularly valuable service in showing how the scope of the capabilities approach may be extended to the non-human world. Indeed, he makes the point that a human/non-human distinction should not be overdrawn since flourishing within one's context is integral to the life process.[3] We therefore need to go beyond the limited ambition of Sen and Nussbaum, the former focusing on future generations and the latter on the sentience of individual creatures. Instead, we should raise our sights to the 'macro' level of species and ecological systems, he argues, recognising how these too can either flourish or fail to flourish. Systems are themselves agents that enable their parts to function. So, rather than Nussbaum's reliance on an anthropocentric language of dignity, a notion derived from human psychology, we ought to ally capabilities to a conception of 'integrity', something which all life requires, sentient *and* non-sentient. In short, Schlosberg's critique is that the capabilities approach has been anthropocentric but can be reworked in an ecocentric direction.

Schlosberg's defence is thus highly ecocentric and anti-universalist. In fact, it is anti-universalist *because* it is so ecocentric. Universalism, he claims, only seems possible and desirable if we either (1) limit our attention to humans or (2) apply human categories (such as dignity) to those non-humans that share some vital human characteristic (such as sentience). But if we ought to extend our ethic more fully to the non-sentient world, including holistic entities such as species and ecological systems, then universalism breaks down, he believes. We cannot (yet) speak meaningfully of that which applies to *all* forms of life. Instead, we need to develop capabilities sets for each species and ecological system, while also exploring the extent to which these sets overlap, so that we may eventually come to appreciate what flourishing might mean for all forms of life. Over the course of time, this implies altering humans' understanding of what it means to be human. Developing an overlapping consensus of capabilities sets is a long-term, interdisciplinary process (and not one that can occur by plucking narrow, anthropocentric concepts from the human context and treating them as universals). For now, it means making much greater room for non-humans and nature in our decision-making processes.

Schlosberg's account therefore splits into two directions. On the one hand, he enjoins us to develop an ecocentric ethic, which will involve allowing capabilities sets to overlap and merge. On the other, we need to attend to the practical business of reforming existing institutions. These two directions may well converge in the far future, as Schlosberg anticipates. However, since he himself acknowledges that we are limited to a human frame of reference, some degree of anthropocentrism seems unavoidable. Like Nussbaum, Schlosberg (2007, pp 154-7) admits that paternalism is inherent to how humans think about and act towards non-humans.

This is a rather grudging concession, an admittance that the two roads Schlosberg would have us walk down may never converge perfectly. Does this schism in Schlosberg's analysis occur because he is irrevocably committed to the view that anthropocentrism is too narrow and unreformable? If so, then is it worth starting from another premise, one which is not so pessimistic about anthropocentrism and which sees little need to allow the ethical to diverge from the practical? We could then speak a language of universals while also acknowledging that the language can improve over time as our relationship to non-human nature changes. Indeed, Schlosberg (2007, Chapter 8) makes room for liberal individualists in his account of 'ecological reflexivity'. As such, universalist values and categories may be indispensible, even ones limited to humans and human-like frames of reference. After all, the human context *is* our context, implying that while the human/non-human distinction can be reconfigured, it can never be entirely dissolved.

In contrast to Schlosberg, Holland has also applied the capabilities approach to questions of environmental justice while being more comfortable with a revised anthropocentric framework.

Holland (2008, p 320) argues that the environment is a 'meta-capability' because it consists of the material properties (for example, shelter, nourishment) that enable us to flourish. The environment is the capability that makes other capabilities possible:

> Being able to have good health and nourishment requires that ecological systems function at a level that can sustain the provision of soil, water, and atmospheric temperature that enable agricultural production and the absorption of human produced waste (pollution). Similarly, the adequacy of human shelter is partly contingent upon the extent to which whole ecological systems can maintain the chemical composition of the atmosphere in a way that stabilizes temperatures

and ensures environmental change occurs on time scales to which humans can adapt. (Holland, 2008, p 323)

A just society is that which maintains those ecological systems at a level that enables people to achieve a threshold level of the central capabilities. The functioning of ecological systems is therefore more essential than the 'human-created environments' of social, political and economic systems,

> For it is possible to exercise at least some of the central human functional capabilities outside or independent of social, political, and economic systems, while it is not possible to exercise the central human capabilities outside or independent of functioning ecological systems. (Holland, 2008, p 324)[4]

There are limits to Holland's approach. Importantly, Holland follows Nussbaum and many other capabilities theorists in downgrading the importance of income and wealth. As the quote above reveals, she divides ecological systems from what she calls 'human-created environments' in the course of making the former central to her 'meta' account of capabilities. In order to prioritise the natural environment as a meta-capability, social, political and economic systems are effectively relegated – the former needs the latter more than the latter needs the former.

Holland's categorical dualism is overstated, therefore. In some primitive state of nature we can just about imagine humans achieving capabilities without accompanying social, political and economic systems, but this hardly provides meaningful guidance for the promotion and operation of justice in contemporary societies. Thus, if the natural environment is a meta-capability, it is not one that we can afford to separate from so-called 'human-centred environments', if only because the social and the natural are highly interdependent (see the Introduction earlier).

Additionally, if income and wealth *are* central, and if they point us towards a critique of capital, as argued in previous sections, then such a critique is indispensible to the convergence of social and ecological justice. Perhaps what Bangladesh needs are enforceable property rights to prevent the violations of its ecological space made when other countries exceed the threshold level of capabilities. In less rarefied language, this is equivalent to not allowing your neighbour to extend their home at the cost of your property. And if such rights are available to all on an egalitarian and democratic basis, the Bangladeshi poor would be less vulnerable to the infringements of their ecological space and capabilities made by others, including the Bangladeshi rich.

To sum up, Holland's approach to the capabilities approach therefore seems more immediately persuasive than Schlosberg's since it envisages the development of capabilities through the meta-capability (that which makes other capabilities possible) of the natural environment. However, Holland's notion of a meta-capability assumes an overdrawn distinction between ecological systems and human-centred environments, in the course of repeating what I have repeatedly insisted is a mistake of the capabilities approach: the downgrading of income and wealth (including capital and property), material resources, economic power and the distributive paradigm.

In short, if human capabilities are made possible by the web of human/non-human, social-natural interdependencies to which we belong, we should not be so quick to dispense with a distributive, resources-based account.

Conclusion

The capabilities approach is valuable. A distribution of material resources does not, in and of itself, say anything about substantive freedoms, that is, what people are able to do and to be, but does this mean abandoning a material-distributive framework? Few capabilities theorists probably believe as much, although some come closer to doing so than others (Sen, 2009, pp 6-27).[5] As such, the capabilities approach risks a certain indeterminacy and slipperiness. Resources such as income and wealth are not 'things' but social relations of power that significantly enable and constrain doings and beings. If we displace the distribution of resources too far from our account of justice, we displace something crucial to the very substantive freedoms held to be important.

So far as poverty is concerned we can agree with those such as Burchardt (2008) when she argues that we should conceive a 'poverty of capabilities'. This suggests a plural, multidimensional framework that, in developing the list of capabilities by asking people what they value, invites participative democracy into the policy process. However, poverty also implies a deficiency in the meta-capabilities that make capabilities possible. Holland is no doubt correct that this makes ecological systems central but, as argued above, we should not thereby downgrade the centrality of human-centred ones.

The conclusion to this chapter is simple: we ought to focus on the socionatural conditions underpinning the multiple dimensions of poverty. A poverty of capabilities implies *deprivations in those resources central to both ecological and human-centred systems: socionatural resources*, in other words. Thus, an ecosocial understanding of poverty defines it as the deprivations resulting from an inadequate distribution of, and participative access to, those resources that are essential to both natural and social environments.

Notes

[1] As acknowledged in the Introduction earlier, I bypass such questions myself.

[2] Whether such a critique could be accommodated under their third policy about social structures is not a question we can tackle here.

[3] The notion of integrity – of flourishing within one's context – resembles what others would term 'needs'. This book offers no systematic analysis of needs, interests, and so on, but such an account could be developed from what I say in Chapters Two to Four,

for example, the deprivation categories can be re-articulated in such terms. See the work of Hartley Dean (2014) and Ian Gough (forthcoming).

[4] The same is presumably true in a distributive framework: the environment is that which makes social distributions possible. Reciprocally, if distributions do not observe some baseline of social and environmental justice, they undermine their own ecological conditions.

[5] If anything, they may even take the framework too much for granted. In their rush to demote the importance of income and wealth (and capital and property), they risk leaving a political vacuum into which those who would dismiss the distributive aspects of justice altogether are all too eager to step – 'See, the poor don't need money, they need moral lessons about their failings'.

TWO

Resources

The last chapter ended with two observations: we should not downgrade the role played by resources in the distribution of social and economic power; and if capabilities are important, it is against a background of what makes them possible, that is, the interaction of ecological and human-centred systems. By placing these observations together we arrive at the idea that 'socionatural resources' are crucial. This chapter uses this idea to develop a set of basic principles on which an initial definition of ecosocial poverty can be built.

Some propose that existing institutions and practices are largely sufficient: 'ecological modernisation'. I argue, however, that making sufficient room for the intrinsic value of nature requires us to subject our social and economic systems to a more radical critique. This means exploring concepts such as exclusion and alienation, 'domainship' and socialisation. The chapter ends by offering the initial definition just mentioned. Our first task, however, is to understand what we mean by 'resources'. As one of the most recent debates on this theme has concerned 'assets', for reasons that will become clear, I wish to start there.

Assets

Assets include external goods (home equity, property, savings, shares, inheritances and arguably jobs) and internal goods (education and training qualifications, skills and talents, confidence and motivation, work experience, cultural capital). Assets are thought to improve economic security, facilitate financial literacy, enable individuals to cope with risks, enhance personal development, encourage savings and other responsible habits, provide everyone with a stake in their society and invigorate social networks (Belsky and Retsinas, 2005; Paxton and White, 2006; Fitzpatrick, 2007, 2011a; Prabhakar, 2008).

Over the last quarter of a century assets have become crucial to many discussions of poverty (Oliver and Shapiro, 1990; Sherraden, 1991, 2002; Kober and Paxton, 2002; Schreiner and Sherraden, 2007; McKernan and Sherraden, 2008), because purely income-based approaches have been increasingly regarded as inadequate measures of deprivation. Resource 'flows' (income) may not fully capture a person's circumstances, that is, the overall 'stock' of resources they have available. In arguing for a broader conceptualisation of wellbeing, the capabilities approach converges with the view of those who defend 'asset-based' models (Sherraden, 2003, p 28).

'Asset poverty' is therefore a compelling concept that carries many implications for social policy (Haveman and Wolff, 2005, p 64). Most of those who recommend asset-based solutions to poverty do not advocate the dismantling of income-based policies. Wages, income supplements, benefits and tax credits remain crucial sources of wellbeing and social participation, such as, for example, collective bargaining, employment rights and broader labour market reforms. Indeed, as Bernstein (2005, p 357) notes, since the Right often wish to take the emphasis away from redistributive cash transfers (Niemietz, 2011, pp 124-8, 167), asset-based strategies may give them the perfect excuse. In the UK in the 1980s, the privatisation of public utilities, the Poll Tax and the revolution in council housing were introduced by the Conservative government as a means of spreading wealth and ownership, yet each reform helped to exacerbate social inequalities.

In short, there is already plenty of evidence that asset-based strategies can generate *inequalities*. By contrast, if assets were deployed to complement other measures designed to implement distributive justice, then their potential may still remain untapped. Assets might revive elements of mutualism that, emphasising the importance of savings and insurance through friendly and cooperative societies, predated the welfare state, without having to lose the progressive, universalist and comprehensive aspects of the latter. Such reforms could even revitalise a politics of social ownership (Blackburn, 2002; cf Paxton, 2003, p 3).

Whatever the strategy adopted, the ecological dimensions of justice are surely relevant, it being clear that the natural environment is replete with assets. It is the store, the treasury, the stockpile from which all forms of wealth ultimately derive and on which they depend (Sarkar, 1999, Chapter 4). Yet social policy debates about assets have not yet taken sufficient account of the natural environment.

One possible exception comes in the form of 'natural capital' which is sometimes added to 'social capital' (networks, contacts, reciprocity, trust) and 'economic capital' (qualifications and skills, work experience, education) as that which is essential to social inclusion and wellbeing.[1] However, there is a question mark – first, over whether it is appropriate to bolt nature on to social and economic capital in this fashion, as in Figure 2.1. Does Figure 2.2 offer a more accurate model of our reliance on natural capital? Furthermore, should we even be using the vocabulary of 'capital' when we speak of nature at all? We consider such issues shortly.

There are two debates that substantiate my basic claim about the neglect of the natural environment.

Asset poverty

A scope of the asset poverty literature (see, for example, Sherraden et al, 2004) suggests that its authors have failed to explore a connection between poverty and natural resources. As a typical example, Lerman and McKernan (2008, pp 182-200) detail at some length a range of financial assets (bank accounts, stocks and bonds, pensions) and non-financial assets (homes, cars, small businesses and self-employment) that they link to various forms of wellbeing (see Table 2.1).

Figure 2.1: Types of capital 1

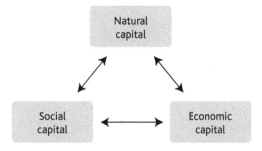

Figure 2.2: Types of capital 2

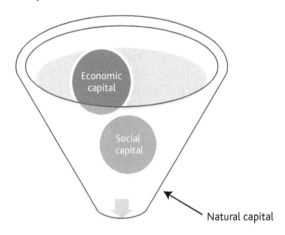

Natural capital

The interdependencies of society and nature certainly lurk within these categories. It is hard to conceive of physical, mental and emotional health being achieved in an environment of pollution and scarce, depleted resources, for instance (Verrinder, 2011). The argument of the environmental justice movement is precisely that the poorest do not achieve a sufficient and equitable state of wellbeing because the quality of their lived environment is degraded due

Table 2.1: Wellbeing and assets

Wellbeing	Examples of assets
Economic	Income, consumption and self-sufficiency
Social and civic	Household and residential stability, social capital, political membership
Child	Gifts and bequests, educational and extracurricular, emotional, cognitive and behavioural development
Health and psychological	Health, future-orientation, feelings of security and satisfaction

to social inequalities and policy processes that disadvantage them. Nonetheless, the literature on asset poverty has remained largely deaf to that dealing with environmental justice.

This allegation is perhaps less fair when applied to development studies. Those who advocate microfinance and microcredit schemes sometimes argue that in addition to enhancing personal savings and aiding social projects, they enable the poor to exert greater control over their natural environment (Mahajan, 2007). Thus, Moser (2007, pp 92-4) proposes the 'financialisation' of natural capital (forests, air and pollution).[2]

Development studies aside, however, the literature on asset poverty in the *developed* world seems to have paid insufficient attention to the ecological dimensions of poverty.

Social justice

Philosophical debates about social justice and the natural environment are more developed (Dobson, 1998, 1999; Bell, 2004; see also Nussbaum, 2006). Interest has centred on whether nature is substitutable, whether it possesses intrinsic value and how humans should relate to the rest of nature. We investigate some of these themes below. *Social policy* debates concerning social justice and nature are less advanced, however – for example, Rowlingson and McKay's (2012) research on wealth and assets barely mentions environmental resources. Some academic research is only gradually developing (see Aldred, 2011; Fitzpatrick, 2011b).

Certainly, at the level of government there has been little work on how and why natural assets might shape the social policy agenda. For instance, in 1998 the New Labour government specified 15 'headline' indicators from a wider set of sustainable development indicators, data about which would be published each year (Hewett and Rayment, 2000). These signalled that recognition of environmental concerns – including river quality, bird numbers and air pollution – deserve to sit alongside familiar issues of health, education and economic growth. However, although such initiatives were welcome, they were never properly integrated, and New Labour never provided an answer to the sceptic wondering what bird numbers had to do with jobs and wages. Furthermore, most of its initiatives emerged at the tail end of its period in office – the Department of Energy and Climate Change (DECC) was only established in 2008. New Labour also tended to think in technocratic and consumerist terms that avoided making the political connections between environmental and social policies.

Overall, then, New Labour's approach was one consistent with what has been called 'ecological modernisation'. Does ecological modernisation nonetheless offer a way of bringing together various issues – assets, social policy, justice and poverty, and the natural environment?

Ecological modernisation[3]

Ecological modernisation is the idea that economic growth and environmental damage can be decoupled using new technologies, market incentives and reforms to existing institutions, thus transforming growth into decarbonised 'green growth' (Mol et al, 2009). A key assumption is that we *are* permitted to conceive of natural assets as *natural capital* to be bolted on to other forms of capital, as in Figure 2.1. There are various reasons for defending this strategy.

First, there is a pragmatic consideration. We have to start from where we are, and that means acknowledging the extent to which market exchange dominates current social and economic thinking. We cannot preserve what we have not measured. Certainly, we may value it for additional reasons and in additional ways, but unless we first render nature into calculable dimensions, we cannot incorporate it to our socioeconomic practices. *Natural capital is thus the stock of environmental assets, including land and soil, forests and jungles, oceans, rivers and wetlands, potable water, minerals and the atmosphere.*

Second, there is a more principled, philosophical consideration. If humans are indeed woven into the web of natural interdependencies, there is nothing inherently objectionable about the desire to develop and improve nature. What humans do is merely a more sophisticated version of what ants do when they construct a lair, or what beavers do when they build dams and lodges. All species alter and adapt their environment in order to serve their needs and interests. Just as nature has worth for non-humans, so 'natural capital' captures the worth that the rest of nature has for us (HM Government, 2011, pp 35-43). Nature is a resource for humans that we are perfectly entitled to utilise, it being legitimate for us to consider productive capacity of natural capital (see UK National Ecosystem Assessment, 2011).

The implication is that we can bring issues of poverty, justice and sustainability together without a major revolution in our thinking. The causes of and solutions to poverty in a green society will largely be similar to those in a non-green one. In short, the equitable distribution of green growth will be *the* means of addressing poverty in an era of climate change. If assets (including natural capital) are a means of ensuring such equity, then useful synergies between ecological modernisation and an asset-based approach can be developed.

Intrinsic value

Are such arguments persuasive?

The pragmatic consideration is seductive but risks allowing business-as-usual assumptions to overwhelm moral considerations. If we stray too far away from today's realities, our utopian dreams may be so powerful that they lull us to sleep. Yet if we do not imagine a future different from the present, we only populate that future with endless replicas of today's errors. Social democratic politics has trapped itself in that loop for far too long.

The principled consideration is harder to challenge. All living beings do indeed use their natural environments in ways that serve their needs. Yet are humans limited to such instrumentalism? Is there something to nature beyond 'natural capital'? What about the intrinsic value of nature (Sandel, 2012, pp 72-84; see also O'Neill, 1993: Chapter 2)? Are we capable of recognising and protecting intrinsic value, even when doing so does not serve, and may sometimes even harm, our interests? To what extent should intrinsic value be part of our moral, social and political thinking? Let me make two points in response to these questions.

First, although they may sometimes conflict, we should not imagine that intrinsic value and instrumental value are always and necessarily in opposition to one another. The argument was famously made by Kant (1991, p 91):[4]

> Act in such a way that you always treat humanity, whether in your own person or in the person of any other, *never simply as a means*, but *always at the same time* as an end. (emphasis added)

We are allowed to treat others as a means to our own ends so long as, first and foremost, we also respect them as ends-in-themselves (Fitzpatrick, 2008a, Chapter 3). Therefore we could follow Kant in giving moral priority to intrinsic value. The value of x is instrumental in so far as it serves y in some capacity, but it is intrinsic in so far as x's essential worth persists regardless of the extrinsic presence of y. Thus, it is both the case that (1) synergies between the intrinsic and the instrumental can be imagined, yet (2) intrinsic value is more important because it expresses the essential qualities of x.

If so, what about instances where they do conflict? Should intrinsic value always have priority? Are we always required to sacrifice our instrumentalist interests when something of intrinsic value is threatened? In one sense it seems ridiculous to imagine so. An ant may have intrinsic value, but if an ant colony prevented the development of a building project that would provide jobs to thousands, then would we allow that intrinsic worth to stand in our way? One possible response to such dilemmas is to ponder why such conflicts would exist in the first place.

Nature is the source of life because it transforms solar energy into the plants on which humans and non-humans depend for food and oxygen (Soper, 1995, pp 130-45, 149-60; Franklin, 2002, pp 39-47). By eating food we are using those natural resources without thereby disrespecting their intrinsic value, for in the absence of humans and non-humans, plants would either have no value, or at best, a value that lies inert and unactivated.[5] Certain forms of use will activate nature in ways that respect and preserve its intrinsic value, while others will not. Therefore, the extent to which instrumental value does or does not conflict with intrinsic value depends on the *means* and the *justifications* by which nature is transformed by living beings, *not the fact of transformation itself* (Barry, 1999, pp 114-15).

For instance, imagine that you are the last human left alive (see Carter, 2004). Would it be morally acceptable for you to burn down the forests and slaughter millions of animals for sport because there is no human left to reproach you? One reason for thinking otherwise is because nature continues to consist of non-human beings to whom we possess obligations as members of the interconnecting web to which even the last human continues to belong. As such, we must be able to legitimate our actions within any moral court in which they (and not just other humans) were judge and jury.[6] According to this view, you have an obligation to leave the Earth in at least as good a state as you found it, regardless of whether any human inhabits it after you. You can use and transform the forests so long as you recognise that they belong to non-humans too.

Therefore, the uses that respect and preserve nature's intrinsic value are those that do their best to recognise and nurture that interconnecting web. In other words, life has a responsibility to life. Animal *a* attacks animal *b* because it sees animal *b* as food. Yet the drive to eat or be eaten still respects the interconnecting web of nature in a way that is not true if animal *a* killed for no purpose or for frivolous reasons (sport or fun) or in ways that were predominantly cruel, or if species *b* risked becoming extinct. Of course, given our status as highly developed social beings who must make often complex value judgements, there is no easy way of distinguishing activities that recognise and nurture life's interconnecting web from those that do not. Does a meat-eater respect intrinsic values by only eating animals that died of natural causes or were killed painlessly? Do vegans occupy a stronger moral position than vegetarians?

That is why I added the modifier 'do their best'; there is no guarantee we will always get it right. Respect for intrinsic values and for life's interconnecting web is a guide, not a guarantor. It is difficult to judge which bits of nature to leave alone, which bits to transform and which bits to sacrifice. No credible environmental ethic can pretend otherwise.

Nonetheless, my first point is that where intrinsic and instrumental values conflict, our main duty is to alter our activities and interventions – to debate how that conflict can be reduced – rather than to treat non-intervention and the withdrawal of human activity as the default response. As argued below, rather than withdrawing from the non-human realm and sacrificing human wellbeing, we ought to rethink the types of interventions we make, the features of human wellbeing and the methods of enhancing that wellbeing.

My second point, therefore, is that our economic systems must be judged and reformed accordingly. Debates about intrinsic value are vitally important, yet these are debates that our market-dominated societies, based on self-interest, the maximisation of preferences, competition and possessive, acquisitive forms of individualism, have been very poor at initiating. Humans do indeed use nature, as do ants and beavers. But some activities are undoubtedly more consistent with the intrinsic value of life's interconnecting web than others. The building project is easier to justify if unemployment can be shown to be environmentally destructive and if there are no other ways of creating jobs. And it is easier to justify if they are green jobs designed to enhance environmental sustainability.

Thus, by attaching itself so firmly to prevailing orthodoxies, ecological modernisation may fail to subject existing systems to the required amount of critical attention, that is, to base our ethical principles and judgements around the notion of intrinsic value. As I demonstrate throughout this book, tackling poverty is not simply a case of mechanically redistributing resources, but of encouraging new relations between humans and their natural world, ones that embody new social habits, practices and perceptions.

Of the possible objections to my argument, let me mention two. First, there are some who will object that instrumentalist values distract us from what is truly significant about humanity and natural life in general (see Lu, 2010). My reply is to acknowledge that there is a danger here, but to insist, as noted above, that forms of instrumentalism are permissible in so far as they serve *intrinsic* values. If it can be demonstrated that intrinsic values are served more by the presence of instrumental values than they are by the latter's absence, we would only be damaging intrinsic values by ignoring them.

A second, related objection is that my entire position (as defended here and in Chapter One) is too anthropocentric. Take the following possibilities:

(1) A world without any life whatsoever possesses intrinsic value.
(2) A world with life but without conscious life possesses intrinsic value.
(3) A world with conscious life but without sentient life possesses intrinsic value.
(4) A world with sentient life but without human life possesses intrinsic value.
(5) Only a world with human life possesses intrinsic value.

A strong anthropocentrist will prefer (5), while a strong biocentrist will prefer (2).[7] I see no way of resolving the issue here except to state that most of us would locate ourselves somewhere between (2) and (4). This reflects back on the last human argument (and see note 4). Would the last human have an obligation to sentient life, to non-sentient conscious life or to life *per se*? My view tends towards (2), but the debate is far too complex to be settled here.

To sum up: the principled justification for ecological modernisation is strong but can be challenged by arguing that our approach should be framed more firmly around the intrinsic value of nature, the value of life's interconnecting web and the interdependencies that flow from it. Therefore, neither the pragmatic nor the principled consideration entirely succeeds. Debates about intrinsic value should be at the heart of social reforms to an extent that the technocratic, business-as-usual tendencies of ecological modernisation ignore. So yes, humans alter their environment just as non-human animals do, but this does not mean that all forms of alteration are justified, or that natural capital is morally equivalent to economic and social capital.

Where might such considerations take us?

Beyond ecological modernisation?

The above claim that we ought to respect both intrinsic and instrumental values resembles and inspires the view that nature can be *both* decommodified *and* commodified. The idea here is that respecting nature is not the same as withdrawing from nature. If our economic system is degrading nature, we ought to improve the system rather than adopt a philosophy of non-intervention. Let me explain why.

As traditionally understood (see, for example, Marx, 1976, pp 128-31), x is commodified if the meaning, identity, value and status of x is defined exclusively or largely in terms of its exchange-value, that is, its capacity to be transformed into money, or equivalents, and circulated within a market system whose overriding purpose is the accumulation of more exchange-value. This is in contrast to the use-value of y, where y is subject to use (consumption, gifting, enjoyment) without it being dependent on circulatory exchange or market systems. In this sense, y is decommodified.

One problem with this distinction is that it tempts us to contrast commodification and decommodification as stark, dichotomised opposites. This easily misses the extent to which they may coincide. The photos I ask a professional photographer to take of my wedding have use-value for me but exchange-value for him. He earns a wage which on that day he could have earned by taking photos of something else; by contrast, the meaning of those photos to me resides in the fact that they are of this specific event, one that cannot be substituted. By being both 'price-less' and yet also the objects of a market contract, the photos are simultaneously decommodified and commodified. Therefore, it may be that commodification and decommodification are often concurrent. Furthermore, it is all too easy to idealise decommodification as superior to commodification. This, too, assumes that the terms have a water-and-oil quality, with all of the virtues residing in the former.

This is why we should be cautious about how we map the two sets of concepts discussed above. It is tempting to propose the following. If decommodification implies use-value where the value of p resides within itself, then surely that implies it is equivalent to intrinsic value. And if commodification implies exchange-value, or treating q as a commodity whose value is only circumstantially related to its innate qualities (other objects could potentially substitute for q), then that surely implies it is equivalent to instrumental value. Accordingly, the conceptual map would resemble Figure 2.3. But if, as argued above, the intrinsic and the instrumental are more intricately related than this, and if commodification and decommodification are not necessarily in opposition to one another, this complicates the picture. It could imply a more intricate series of interrelationships, as in Figure 2.4.

Here the vertical relationships are potentially as important as the horizontal ones. Of course, we lose something by making this move; namely, the idea that we should regard nature as somehow morally and spiritually 'higher' than the corruptions and compromises of our all-too-human economies. A vision of nature as being beyond markets, profit, money, competition and consumerism is deeply alluring. Nonetheless, as already argued, we do not necessarily serve nature by

Figure 2.3: Commodification and decommodification 1

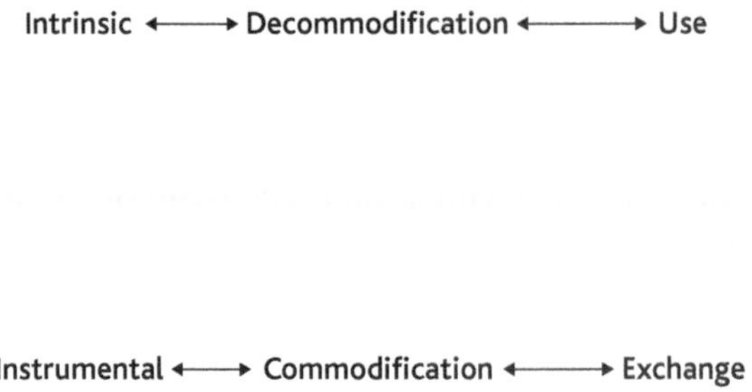

Intrinsic ◄──────► Decommodification ◄──────► Use

Instrumental ◄──────► Commodification ◄──────► Exchange

Figure 2.4: Commodification and decommodification 2

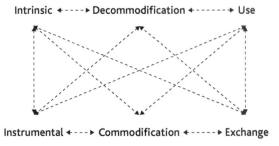

Intrinsic ◄------► Decommodification ◄------► Use

Instrumental ◄----► Commodification ◄-----► Exchange

treating it as a no-go area into which the language of instrumentalism (and so of commodification and exchange) is necessarily unwelcome.

Therefore, rather than emptying the natural of socioeconomic concepts and principles, we ought to be *revising* those concepts and principles so that they are less threatening to the present and future wellbeing of the natural environment. According to ecosocialism, for example, the problem is not economic relations *per se*, nor even 'the market' necessarily, but a capitalist system whose 'creative destruction' has eroded the natural foundations of social and economic life (Pepper, 1993, 2010; Benton, 1996; Sarkar, 1999, 2010; Huan, 2010). Sustainability therefore requires a new system of social ownership, social economy and community property. We should not shrink from conceiving of nature as a set of assets and resources so long as we also do our best to respect its intrinsic value.

The choice is this, then. If we adopt an ecological modernisation approach, particularly in the context of deregulated, hypercapitalist economies, we risk conceiving of nature largely in commodified, instrumentalist terms. But rather than stripping economic concepts away from nature, the best alternative is to revitalise social understandings of the economic. Only through an economy that stresses our social interdependencies can the interconnections and interdependencies of society and nature be developed in a way that is both mutually advantageous and morally desirable.

Drawing in part from the ecosocialist account, the social interdependencies I have in mind make reference to concepts of alienation, exclusion, stewardship and ownership. We now explore these in order to formulate the principles underpinning an 'ecosocial understanding of poverty', that is, poverty understood as a malfunctioning of our social-natural interdependencies.

Towards an ecosocial understanding of poverty

Exclusion and alienation

The current system of property and resource ownership generates a 'dual injustice': (1) the exclusion of the poorest from possession of, and the opportunity to accumulate, social wealth, and (2) the alienation of most of us from the main source of social wealth, that is, the resources of the natural world.

By (1), I mean what commentators on the Left have traditionally meant. Free market capitalism:

- condemns millions at the bottom of the income and wealth scales to poverty, squalor, disrespect and the inability to participate fully in their society;
- demands that we think of wealth, growth and progress largely in individualistic and materialistic terms, for example, as purchasing power, the consumption of private goods and private affluence;
- estranges social groups from one another, so that others are regarded as competitors for scarce resources (although this is a 'manufactured scarcity' since capitalism thrives best when people chase positional goods, as we shall see later in Chapter Eight).

It inhibits people from flourishing, both as individuals (capitalist societies are not as free as they think they are) and as members of shared, cooperative enterprises, nurturing relations of solidarity and mutuality away from the market's relentless treadmill.

By (2) I mean that we miss the extent to which the sources of social wealth reside ultimately in a natural environment with which we are interdependent and interconnected. Modernity has encouraged us to regard nature as both an account to which an endless overdraft is attached and as a bin that will absorb anything we throw into it. Nature is constructed largely as a site of profits to be exploited. Stiglitz (2012, pp 212-15; see also Berners-Lee and Clark, 2013, p 93) highlights the extent to which we give natural resources away to corporations who then charge us excessive amounts for the resulting service. Paradoxically,

> ... among the countries with the greatest inequality are those with the most natural resources. (Stiglitz, 2012, p 40)

This is less an economic rationality than an economic irrationality, yet it continues to dominate. Arguing against running a motorway or high-speed railway through areas of natural beauty is rarely done without calculating the implications for economic growth or national competitiveness. As such, the cost to the economy is invariably rated higher than those intrinsic costs that ultimately evade quantification. The attempt to reconcile intrinsic ecological values with *laissez faire* capitalism's demand to endlessly expand everywhere has, not surprisingly, defeated even those who have approached the problem with good intentions. By being estranged from the natural environment to which we belong, we are thereby estranged from ourselves.

Therefore, an ecosocial account argues that (1) we lack an equitable distribution of, and sufficient control over, both socioeconomic and natural resources, and (2) we lack adequate synergies *between* socioeconomic and natural resources, such that (3) addressing one is counterproductive unless we also address the other. The implications of this for poverty debates are relatively straightforward.

Traditionally, socialists proposed that alienation implied alienation from the products of our labour (due to expropriation through the wage contract) and from each other (due to a lack of self-organisation within the workplace and a competitive consumerism). For socialists, then, poverty is not only a relative lack of money and goods, but also a deeper impoverishment and estrangement, one that affects poor and non-poor alike. The ecosocial starts from a similar intuition but emphasises more firmly that wealth is a 'socionatural resource' (defined below).[8] This is why we need that paradoxical language of commodification and decommodification, of instrumentalist and intrinsic value. We must approximate the ownership and control of something that, ultimately, we can never own or control. This is to follow Polanyi (1957, pp 72-3) when he described land, labour and money as 'fictitious commodities'. They may be fictions, but they are necessary fictions.

Understanding poverty therefore necessitates understanding how the degradation of the natural environment, caused by the untrammelled pursuit of wealth, impoverishes us all, alienating us from the intrinsic value of nature, and so excluding us from recognition of that value, an exclusion that inhibits the flourishing and fulfilment of human wellbeing.

The non-poor are at least more able to seek compensation for this through simulated activities. In short, they buy proxies for what has been lost: large houses, land and gardens, exclusive residential locations, convenient access to the countryside and wildlife, wilderness holidays and other privatised enclaves. The poor are those who bear the brunt of environmental injustices (inferior housing, inadequate heating, health and food, political disempowerment over planning decisions) without being able to purchase private forms of compensation.

An ecosocial approach also draws on older traditions of the common good. Campaigns to give people access to allotments and community gardens, the establishment of public parks and zoos, and granting rights-of-way across private land, have represented embryonic forms of socionatural distribution which, in some cases, go back centuries. According to an ecosocial approach, the response to poverty must go further, involving universal repossession of our common possessions, a re-inheritance of a shared heritage.

Addressing the causes of poverty therefore requires not only the socialisation of natural capital, but also the 're-naturing' of our economic and social institutions and practices. This means attending to natural realities instead of the fantasy economics on which free market capitalism has come to rely. The financial bubbles that eventually burst in 2007-08 were inflated by the view that so long as we make future generations rich enough to pay off the debts we are accumulating, all will eventually be well. But the 'carbon bubble' that we have created signals that the party is over for such assumptions (Berners-Lee and Clark, 2013). Either we burn all the fossil fuels available, and create levels of global warming that future generations cannot 'pay off', or we leave four-fifths of those fuels in the ground and must find other ways of creating and sharing wealth.

Re-naturing and socialisation

Protecting the commons is thus an ethical matter of re-socialising the economy and of re-naturing the social. These concepts relate to an important distinction:

- *Domainship:* what are we allowed and not allowed to do with nature? What is our domain, our legitimate sphere of action and intervention? What limits should we observe?
- *Control and ownership:* what forms of property, control and ownership should we prefer? What legal, political and social rules and institutions are required?

These dimensions should not be confused. Socialist forms of control and ownership could be environmentally destructive if, like their capitalist counterparts, they treat nature purely as a store of wealth to be exploited. This might be less desirable than a green capitalism that is more respectful than existing capitalism of ecological limits and values.

Re-naturing is therefore a principle of domainship. It rejects an ethos of 'full domainship' in which we assume that there is no part of the world that is not ours to possess, control and dispose of, however we wish. That would risk neglecting the intrinsic value of nature. Yet nor should we adopt an ethic of 'non-domainship'.[9] That would reflect the philosophy of non-intervention that I argued against above. Given the power we possess to affect the fates of non-humans, it is better to tie that power to an ethic of responsible intervention rather than imagine we can withdraw into some primitive state of pre-civilisation. In short, re-naturing implies an ethos of 'partial domainship', of self-limiting interventions into the natural environment to which we ourselves belong.

An ethos of partial domainship distinguishes between:

(a) non-renewable resources we can use (even though once they are gone, they are gone forever);
(b) non-renewables we are *not* allowed to use;
(c) renewable resources that we are allowed to use *if and only if* such use is sustainable.

To this, however, we must add the respect for intrinsic value defended earlier. Therefore, even in the case of (a) and (c), we are not permitted to use *at will*. We are not allowed to deplete non-renewables without thorough consideration of the impact on other species and the natural environment. Nor are we permitted to use renewables without a similar assessment. It is not sufficient to cut down a forest one year so long as we replace it the next if, in so doing, we destroy natural habitats that it is beyond our capacity to renew.

An ethic of '*qualified* partial domainship', then, is one in which we exercise both sovereignty and non-sovereignty over natural resources. Nature is both commodified in so far as we must devise ways of generating and organising social wealth while protecting the natural sources of that wealth. It is decommodified in so far as the elements of nature belong to one another organically. To alter one part is potentially to alter everything else. We may indeed intervene, but only with an overarching, respectful attendance to the interdependent web into which we ourselves are organically woven. Our ownership is fictitious but this, too, is a necessary fiction. Re-naturing therefore implies recognising the ecological bases of social wealth through an ethic of qualified partial domainship.

We are therefore entitled to use non-renewable resources (coal, oil, gas) if the long-term environmental impact can be minimised and if we do so as part of a rapid transition to an economy of renewable energy. The intuition here is one in which we are privileged to *borrow* the natural world, subject to certain conditions. We are entitled to receive the yield, the dividends, of natural assets if and only if we preserve the real, intrinsic value of the world as a whole. Arguments about peak oil, shale gas or the longevity of coal reserves risk missing the point of our responsibilities to the non-human: (1) a self-limiting recognition of the extent to which we belong to the world but do not possess it, and (2) the 'ethical reinvestments' we should make to revitalise an environment that previous generations have degraded.

In short, we are obliged not simply to get our distributions of resources right, but to organise those distributions in such a way that we reconnect people to the natural environment on which they depend but from which they often separate themselves.

This takes us to the issue of socialisation. What should the socialisation of natural capital imply? I adopt a minimalist stance in this respect, and do not over-prescribe the property regime implied by 'socialisation'.[10] I assume that qualified partial domainship implies that (1) we should not regard nature as an endlessly exploitable resource, and (2) it can only be used in ways conducive to the common wellbeing. This is to reject the *laissez faire*, winner-take-all approach that has long characterised our economic systems. Therefore, no system grants an absolute, exclusive right to dispose of a resource without reference to the environmental *and* the social consequences for the common wealth and wellbeing. Thus, in an ecological age, even free market capitalism must be socialised to some extent.

Imagine a group of us are stranded on a desert island, with limited access to food. You stumble upon a buried treasure trove of food and use your ingenuity to haul it out of the ground. The economic liberal might argue that you then have an exclusive right to dispose of that food as you wish: to sell it at extravagant prices or even to throw it all into the sea. An alternative is to argue that, while you might deserve a fee for finding and extracting the resource, because you did not create the food, because you were lucky in stumbling across it, and because the rest of us have a basic need, you do *not* have the right to dispose of the food as you wish. And if use of the extracted resource has implications for other people on other islands, then arguably control of that resource should be global. If use of that resource has implications for future generations and/or non-humans, then this, too, should be part of the decision-making process. (For a slightly different application of this example, see Fitzpatrick, 2005a.) In short, even a minimalist approach to socialisation implies that systems of private property should be more closely attuned to social contexts and ecological consequences than is permitted by the deregulatory mania of free market capitalism – in other words, a principle of stewardship.

But beyond that, we should be wary of over-generalising about which model of control, governance and ownership works best. As Ostrom (2012, p 70) observed:

> There are certainly very important situations where people can self-organise to manage environmental resources, but we cannot simply say that the community is, or is not, the best; that the government is, or is not, the best; or that the market is, or is not, the best. It all depends on the nature of the problem that we are trying to solve.

To conclude, re-naturing implies recognising the ecological bases of social wealth through an ethic of qualified partial domainship. Socialisation may entail the social ownership and control of social and natural resources but, at the very least, implies retuning markets to their social contexts and environmental consequences.

Poverty as an ecosocial category

Given the concepts discussed in the last section, what does ecosocial poverty imply?

According to the above argument, poverty represents an alienation of and exclusion from social wealth, which, in turn, implies an alienation of and exclusion from the natural sources of that wealth. This means that the environmental justice movement is correct: social and natural disadvantages are mutually reinforcing. To ensure that everyone has a decent quality of life and the opportunity to flourish, therefore, measures of poverty must incorporate indicators drawn from the natural, the social and the intersection of both (such as access to energy, decent water, air, food and living environments).

All of which is to open some big issues concerning resource *inequalities*. For example, according to Kevin Cahill (2002), 69 per cent of UK land is owned by less than 0.6 per cent of the population, with 160,000 families, or 0.3 per cent of the population, owning two-thirds of British acreage (approximately 37 million acres). Most of Britain's 24 million homes occupy about four million acres. We are in a worse position than we were before the enclosures and highland clearances of the 18th and 19th centuries, when 8 million acres were stolen; to this day, the Land Registry does not even know who owns 50 per cent of UK land (Cahill, 2006). Land ownership is by far the most unequal form of resource ownership.

Therefore, in addition to income and wealth as traditionally understood, we ought to add a stock of socionatural resources. So, continuing to use land as our example, what matters is the:

- ownership of land;
- control of that land within the moral limits set by the relevant communities to which a duty of concern is owed (local, national and global; human and non-human; present and future generations);
- right and the opportunity to participate democratically in the relevant decision-making process;
- capacity to flourish by developing the requisite capabilities (the obligation to value the intrinsic worth of land and so care for and preserve the natural conditions of social interaction).

If we distil each of these down, the component principles appear to be:

(a) *minimum entitlements* to socionatural resources and/or their commensurate value;
(b) *property rights*, as mediated by the needs and interests of relevant communities;
(c) institutions and networks permitting *political voice and democratic representation*;
(d) *obligations to value*, that is, that we recognise, care about and preserve the worth of nature in conjunction with other living beings (human and non-human).

In the language of the Introduction earlier, these principles are broadly distributive *and* procedural: (a) and (b) are entitlements and rights to what gets distributed, which, in turn, facilitates participation in the political and policy-related means of distribution; (c) and (d) concern procedures, but procedures that involve the ownership and control of key material resources and public goods.

It should be possible to take principles (a)-(d) and apply this basic framework to every socionatural resource. What, then, do I mean by 'socionatural resource'?

Socionatural resources can be defined as those that exist squarely at the interface of the natural and social world, such that each is a condition for the production of the other (Swyngedouw, 2004), and both have instrumental and intrinsic values.[11] They denote (1) the material that humans obtain from the natural world and which, through transformation, enables (2) the beings and doings of social interaction, and eventually (3) the waste that the natural world will eventually re-absorb and re-assemble into new forms of matter. Socionatural resources describe the space through which we either sustain, or fail to sustain, the interconnecting lives of humans and non-humans. Thus, in addition to land we might include energy, water, food stocks and the atmosphere as examples. For ecologists, the task is to revise our understanding of wealth so that we put less pressure on the capacity of the Earth to supply resources and to absorb the resulting waste.

Based on this concept and the above principles, we are now ready for a first, tentative formulation of an ecosocial understanding:

> Ecosocial poverty implies falling below some decent minimum access to, ownership of and control over key socionatural resources due to malfunctioning social institutions and systems (including distributions of income and wealth). Ecosocial poverty is thus one extreme manifestation of wider social and environmental injustices where humans can neither adequately flourish qua humans nor fulfil their duties to the natural world to which they belong and over which they possess considerable power. Ecosocial poverty therefore implies inequalities in both rights (the power to command those resources that minimise vulnerability to ecological hazards and permit individuals and communities to adapt to climate change) and obligations (the capacity to care for and cultivate the intrinsic value of such resources so that their production, use and replacement is sustainable).

There are many questions left begging here, not all of which we will be able to address in the course of this book. Nonetheless, this is the basic definition that we will return to and develop over the next couple of chapters.

Conclusion

Our task in this chapter has been to conceptualise resources. I began by arguing that natural assets have not been given sufficient attention in a range of literatures dealing with assets, poverty and justice, and social policy. I then critiqued a principled justification for ecological modernisation by proposing that intrinsic value should be at the heart of social thinking and reforms. This was taken to imply that we should look beyond ecological modernisation to more radical approaches, albeit ones still rooted in the pragmatic need to apply economic categories and ideas to the natural world. This then inspired the first elements of an ecosocial account via a discussion of de/commodification, alienation and exclusion. This account argues that we lack sufficient control over socioeconomic resources and adequate synergies between socioeconomic and natural resources; it proposes both the socialisation of natural resources, and also the 're-naturing' of economic and social relations through an ethic of 'qualified partial domainship'. This led to the idea that 'socionatural resources' should be subject to the principles of minimum entitlement, property rights, political voice and democratic representation and obligations to value. The chapter closed by offering a preliminary definition of ecosocial poverty.

Our next task is to consider concepts of space and of time in order to conceptualise and refine this definition further. We begin in Chapter Three with space.

Notes

[1] 'Economic capital' is often called 'human capital', but due to my use throughout this book of a human/non-human distinction, I refer to 'economic capital' to avoid confusion.

[2] However, some, like Bateman (2010, pp 201-10), deny that such measures have been effective. First, rather than offering an emphasis on human-centred economics, justice and ecological sustainability, microfinance has been driven by an economic liberal agenda of possessive individualism, profits and self-interest. Second, commercialisation, entrepreneurship and self-help have been promoted in order to alter the behaviour of the poor (on the assumption that social problems are caused by behavioural irresponsibility). In short, microfinance amounts to a 'local economic liberalism' in which the poor are seduced into becoming entrepreneurs.

[3] As Ian Gough observes (private correspondence), I use the term in a broader sense than is usually applied, for example, green reforms to existing social, economic and political institutions. Here, and more broadly, ecological modernisation denotes a social philosophy about how humans relate to the non-human world. The pragmatic and principled justifications inform the view of those who believe that the 'greening of capitalism' is all we need to contemplate. In truth, as Christoff (1996) once observed, there may be versions of ecological modernisation that incorporate more radical social, economic and political changes. Whether the ecosocial approach being defended in this book is compatible with them is a question I leave open.

[4] See also Skidelsky and Skidelsky (2012, pp 139-40). For a critique of the Aristotelianism and republicanism they support, see Fitzpatrick (2010, 2014).

[5] I am clearly bypassing big questions about the nature of sentience and the value of non-sentient life hdfd, but see below and note 6.

[6] As Nussbaum (2006, pp 361-2) observes, there is the problem here of drawing a line; for example, do we only treat sentient beings as moral agents? If there were no more humans or non-humans after your death, would you still have an obligation to respect the forests? See the brief discussion of anthropocentrism in the next paragraph.

[7] I am not sure what to call someone who would support (1).

[8] Now that I am about to use the term 'socionatural' more frequently, it is time to state that it and the 'ecosocial' are similar, but the terms capture slightly different emphases. The ecosocial highlights the ecological nature of that which has to date largely been defined through social frames, for example, poverty. The socionatural highlights the

social nature of that which has to date largely been defined through natural frames, for example, land or air. The concepts are therefore practically synonymous but, given their genesis, I think a slight variation in terminology is warranted and shouldn't be confusing.

[9] The classic statement against all forms of property can be found in Proudhon (1994, pp 51, 66, 73), although he also expresses something close to my position when he distinguishes between property in products and property in raw materials and the natural means of production (Proudhon, 1994, pp 84-94).

[10] My own politics is one that makes considerable room for social ownership, and in many countries this is what socialisation will imply. But an ecosocial approach is not only a distinct political position (see Table 5.1 if you want a sneak preview); it is also that which attempts to alter the terms of the debate across the political spectrum. We need to appeal not only to socialists and social democrats, but also to social liberals, social conservatives and to those who don't see themselves or the world through political eyes at all. So, just as an ecosocial politics is more than green social democracy (see the Introduction earlier), it is more than ecosocialism too.

[11] For a longer, more nuanced account, see Schuppert (2012, pp 218-23), although this is limited to basic rights and does not consider questions of distributive fairness.

THREE

Spaces

Socionatural resources occupy geographical space. They *take up space, border space* and *interact with space*. But those resources are social, too, in that they must be used and exchanged within a system of social relations. The meaning and significance of any resource alters according to the distributive in/equalities and stratifications of the social system to which it belongs. Which is to say that since all social systems are structural, enduring across time and shaping the lives and opportunities of social agents, resources are structural too. Resources *both structure and are structured by* the spaces of social relations. Thus, while resources are distributed between individuals, it is also the case that *individuals are distributed between resources*.

Like socionatural resources, then, space represents an interface of the physical on the one hand, and the social on the other. As a result, the concept of space is necessarily open, dynamic, contested and, indeed, political.

To make sense of this, and its significance for the concept of poverty, we begin by reviewing various literatures dealing with space: social policy and environmental sociology. We then apply key elements of these debates in order to develop the definition given at the end of Chapter Two.

Social policy

Social policy is also *spatial* policy. Space affects, and is affected by, the delivery and regulation of services and the experiences of service users. Research into health, housing and labour markets often makes this clear, in relation to urban/ rural boundaries, for instance (see, for example, Woods, 2006). Furthermore, in an era of global social policy, welfare services resemble 'nested systems' that stretch across several spatial borders.

From Booth and Rowntree onwards, it has long been understood that poverty has significant geographical dimensions (see, for example, Coates and Silburn, 1970; Townsend, 1979, Chapter 14). Within any particular territory there will be inequalities in access to decent housing, schools, shops, transport and other facilities necessary for social participation, quality of life and self-esteem. At the same time, the composition of a place – its wealth and distributions of that wealth – will be shaped by its relation to other relevant places. In short, social-spatial inequalities are both intra- and inter-territorial. But what do we mean by 'relevant places'?

The difficulty is that the meaning of territory and place is always evolving. Over the last century we have shifted from an imperial era, to a Cold War era, and then to a hyperconnected, post-national world of multiple axes (dominated by free market capitalism) in which globalities and localities infuse one other. It sometimes seems we can no longer easily relate what happens inside a territory to what happens outside it, as our very notions of internal and external are highly mutable.[1] Spaces and places are permanently coalescing *and* dissolving.

The natural environment adds another complicating dimension. We belong to the natural world as organisms who eat, sleep, defecate, fuck, and eventually decay; yet we are also the bearers of particular social and cultural contexts. In one respect, nature seems to stabilise what we mean by place, as rivers, woods, oceans, deserts and hills provide natural borders, yet boundary-drawing is always a socially constructed activity (Massey and Denton, 1993). Natural places, too, may be simultaneously solid and yet mutable.

If the social, spatial and natural pervade one another, therefore, how might we understand poverty?

Dorling's maps

One method cuts straight through this complexity. We might conceptualise a territory based on existing governmental practices, for example, local authorities, wards, parliamentary constituencies, postcodes, and so forth. Each area can then be studied through the lens of multiple indicators of deprivation, including environmental ones. Those households living close to busy roads, and having less access to parks and gardens, are more likely to suffer from air pollution (Mitchell and Dorling, 2003; Pearce and Kingham, 2008).

The work of social geographer Danny Dorling (2011, Chapters 5-6; 2012, Chapters 4, 29, 36, 37, 40; see also Dorling and Ballas, 2008) provides invaluable maps of such socio-spatial deprivation.

Dorling et al (2007, p 31) show that UK poverty tends to be concentrated in central London, the North of England, Wales and Scotland. The dispersal of poverty became less concentrated during the 1970s but, as overall poverty levels began to rise again in the 1980s, such concentrations reappeared in the form of 'urban clusters' that were highly pronounced, a polarisation that has subsequently continued. Thomas and Dorling (2007, pp 294-6) confirm the bipolar nature of geographical advantage in contemporary Britain, one that has effectively returned us to the 1930s. This contrasts with the bell-shaped distribution of the 1940s-1960s when there were more 'in-between' neighbourhoods establishing a continuum between rich and poor, and so a feeling of shared fate and common purpose. By the final decades of the 20th century, that bell-curve had split into two peaks, a bifurcation not only of assets but also of life chances and opportunities in which two parallel social worlds increasingly fail to inhabit a shared moral and cultural space of mutual respect and understanding.

This suggests something of a 'multiplier effect', where the dis/advantages of geographical separation are magnified the longer they persist (Dorling, 2010, pp 116-24). Once the best schools and the most expensive neighbourhoods are monopolised, they *stay* monopolised by being inherited from generation to generation. Thus, reversing the effects of sociospatial deprivation becomes *harder* the *longer* relative dis/advantages remain entrenched. Organisation for Economic Co-operation and Development (OECD, 2010, Chapter 5) research confirms that there is a strong link between inequality and a lack of social mobility. The Marmot Review (2010) and the National Equality Panel (2010) showed that among adults in the most deprived 10 per cent of areas in England, 30 per cent had no qualifications at all and fewer than 8 per cent had degrees. In the richest 10 per cent of areas, these figures were reversed.

Dorling and Thomas (2011, Chapter 6) have also mapped ecological factors in the form of transportation, domestic and industrial pollutants. Thus, by the time children are 10 years of age, cars are the greatest environmental risk faced by them; and cars obviously cause higher levels of air pollution in cities, especially in those areas where a lack of green spaces means that pollutants take longer to disperse. UK children from poorer communities are five times more likely to be killed in road accidents than children from more affluent communities; and half of all carcinogenic emissions occur in the top 20 per cent of deprived wards (Adebowale, 2008, p 263). Domestic pollution (from the heating of homes) offers a double whammy. The incomes of the poorest are the most adversely affected by rising prices, and remain the most susceptible to the resulting pollution. And the poorest households are the most likely to live near industrial sites and plants that affluent individuals can afford to avoid.[2]

Nuances of place

Yet such 'God's eye' maps may miss significant 'ground-level' nuances. As Powell and Boyne (2001) suggest, not all spatial inequality is necessarily bad, just as not all spatial equality is necessarily good. Much depends on local circumstances and local autonomy. That said, we might be advised to *supplement* a broad-brush approach rather than abandon it. If there are long-term patterns in the degree of spatial equalisation or segregation, then, subject to further examination, we are entitled to treat these as *prima facie* evidence that something capable of overriding local circumstance and autonomy is at work.

Within this context, many researchers make a distinction between the following types of poverty (Room, 1995; Flaherty et al, 2004, Chapter 9; Lister, 2004, pp 69-72; Spicker, 2007, Chapter 5; see also Alcock, 2006, pp 151-3, Chapter 16):

> ... people poverty occurs where low-income people occupy certain parts of a city by virtue of their low income, but their money incomes are not low *because* of where they live. On the other hand, place poverty emerges when other benefits or penalties *compound* the advantages or disadvantages of particular groups by virtue of where they live. (Powell et al, 2001, p 247; emphasis added)

First, 'people poverty' implies forms of concentration (where households are more likely to cluster together with other households at similar levels of wealth), segregation (in which clusters are socially and spatially divided from each other) and polarisation (in which those segregations intensify over time). As neighbourhoods drift apart, so it becomes less likely that their inhabitants will share the same experiences, opportunities and ambitions.

The US has long typified this process. Sociologists such as Davis (1990) and Wilson (1987) highlighted the way in which, through a malign interaction of individual choice, social conditions and punitive social policies, urban spaces bifurcated into dual ghettoes of affluence and poverty, each of them no-go areas for outsiders. Poor spaces are then policed and surveilled to ensure that the pressures of poverty are internalised onto the poor themselves and do not erupt into the public sphere (Wacquant, 2009). And when riots do occur – such as in Los Angeles in 1992, or London in 2011 – efforts are made to depoliticise the eruption by representing it as simple criminality.

Second, 'place poverty' captures the extent to which locations take on distinct characteristics in terms of transport links, leisure facilities, housing, medical services, schools, shops and basic design (Hanley, 2007). These characteristics then affect the opportunities of those living there, with those on low incomes being disadvantaged *because* of where they live. Living in inadequate housing without good shops nearby may exacerbate levels of stress and anxiety that affects health and so intensifies the other problems that people in such areas face, for example, it reduces the capacity to take the jobs that are in short supply anyway. Poor resources lead to poor spaces, which, in turn, exacerbate the quantity and quality of the public and private goods available (Power et al, 2011, Chapter 4).

The people/place distinction is one on which social ecologists have long drawn (see, for example, Gunter and Kroll-Smith, 2007, Chapter 5). 'Environmental injustice' captures the notion that environmental problems have disproportionate impacts on low-income communities and other disadvantaged groups (Cutter and Solecki, 2006; Walker, 2010, 2012). Since income determines the quality and location of the housing a person can rent or purchase, those who can afford to will tend to live away from major roads, industrial sites and other sources of pollution. Inhabiting poorer areas will often exert adverse effects on physical wellbeing (due to the consequences of pollution for respiratory systems, for example) and mental wellbeing (since an undesirable lived environment may aggravate feelings of stress, confinement and despair). Those effects will exacerbate the range of disadvantages that characterise poverty and make it that much harder for individuals to leave such circumstances. And, as Schlosberg (2007) argued (see Chapter One), this interaction of 'people' and 'place' is not just about distribution, but about participatory recognition and voice (we return to this point later).

The people/place distinction suggests that space is not merely something that contains resources, but *is itself a resource* such that those who are disempowered by social structures are 'spatially deprived' in two senses: deprived *within* space and deprived *by* space. This recognition helped drive the anti-poverty measures during the period of New Labour, with its area-based initiatives and strategies for neighbourhood renewal (for an analysis of health-related initiatives, see

Sullivan et al, 2006). The association of poverty with place may often reinforce the problem, for example, those living in certain areas may have to pay higher insurance premiums because high crime statistics suggest that the risk to the insurer is greater. But even well-motivated government initiatives, by parachuting in experts and agencies from 'outside', may reinforce the perception of some areas as lacking the capacity to organise things for themselves.

So, although people poverty and place poverty should not be confused,[3] they clearly intersect. Not only do people define the places they occupy, places come to define their inhabitants – what they mean to themselves and their value (or lack of) to others in other places (Sibley, 1995, pp 55-9). Space is a resource that distributes individuals across itself. Individuals are shaped not only by the territories in which they live and work, but also by *perceptions* of those territories, their sense of where they do and do not belong. The inter-territorial nature of spatial inequality means that those who are living in more affluent areas get to define the worth of low-income neighbourhoods. The prevailing underclass discourse of 'sick estates' and 'chavs' collapses people and place into a sense that some individuals and groups are inherently dangerous because they embody those zones that are perilous and risky (Jones, 2011). Personal characteristics and situational circumstances are merged, with the poor constructed as wild, feral outsiders, barely distinguishable from wastelands, urban wilderness and no-go areas (Davis, 1998).[4]

In my own city, Nottingham, some estates are physically close to commercial and business districts and yet effectively occupy a different social world. St Ann's is adjacent to the city centre but a world away from it, characterised by high unemployment and high crime rates, and stigmatised both locally and nationally, such that 'social problems' becomes code for 'problem families' who have supposedly excluded themselves from 'normal' society. A former doctoral student of mine would report that for some living in St Ann's, a trip to our university campus of only a few miles was like going on holiday.

McKenzie (2009) also stresses how and why the face we present to the world, to represent what we *are*, is contrasted by what *we are not*. To go from one territory into another may involve forms of concealment (in which you dress and behave in ways designed to disguise your origins and appear as non-threatening) or of stridency (in which you proclaim your difference in order to occupy the alter-territory and reshape it to yourself). Within the home territory, some people internalise the stigma while some construct forms of local pride and association – new ways of being an insider, where it is the well-off who become outsiders. Either way, feelings of otherness frequently persist, as do the socioeconomic inequalities that generated them. The worth of the affluent is maintained by keeping a social and symbolic distance from the worth-less.

Relational social spaces

As Lister (2004, p 69) says, then, 'geography both contributes to and mediates poverty.' Available income and assets will determine where that household is located; in turn, locations will themselves contribute to the distribution of socioeconomic advantages and disadvantages. The growth in poverty levels since the 1970s represents a spatial *re*-segregation following the post-Second World War experiment in egalitarian universalism (also Wilkinson and Pickett, 2009, pp 162-3). In the era of social and local authority housing, households with differing occupations and incomes were more likely to share the same kind of neighbourhoods and communal facilities. But with the explosion in owner-occupation, the evisceration of social housing and the rise of the private rented sector (and private rents), the housing market has both reflected and helped to drive the rise in UK inequalities. Affluent parents can effectively 'buy proximity' to the best schools ('selection by estate agent') (Leech and Campos, 2003).

None of which is surprising to those who advance relative explanations of poverty and exclusion. Indeed, this is a fairly tepid word that allows its critics to dismiss unequal social conditions as *merely relative*. For conservatives, if 'relative social position' does not matter, the agency of those on low incomes is substantially the same as those on affluent incomes; their poverty can then be safely attributed to laziness, lax morals and malfunctioning cultures (Mead, 1997).

But relative conceptions are, more properly speaking, *relational* ones in which physically distant spaces interpenetrate socially and symbolically (Harvey, 1996, pp 261-4).[5] This means not only that what happens here affects what happens there, but that the value of a territory – both to its inhabitants and to outsiders – is intimately associated with its comparator groups. In a country like the UK, whose wealth has long been dependent on house prices, this is what can make boundary changes, housing developments and other construction projects such a politically charged issue. Geographical space is always symbolic of how we view ourselves in relation to how we view others.

The polarisation of space within the UK has made it easier for the non-poor to dismiss poverty as a self-inflicted wound committed by those from whom they are morally and culturally dissimilar. With this increase in symbolic and economic distances, there has also been a moral estrangement.[6] Those who are not like me are *other*, possessing an inferior status. Those who inhabit or travel through the same territory as me can nevertheless appear as trespassers, or squatters, occupying a space they haven't really earned. Thus, citizenship rights atrophy, becoming highly conditional on the repeated performance of duties – defined by affluent individuals' image of themselves as hard working, rather than the lucky recipients of inherited advantages – to prove one is deserving (Kahneman, 2011, pp 199-201, 216). So what conservatives attribute to human nature is really a reflection of the moral alienations and estrangements deriving from socioeconomic priorities, political decision-making and cultural constructions.

The following makes clear that this 'relational' analysis is suited to sociological and ecological critiques that emphasise the extent to which natural and social spaces are mutually interactive.

Environmental sociology

Before dealing with environmental sociology, the centrality of space to climate science should be noted, the most famous contribution being the 'ecological footprint' (Agyeman, 2013, pp 46-54, Chapter 3 *passim*). The ecological footprint initially referred to the size of the 'hinterland' needed to support an industry or population. Generalised, it refers to the amount of capacity needed to support humanity as a whole. In popular and media accounts this is sometimes expressed as the number of Earth-like planets we would need to sustain our present production and consumption habits, or as that point in the calendar year when humanity begins to exceed the 'carrying capacity' of the Earth:

> If everyone in the world wanted to live like people in the UK ... we would need over three planets like the earth and head into deficit in early April. (Simms, 2009, p 215)

The genesis of such thinking arguably tracks back to Malthus's (2004) belief that population growth inevitably outstrips the supply of food. If there were ample food and space, then life forms would fill millions of worlds in just a few millennia, he observed. But in the absence of such surplus, nature 'checks' the growth of populations by effectively killing off those who cannot find enough food to survive. This idea directly influenced Darwin's (1887, p 83) formulation of 'natural selection', in which those life forms most suited to their environments thrive and evolve accordingly.

Not surprisingly, Malthus and Darwin have been interpreted (by critics, but also some supporters) as thereby facilitating a brutal social ethic. Malthusianism, they say, must propose that starvation, epidemics and destitution are welcome means for dispensing with what Dickens satirically referred to in *A Christmas carol* as the 'surplus population'; Darwinism must advocate a 'survival of the fittest' in which beings compete against and kill one another.

Yet such interpretations easily mislead. In later editions of his *Essay on the principle of population*, Malthus (2004, p 128) acknowledged that population growth could be brought under control through 'moral restraint' and thus reconcile two desiderata:

> ... a great actual population and a state of society in which abject poverty and dependence are comparatively but little known; two objects which are far from being incompatible.

And for Darwin, humans have developed moral instincts, kinship relations and social-cultural structures through which cooperation can be effected (Fitzpatrick, 2005b, pp 116-21; 2008a, pp 17-21).

In short, ecological space is continually reshaped by social practices. The ecological footprint, then, is more than a statistic generated by number-crunching scientists. If our moral judgements, social practices and political interventions matter, the footprint is not set in stone, being as much a social and qualitative category as it is a scientific and quantitative one. This idea of the footprint as being both solid and yet fluid, both fixed and yet flexible, is a particular instance of the contribution that environmental sociology has made to attempts to understand the interweaving of the ecological and the social.

Space is a central sociological concept (Scott, 2006, pp 158-63). Beck (2002), Bauman (2000), Castells (1999) and Giddens (1991, pp 16-27) all suggest that space has disconnected from localities, spreading along diverse geometries. Boundedness has melted, to be replaced by movements and networks that are always multidimensional and always changing. People still seek sites of stability, community and solidarity, but those sites are 'social mirages', forever being dissolved and recombined. In short, the predictabilities, certainties and regularities that formally characterised space have been replaced by indeterminacy, randomness and volatility.

For these authors, inequalities and stratifications are subject to similar tectonics, such that simplified models of hierarchies and structures no longer apply. Family background, class and gender, and so on still matter, but what they mean and how they manifest themselves is far more complex than was once imagined.

Where does nature fit into the picture? For Eckersley (2004, pp 122-6), there is a 'pre-discursive nature', but one that we can only understand through a shared, critical discourse; for Beck (1999, pp 145-8), there is no such thing as nature 'in the raw', for how can nature be encountered except through the social understandings of those encountering it? Whatever the subtleties at work in such debates, environmental sociology has reintroduced sociologists to the 'givenness' of nature, that is, the extent to which nature may form a distinct yet interdependent material substance that causes and shapes social productions (Hannigan, 2006, pp 29-35).

If there is a degree of consensus here, it arguably resides in the acknowledgement that nature imposes limits on what humans can do, twinned with a view that those limits are not necessarily fixed and immutable but are always reconfigured by social practices and economic developments. (This notion of 'flexible limits' is one that I invoke below.) Society mediates the natural and nature mediates the social (Irwin, 2001). The nature we encounter is never untouched by human hands as there is no longer any primordial wilderness, but it *is* nature and not just another social production, representation or simulation. Inevitably, then, social-ecological relations are deeply symbiotic (see Dunlap and Catton, 2002; for a useful review of other key literatures, see Manuel-Navarrete and Redclift, 2010).

David Harvey and John Urry

For illustrations of how we might understand that symbiosis, take the work of David Harvey and John Urry.

According to Harvey (1996, pp 150-7; 2000, p 177), free markets have left us with both spatial inequalities and ecological degradation. The free market represents a fetishism of 'process' in which the means (monetary exchange, market contracts, profit-making) always justify the ends. Capital constructs whatever social and geographical landscape it needs in order to function, and then destroys those landscapes again (and again and again). In this way, new opportunities and needs are created, and the cycle of capital accumulation is kept in a devouring, perpetual state of motion. As Marx and Engels observed, it creates a world after its own protean and self-consuming image (Marx, 1977, pp 224-5).

This is why social politics has to be ecological and ecological politics has to be social:

> The concept of sustainability ... points to spatiotemporal horizons different from those of capital accumulation. (Harvey, 2000, p 194; see also pp 221-3)

These horizons require mediating institutions that will facilitate (1) risk prevention and reduction, and (2) the restoration and control of resources, 'in which the working class, the disempowered, and the marginalised take a leading role' (Harvey, 2000, pp 223, 241-4; see also 1996, pp 434-8). This would be a new utopianism of both process and space. For Harvey, the utopia of process implies democratic processes that regulate and limit the operation of market forces; the utopia of space implies a socialisation and (in my vocabulary) the re-naturing of capital.

Echoes of Harvey's position can be found in the recent publications of John Urry.

Urry (2011, pp 50-2) advocates what he calls a 'post-carbon sociology'. By being 'carbon-blind' sociology has failed to fully comprehend the resource and energy bases of social and economic life (cf Foster, 1999). Capitalism alienates us from natural environments and social processes by annihilating space in favour of time. It liberates people from the restrictive geographies of feudalism, but eventually sets them adrift in a world that lacks solidity and stability. Nature comes to be mastered by the interdependent systems of movement that occur 'over, under and across it'. High carbon systems came to dominate capitalist practices due to the 20th-century hegemony of the US: electric power generation, cars and oil-based infrastructures, suburban housing, commuting and consumption, networked and mobile technologies.

So, throughout the last century, the scale and speed of our work, leisure and family relationships involved the elongation and urbanisation of social space, in a metabolism that requires us to live increasingly 'beyond neighbourhood' (Urry, 2011, pp 55-9, 63-76). Places become defined by the physical and symbolic distances between them. The modern self is always a mobile self, where we constantly track and are tracked by others:

> … high carbon lives involve much movement beyond neighbourhood, because of fast-moving objects, signs and people. (Urry, 2011, p 58)

Like Bauman (1998, p 113), Urry is suggesting that immobility becomes a form of exclusion so that, unless we are constantly on the move (upwardly mobile, productive, touristic, networked, fully downloaded and updated), we risk being left behind. Economic liberal capitalism engenders this feverish, positional competition in which the solution to the frustrations created by movement is always more movement.

Urry's (2011, Chapter 9) preferred solution is a 'resource capitalism', in which space is reinvented as natural and localised space. He rejects the view of those who would establish a green society on isolated eco-communities, but anticipates that a post-economic liberal era would have to address social inequalities by allowing the greater communalisation of life, work and leisure based on denser neighbourhoods. But such a social restructuring would be dependent on, and would therefore accompany, the continued digitalisation and virtualisation of space since, to put it simply, if you want less physical travel, then people will have to access better forms of virtual travel. Resource capitalism would therefore be low carbon and smart-tech.

For both Harvey and Urry, then, free market capitalism has 'de-socialised' systems of production, distribution and consumption. The task now is to re-socialise these systems and to ensure that this is compatible with ecological imperatives.

Ecosocial poverty revisited

How might such insights influence our understanding of poverty?

Harvey and Urry both suggest that a green society requires new connections between process and space. For Harvey, the former implies a democratic dialogue and openness that is never finalised but always receptive to new developments, while the latter demands an equalisation of the resources that determine the opportunities and life course of different social groups. For Urry, process refers to practices of digitisation and technological innovation that surmount geographical distances, while space refers to the communal densities needed for sustainable production, transportation and consumption.

On both accounts, what is process and what is space, what is fluid and what is solid, is never finalised. Each morphs into the other. As such, a green society has to be constantly remaking itself as a response to the ever-changing and often unpredictable effects of human interventions into the natural environment. The givenness of natural space collides with the indeterminacy, randomness and volatility of social space. The notions of symbiosis and metabolism capture this idea that socionatural interdependencies are never fixed and frozen. The institutions, networks and relations of a green society therefore have to be correspondingly resilient (Adger et al, 2011).

A green society, in short, has both to reconcile itself to natural limits while enabling its citizens to cope with instabilities emanating from the interactions of society and nature. This means not simply trying to diminish the shocks to the ecosystem that global warming is producing, through policies of mitigation and adaptation; it means that mitigation and adaptation are themselves sources of uncertainty that may create unintended consequences to which we have to respond rapidly and pragmatically. We need to live within our resources and distribute those resources such that individuals and communities are empowered to cope with ever-evolving uncertainties. We need to construct 'institutional shock-absorbers' so that the impacts of society on nature and nature on society can be managed imaginatively and quickly. The quality of social relations are woven into the texture of our natural world just as, reciprocally, the natural world can only thrive if the socioeconomic system it supplies is attuned to its needs.

Take the recent proposal for redistributive 'personal carbon allowances' (PCAs). The idea is to reduce overall carbon use by setting personal quotas while boosting the incomes of the poorest because, as those typically with low net emissions, the more affluent would only be able to feed their carbon habit by buying permits from the poorest (Hansen, 2009, pp 209-21; Seyfang et al, 2009). Such a system is only workable via highly complex technological systems, but the central principle is sound as a solution to the following dilemma: low-income households in the UK occupy too little social space, in the sense that they are spatially deprived relative to others, yet as inhabitants of the developed world, they disproportionately contribute to an ecological footprint which is unsustainable.

The main defect with this proposal is that it would be a consumerist, end-of-the-pipe solution that emphasises private incentives and self-interest. If to such policy agendas we add Schlosberg's emphasis on participatory recognition and voice in a public context of shared power and responsibilities, we end up with the view that sustainability is not simply a technocratic question of outcomes (applying quotas, hitting targets, conserving supplies), but of inputs, that is, ensuring that those whose fate is at stake have the greatest possible say in how social and natural resources are governed. If so, this notion of voice also has to make room for non-human interests and the representation of future generations in democratic processes.

Sustainability, therefore, means both living within nature's limits *and* shaping nature so that 'living within limits' implies serving the widest possible range of human and non-human interests, across both present and future. It must straddle both private and public interests. From what has been said in Chapters One and Two and earlier in this chapter, let me speculate what this may imply regarding poverty.

The more poverty there is, the less effective any shock absorbers will be. Anti-poverty policies, in fact, constitute one of the fundamental shock absorbers that we need. Our efforts to effect environmental sustainability will be compromised if measures to address the causes and symptoms of poverty are not made. Unless people participate on roughly equal terms – sharing the burdens of climate change equitably in a society of mutual respect – on fulfilling the tasks of mitigation and adaptation, those tasks are less likely to be fulfilled effectively. And unless people are empowered to occupy more of their lives with something other than the acquisitive materialism of disposable, private goods, transition to a green society of public goods, mutual recognition, shared responsibilities and long-term sustainability becomes harder. The more we obsess about personal wealth, the more alienated from the ultimate sources of prosperity and wellbeing we risk becoming. This possessive individualism is bound together with the inequalities and social-moral distancing that disadvantages and devalues those on the lowest incomes, as people scramble against one another for vital but scarce positional goods (see Chapter Eight, later).

Therefore, in terms of the themes of this particular chapter, ecosocial poverty implies lacking an acceptable level of the resources found at the interface of social and natural spaces. It implies being spatially disadvantaged by those socionatural resources, being especially vulnerable to new uncertainties and volatilities and being excluded from the social processes (the economic and democratic decision-making) that are reshaping nature and through which more robust, sustainable solutions must be developed.

In order to equip ourselves with a model needed to make sense of the topics in later chapters, let us now relate this approach to where we left off at the end of Chapter Two.

Ecospatial deprivation

The end of Chapter Two stated that ecosocial poverty denotes exclusion from social wealth and alienation from socionatural resources. It outlined four principles:

- minimum entitlements
- property rights
- political voice and democratic representation
- obligations to value.

How might these relate to the preceding discussion?

If space is that which both contains resources and which is itself a resource, then poverty also implies *social-spatial deprivations* in which one is alienated and excluded *within* space (kept at a distance from, and therefore deprived of, the goods one needs to live a decent life) and *by* space (estranged from the very places one inhabits). It therefore involves distributive disadvantages and a reduced ability to control the places one occupies. And if nature, society and space are symbiotic, then to lack sufficient socionatural resources means being *ecosocial-spatially deprived*. What I refer to as 'ecospatial deprivation' for convenience implies the following:

(1) *Not possessing enough space.* In one sense this means that the poorer you are, the less living space you will typically possess (Ramesh, 2012). As a glance at any estate agent's window tells us, extra bedrooms mean extra cost. House values and rents usually decrease according to a familiar scale: from detached houses to semis to terraces to flats/apartments. The more floor and garden space a home offers, the more expensive it will generally be. Although regional circumstances can introduce complexities, the essential picture remains.

Quantitative space matters because, to possess autonomy, individuals and families need personal spaces, areas of peace and privacy away from the 'madding crowd'. To relate properly to others in a community or neighbourhood – to share some of our space with them – we need to feel they are not crowding in on us. To maintain physical and mental health, we need to avoid the reduced living space that can adversely affect sleep. To develop cultural capital and fulfil their potential, children need space to do homework and to read.

(2) *Not having sufficient mobility across space.* Although some city centre properties belie the point, by and large the most expensive places also tend to be those far from congested spaces: the suburbs, the commuter towns, the villages really only accessible by car. Transportation and housing costs effectively lock those on low incomes out of such places (see Chapters Eight and Nine). And even within their own localities, to afford transportation, the poorest either have to divert money away from other basic necessities, or they have to severely ration their transportation and so immobilise themselves, effectively imprisoned within open spaces.

Ironically, these spatial patterns can sometimes immobilise the affluent too, especially when compounded by inadequate investment in public transport and infrastructure – illustrating how affluent people gain from social inequalities less often than they imagine.[7] Road congestion, high fares and overcrowded trains all suggest that the spatial distances bought by high incomes can eat into the time available to enjoy them. Yet a politics of sociospatial segregation prevails. Public solutions that benefit all communities have been shown to work, for example, London's Congestion Charge, but they are always vulnerable to a backlash by those promoting privatised solutions to collective action problems.

(3) *Not inhabiting valued spaces.* The above elements ('quantity' and 'mobility') combine to suggest that some spaces are more economically and symbolically valuable than others. Affluent households will typically be closer to the best schools, facilities, transport links and parks, and have greater access to the countryside. The best spaces are those exclusive spaces that allow the affluent to keep their distance from, while still being able to compare themselves to, the less well-off. The type of space you occupy, and the type of 'spatial tribe'

to which you belong, is a sign of your worth because social space is what occupies *you*. Devalued space equates to devalued people.

And recall that the environmental justice movement has long translated this idea of spatial devaluation into ecological terms (see above). If green spaces have therapeutic value – aiding physical health, mental health and social relations (Juniper, 2013, pp 246-54; see also Walker, 2012, pp 173-7) – then their absence compounds other social problems.

(4) *Not being able to control spaces.* Spatial deprivation therefore involves multiple disempowerments in which space inhibits and restrains. Living in deprived areas reduces access to good jobs and wages. Being from a place already marks one out as being more or less than others, leading to divergent feelings of esteem and status. Stigmatised places are those in which social networks are already assumed to be threadbare or malfunctioning. Social problems are individualised in a downward spiral by being attributed to problem estates, problem streets within those estates, and problem families within those streets.

Such disempowerments inevitably also involve political disempowerment. To lack space in terms of quantity, mobility and value is already to lack the political voice needed to make a difference, to succumb to the feeling that things cannot change. Socioeconomic inequalities are always political inequalities. Even well-meaning attempts to target money at 'problem places', and to parachute in experts from public and voluntary agencies, may only exacerbate such obstacles by reinforcing stereotypes in which the well-off think they always 'know best' by virtue of their being well-off. And when the state is associated with bureaucracies operating according to complex rules about which one has little understanding, let alone control, managed by powerful and seemingly unaccountable officials – the police officer, the social worker, the benefits officer – it is then difficult to engage and consult in a genuine spirit of reciprocity and cooperation. The resentful teenager in a 'sink estate', facing a bleak future of few opportunities, already knows more about social power than any politician preaching the virtues of hard work and 'playing by the rules'.

(5) *Not adequately recognising that space is always shared.* The inequalities creating such disempowerments also create various social disconnections. For the affluent, social space is highly commodified, judged according to house prices and equity in a society in which state pensions have withered. For the disadvantaged, taking pride in one's space becomes harder and can manifest as a form of embattlement against a hostile world. Both cases are dissociative, constructing values against a background of deep social divisions.

It is hardly surprising, then, that social disconnections accompany natural disconnections in which people neglect the ecological foundations of their social spaces and their effects on them (Dominelli, 2012, Chapter 3). Natural space, too, becomes commodified ('my garden', 'my tree'), and so detached from the multifarious webs of the ecosystem. A piece of ground is treated as passive, an object of exchange one either can or cannot afford to own. For the affluent, it is unit of possession; for the disadvantaged, it is a further sign of exclusion, of what cannot be possessed. In neither case is the true value of the ground fully recognised: the water it contains, its subsoil minerals and nutrients, its micro-organisms, the breaking down of dead matter, its store of carbon, its role within the hydrologic cycle (Juniper, 2013, pp 27-35).

Our marketised and individualised cultures cannot cope with the extent to which social and natural spaces are collective pools in which we all swim, where the buoyancy and hygiene of the water depends on the wellbeing of all those with whom we share it.

(6) *Not caring for shared space.* And if space is not perceived as shared, then why bother caring for it? The bits of land I own or that I live near have an immediacy that is denied to 'nature' as such. I can object to the wind farm that would spoil my view and needn't worry about the impact fossil fuels have on the natural environment. If something *does not belong to me*, then I can leave it to others. If a space lacks value, familiarity and obvious relevance to me, then I may not recognise myself *as belonging to it*.

But if we wish people to care, exhortation it is not enough. If people are to be asked to use power responsibly, power has to be distributed fairly. People with resources may lack the time and motivation to direct them in favour of those, human and non-human, who are vulnerable to its exercise. Those with few resources may possess the requisite motivations but not the power to realise them. Although you may recognise your place within the web of social and natural interdependencies, you are prevented from participating fully in their continuing and mutual evolution, not being able to protect and nurture the places to which you belong and on which you are dependent.

In this account of ecospatial deprivation I have clearly made reference to land and housing but, with appropriate adaption, they relate to all socionatural resources, as we shall see in later chapters. In terms of energy, for instance:

(1) and (2) the affordability of energy, that is, the supply of energy made available to us ultimately through the extractions from, and transformation of, natural space;
(3) the effects energy prices have on the spending of different households and so on their status regarding relative income and social equalities;
(4) the extent to which we can control the operation of energy companies and markets (as stakeholders and not just as customers);
(5) sustainability of energy usage;
(6) the impact energy usage has on those to whom we bear responsibilities (including non-human species and future generations).

I assume that categories (1) and (2) are fairly uncontentious; (3) and (4) are likely to be acceptable to all those who recognise poverty as a relational category; and (5) and (6) are widely recognised as important and accepted as such in relation to poverty in developing nations. In developed nations, however, they persist much more as ecological categories than as social policy ones. An ecosocial approach to poverty therefore argues that (1)-(4) are incomplete without reference to (5) and (6), and vice versa.

We can now see how they correspond to the principles outlined at the end of the last chapter which, you will recall, I proposed were both distributive and procedural in nature (see Table 3.1).

These are necessarily complex, and it is somewhat artificial to distinguish so schematically between them. Nonetheless:

- 'Minimum entitlements' relate closely to items (1)-(3) in the above list, for example, being entitled to a sufficient quantity and quality of living space and to forms of energy at a reasonable proportion of one's income (so avoiding fuel poverty).
- 'Property rights' relate closely to (3) and (4), that is, having qualified, partial rights to and ownership of the natural spaces and sources of energy on which we depend.
- 'Political voice and democratic representation' relate closely to (4) and (5), that is, having a stake and voice in the firms and organisations that manage, sustain and distribute spatial resources and energy.
- 'Obligations to value' non-humans and future generations relate closely to items (5) and (6), since if space is shared, and to ensure that socionatural resources are preserved and distributed fairly, there is an obligation to nurture, improve and bequeath what we have inherited.

Table 3.1: An ecosocial matrix 1

Distributive	Procedural		
Minimum needs and standards; equity and fairness	Equal citizenship	Quantity	Minimum entitlements
Opportunities and offices open to all	Freedom to realise potential	Mobility	
Empowerment and decommodification	Respect and esteem	Value	
Ownership, democratic institutions and enforceable rights	Participative inclusion and cooperative cultures	Control	Property rights Voice and democracy
Equality regarding common resources	Joint membership of cooperative endeavours	Sharing	Obligations to value
Power to contribute to common goals	Capacity to shape ends and means	Caring	

The initial definition of ecosocial poverty given on page 53 therefore stands. When added specifically to the comments on page 68–73 we arrive at something like the following:

> Poverty is an immobilisation in the spaces that have been residualised and devalued, being trapped in the interactions of 'people and place'.
>
> Ecosocial poverty therefore implies an ecospatial deprivation, that is, an alienation and exclusion from (1) the socionatural resources dispersed across space, and (2) space as a distinct resource that shapes the life course of individuals and the value and distributions of those socionatural resources.
>
> Ecospatial deprivation implies deprivation in terms of minimum entitlements, property rights, voice and democracy and our obligations to value and care for those with whom we share relevant relational spaces.

Conclusion

Chapters One and Two defended the concept of socionatural resources and proposed that this is central to any understanding of ecosocial poverty. Since those resources occupy space, and since space is itself a resource, this chapter has looked at the spatial dimensions of poverty by exploring two subjects – social policy and environmental sociology – and concluded that space is highly relational. Given the interdependencies of society and nature, therefore, we need to devise resilient shock absorbers that enable us to cope with the ever-evolving relations that exist at the interface of these two dimensions. Addressing poverty in general and ecosocial poverty in particular is therefore vital. This means understanding, first of all, the spatial dimensions of socionatural resources and what poverty means in those terms. I defined ecospatial deprivation in terms of various categories and indicators, summarised in Table 3.1 as quantity, mobility, value, control, sharing and caring. This also cross-references these to the principles outlined in Chapter Two and to the distributive/procedural distinction introduced earlier. The chapter ended with another iteration of what ecosocial poverty can be taken to mean.

But the task of constructing a basic model is not yet complete because resources occupy time as well as space. This is the theme of Chapter Four.

Notes

[1] As any parent in an age of social networking and mobile technology will tell you.

[2] We explore all of this in the second part of the book.

[3] Poor households can be found in relatively affluent neighbourhoods, and relatively affluent households can be found in poor neighbourhoods.

[4] Jack London had an evocative term for this phenomenon: 'people of the abyss'.

[5] As indicated later in Chapter Four, by the relational, Harvey means a fundamental intertwining of elements that are apparently at a distance from one another.

[6] Making it easier for the Coalition government to means test space in the form of a 'Bedroom Tax' (since April 2013, households with a 'spare room' have either had their Housing Benefit cut or have been forced to move to smaller properties, which are in short supply). This is in addition to a benefit cap that may well see poorer households forced to relocate to areas of cheaper housing (termed by some as 'social cleansing'). The moral 'othering' of the poor has smoothed the way for such punitive policies.

[7] For a vivid US illustration of this in relation to health and longevity, see Woolf and Aron (2013).

FOUR

Times

Socionatural resources endure through time as well as across space (Giddens, 1984).

Space configures time in that *where* we are in relation to others alters *across* time and changes our experiences and perceptions *of* time. Living in an impoverished neighbourhood causes me depressive anxiety and insomnia. Sleeplessness affects my physical and mental wellbeing. My energy levels, motivation and concentration are depleted, harming my interactions with others and threatening to trap me in a vicious cycle of stress and deprivation.

Reciprocally, time configures space in that the rhythms of time, *when* we are, effects the geographies of social relations. Some individuals are pressed to take jobs with unsociable hours that adversely affect their family life and non-work activities. The value and meaning of time to them differs from its value and meaning to others.

Time, like space, is therefore socially constructed, structuring and structured by socioeconomic inequalities (Bauman, 2000; May and Thrift, 2001). The distribution of resources across space/time both enables and constrains social agents, telling them where and when they may *or may not* interact; the interactions of social agents sometimes conform to the existing contours of space/time (perpetuating existing resource structures), sometimes subjecting them to new processes and configurations.

Below, we look at our key concept and its relation to poverty in the light of three subjects: social policy, sociology and environmentalism. We are then in a position to refine the understanding of ecosocial poverty developed over previous chapters.

Social policy

Time is another central theme of social policy (Fitzpatrick, 2004a; Bryson, 2007, pp 39-43, Chapter 6).

- Social insurance is typically thought of as the socialisation, or pooling, of risks: mutual protection against shared vulnerabilities (Kuhnle and Sander, 2010). Even if you yourself are never ill, unemployed, incapacitated, old, or whatever, you will still have benefited by being insured against such possibilities. Although we cannot predict the frequency and severity of such vicissitudes, nor who they will affect, we can introduce some security into life's lottery. Social insurance smoothes out the life course. Social insurance also represents the socialisation and pooling of time. Consider pensions.[1] Those who die young will be net contributors to a scheme that never supported them; others will be net beneficiaries. We could say that the former have bequeathed some of their time to the latter. But here, too, even the former have gained, both in a *contractualist* sense (being insured against vulnerabilities provided a sense of future security) and in a *solidaristic* sense (as participants within what Bauman, 2005, Chapter 3, called a 'community of fate').

- This idea, in which schemes of mutual security are devised to protect against shared vulnerabilities, is central to the 'classic' welfare state. Take healthcare. In health systems a large proportion of resources are devoted to the final months of life and to those suffering from severe, chronic conditions that need regular care, expensive drugs or other costly interventions (Kielstra, 2009, p 3). The contributor who dies suddenly, and/or before reaching old age, receives little or none of this, having contributed time and other resources that may improve the quantity and quality of the time available to others. Yet here, too, she will have gained, both by a system that would have protected her had her circumstances been otherwise *and* as a participative member of a community that sees it as a duty to care for strangers. The 'welfare community' is one in which the social and moral distances between compatriots and strangers are reduced.

  Yet many inequalities inhabit these systems too. Some inequalities of time are matters of luck, but many are matters of systemic disadvantages that social policies fail to address and may sometimes exacerbate. Domestic labour and unpaid care are activities still performed predominantly by women (Bryson, 2007, Chapter 9; Goodin et al, 2008, pp 178-82), with such work contributing vast amounts to social wellbeing without being recognised in GDP measures (UNDP, 1995, p 6). In effect, such carework is an essential but cheap form of provision whose personal cost is borne by undervalued individuals. The 'breadwinner model' distributes time from women to men. And with less time to devote to jobs and careers, women are more likely to occupy part-time and/or low-paid employment. With more frequent and longer periods outside the labour market, the knock-on effects on job promotion and benefit entitlement are clear (Ginn, 2006; Kan and Gershuny, 2009). Achieving a 'work–life balance' remains much harder for women than men (Fagan et al, 2012, pp 10-12).

- And harder the poorer you are. Think of longevity. People living in the poorest UK neighbourhoods will, on average, die seven years earlier than people living in the richest ones (The Marmot Review, 2010, pp 16-17). Professional men can expect to live to 80 years and unskilled manual men to 72.7 years; for women, the figures are 85.1 and 78.1, respectively (ONS, 2011). In a very real sense, then, inequalities of income and wealth are temporal inequalities too, in which the disadvantaged are deprived of the quantity and quality of life available to the better-off. Gender offsets class to some extent, but the overall pattern is obvious and only partly ameliorated by healthcare policies (CSDH, 2008).

- This, in turn, has implications for public debates about demographic change. With average life expectancy continuing to rise, the prevailing orthodoxy is to claim that because 'we are living longer, we are all going to have to work longer'. So the state retirement age is levered up and defined benefit schemes are closed. Unfortunately, few politicians pay much attention to the 'we' who are living longer or to the 'we' who will be forced to work for more years. The greater your income and assets, the greater your freedom to adapt to such reforms, and retire or flexi-retire early. Most politicians wish to avoid a mature conversation, not only about social inequalities, but also about the many possible ways in which life and work can relate to one another.

Social and temporal inequalities therefore interact and do so in ways that are fundamentally political. The principles of social insurance and universalism have been under assault from economic liberals for decades with variable success (Fitzpatrick, 2012, pp 235-7). For the strict individualist, there are two basic alternatives (Shapiro, 2007, Chapter 4). Either (1) people should be free to take out whatever forms of commercially provided insurance they wish and accept the consequences if they choose unwisely; or (2) there should be compulsion to purchase minimal insurance, backed up by means-tested vouchers for those in genuine need. Option (1) falls to the objection that many on low incomes will either neglect to insure themselves or will be financially impoverished if they do (especially if companies charge higher premiums for individuals perceived to be high-risk). Option (2) is better because it prohibits people from opting-out and helps to compensate for low incomes. However, if the minimal requirement and the vouchers are small, then (2) is barely preferable to (1). We could increase the requirement and the vouchers, but then we are closer to the compulsive, tax-based, redistributive features of social insurance that economic liberals abjure. And option (2) arguably fails to embody the 'welfare community' invoked above.

In conclusion, social policies are capable of socialising time. At their best they counterbalance the 'brute luck' lotteries of birth, inheritance and death, that is, undeserved events that lie beyond the control of individuals. In a world where people face so many uncertainties and insecurities, social welfare systems empower them to control their futures. Social insurance, redistributive taxation and universal provision *connect your present self to your future self by connecting individuals to one another*, enhancing communal and individual wellbeing and liberty. But social policies also struggle to make much difference in the face of broader inequalities (such as health inequalities) and can sometimes make things worse (by failing to recognise carework, or by raising the retirement age without sensitivity to class inequalities). All too often, 'time poverty' continues to characterise welfare states:

> You are time poor to the extent that you have little time left over after what you need (not after what you choose) to spend your time on. (Goodin et al, 2008, p 84)

Goodin et al (2008, pp 149-50) found that the more economic liberal the system, the more likely it is to embody social and temporal inequalities, while social democracies are more equal in both respects (cf Gershuny and Sullivan, 2003, pp 214-25).

So in terms of the politics of time, social policies constitute something of an ambivalent 'counter-lottery', an assemblage of conflicting tendencies. How might we explain that ambivalence?

Sociology

Sociologists and social philosophers look at time from numerous angles (Zerubavel, 1981; Adam, 1990, 1998, 2004). The following summarises the analyses in Fitzpatrick (2004a, 2004b).

David Harvey redux

Harvey (1973, pp 13-14; cf Whitehead, 2004, pp 33-8) offers a threefold distinction. There is an *absolute* space that exists independently of matter: space as a neutral container of that which is enclosed within it (Whitrow, 1988, pp 128-31). There is the *relative* space of the relationships between objects. And there is *relational* space within which space and objects are fundamentally entwined and less easy to distinguish. How can these categories be applied to time?

- Like absolute space, absolute time exists independently of those who are contained within it and would continue to exist in their absence; it would be measurable even if there was no one here to measure it (see Mumford, 1963, pp 12-18, 197-9, 269-73).

Relative time is, first, spatial since the position of agents vis-à-vis one another begins to matter. As people move through space they move through time too, and *vice versa*. Relative time fluctuates as the motions and positions of agents alter. Second, therefore, relative time is complex, multiple and only fully understood within a *social* context. Third, relative time is intersubjective, interactive and performative as it is shaped by those who move within it. Relative time is thus a social, spatial category. But social relations are not just external connections *between* agents; they are 'internal relations', connections that configure the identities and practices of agents. 'Social time' is therefore an amalgamation of the relative and the relational.

Relational time goes even further in collapsing the distinction between medium and agent. Here, there are no time-less agents or agent-less times. It is a flowing, embodied, intra-subjective time of perception, reflection and memory. Whereas with absolute time – and to some extent, relative time – we can achieve a scientific distance from what we are mapping, with relational time there is no God's-eye view to which we can ascend. Relational time is therefore never completely fixed because it is always destabilised through struggles, conflicts and contestations.

Yet relational time is also structural, because the conflicts that occur are not random and chaotic. Mental, emotional and physiological rhythms do not simply follow individual streams but the collective tributaries into and out of which those streams flow. Conflict runs across collective gradients of power and domination. Perceptions, reflections and memories are always shaped by cultural practices and traditions (Fitzpatrick, 2009). Relational time is therefore intimately political.

In sum, social time is a mutual configuration of two sub-categories; it implies the inter-subjective and intra-subjective relations of, respectively, relative and relational time (see Figure 4.1).

A person is distributed across all three dimensions of time: *we age in* absolute time, *we live through* relative, interactive and intersubjective time, and *we embody* relational and intra-subjective time.

What these categories suggest is both a new *and an old* approach to the politics and social policy of time.

Figure 4.1: Dimensions of time

A radical politics of social time

The trick performed by capitalism is both institutional (it freezes space) and hegemonic (it compels us to believe that space cannot be unfrozen). 'There is no alternative' is the enduring slogan of a corporate-dominated capitalism in which markets follow an 'iron law' and economic gravity flattens everything onto the same surface. According to Harvey (1996, pp 329-33), radical politics must therefore be rooted in a notion of social space since only this expresses the collective power that agents have to shape the spatial environments to which they belong and out of which their identities are shaped. A truly social space is never frozen, because those who inhabit it always have the power to reconfigure it. Rather than being immobilised, the agent is that which always embodies and brings forth new spatial relations.

If we follow Harvey's lead, a radical politics must also be rooted in the concept of social time, that is, in the struggles to control time and the ways in which time is valued (Schor, 2010, pp 100-14, 178-9). To unfreeze space we must unfreeze time, and *vice versa*. Rather than being immobilised by the 40-hour working week, multiplied (typically) across approximately 48 weeks per year and 40-50 years, and rather than accept the dominance of the productivist work ethic in which labour, or 'wage-dependency', is regarded as the most virtuous form of activity (Beder, 2000), a radical politics seeks new spatial and temporal geographies:

> ... a radical shift from the historically prevailing tyranny of necessary labor-time to the conscious adoption and creative use of disposable time.... (Mészáros, 2008, p 344; see also pp 177-8, 344-8; Negri, 2005, p 9)

In particular, radicals have long sought to reduce the length of the working week (Kropotkin, 2007, pp 133-41; Schor, 2010, p 163-8). A slogan used by some trades unions – 'From the people who brought you the weekend and the holiday' – captures the extent to which discretionary time had to be wrestled away from the grip of political and economic elites.

This was necessary for the reasons Thompson (1991, Chapters 4, 5) highlights in his famous account. While in the 'moral economy' people only laboured for as long as was necessary to provide them with necessities (once their duties to landowners were fulfilled), industrial capitalism required people to labour for as many hours as possible in order to produce the surplus needed for the further accumulation of capital (Thompson, 1991, pp 274-84). And having been obligated to produce that surplus, people must then be enjoined through advertising and psychocultural norms to devour its consumer goods, to need what they are compelled to want. 'More, more, more' becomes the mantra of modern economics (Gorz, 1989, pp 112-13).

The welfare state, as indicated above, represents a partial victory. The power of capital is partially regulated and social wealth is subjected to fairer distributions than would prevail otherwise. Battles over time were central to this settlement. The working week was gradually reduced in length, holidays were lengthened and the right to free time was enshrined in the 1948 United Nations Declaration of Human Rights.

But this was always an uneasy and ambivalent compromise. State welfare and the Keynesian mixed economy still obeyed a capitalist logic. Even during the relatively egalitarian politics of the 1950s-1970s there were limits to the fairness of social distributions. Time was partly socialised, but only within fairly narrow confines. And once capitalist elites found a way of breaking free of that post-Second World War settlement, they did so.

So from the 1980s onwards this shift propelled the dominance of an economic liberal agenda that served corporate and business interests by swinging distributions away from wages and benefits and back towards profits and shares.[2] Thus was forgotten the battles about time that had characterised earlier periods of political radicalism. There have been important skirmishes, such as social democrats' insistence on enhancing paternity leave and work–life balance (Gornick and Meyers, 2008), but to argue for a shorter working week today is to risk looking like an ideological dinosaur. 'Don't you believe in the work ethic? Think of the mischief the underclass will cause if their time isn't being constantly filled and monitored.'

So far as poverty, inequality and injustice go, one of the biggest elephants in an already crowded room is that of time (Stewart et al, 2009, pp 8-16). What matters is not simply poverty, but how many hours people have to work in order to avoid poverty, and the type of jobs to which the disadvantaged have access (Goodin et al, 2008, pp 16-19). We might applaud a country for having low poverty rates but condemn it if the least well-off have to work an average of 60 hours per week in jobs that are repetitive, trivial and unfulfilling. Goodin et al also observe that the combined 'time-or-money poverty rate' is between two to five times higher than the 'money poverty' rate in Germany, France, Australia and the US. Of the countries they researched, only in Sweden and Finland are the rates broadly similar. In other words, poverty research must make reference to both income and time (Leisering and Leibfried, 1999, pp 240-3; Kuchler and Goebel, 2003, p 364; Whelan et al, 2003; Gough, 2013, pp 208-9).

In conclusion, a radical politics of social time has to make structural, systemic disadvantages central to its analysis if new spatial and temporal geographies are to emerge.

Environmentalism

This is all complicated by another dimension. Environmentalists believe that the timescale with which economic and social policies are typically concerned is too short, neglecting the interests and needs of, and our obligations towards, future generations (Fitzpatrick, 2003, Chapter 7; Page, 2006, Chapter 2). A longer timescale should encompass not just humans but future generations of non-human species too, giving rise to some knotty philosophical and political problems (Carter, 2011).

Let's consider one of the principal ones. Why do most environmentalists challenge the short-term anthropocentrism which, favouring the present generation of humans, dominates our systems of governance? One reason is that such short-termism is seen as counterproductive.

Imagine a hedonist, Jeffrey, who lives each day as if it was his last. On Monday he drinks excessively, injects copious drugs and gambles all his money. Unless Jeffrey is very lucky he won't experience too many days like this. The person who lives for today exclusively will quickly burn out. In other words, the shorter the periods of time that the short-termist regards as valuable, the fewer such periods are likely to be available to him. So, if there is difficulty in estimating the scope and nature of our long-term obligations, there is as great a problem in restricting ourselves to the very short term. Even short-termists have an interest in lengthening their lives.

For economists, the problem occurs in debates about the discount rate (Gollier, 2012; see also Fitzpatrick, 2003, pp 137-40). Let's say that a malevolent economist offers you a series of choices:

You can either receive £100 today, or receive £1,000	20 years	in the future
	10 years	
	5 years	
	1 year	
	6 months	
	1 month	
	1 day	

Clearly, the shorter the period of time before we receive the higher sum, the more likely we are to defer gratification. Furthermore, the higher the sum, the longer we might we willing to wait in order to receive it.

You can either receive £100 today, or receive £1 million	20 years	in the future
	10 years	
	5 years	
	1 year	
	6 months	
	1 month	
	1 day	

The higher the discount rate, the more we favour present-day benefits over future ones, and the more we prefer to avoid burdens today and, instead, defer them to tomorrow. In environmental terms, a high discount rate means prioritising the interests of the present generation; a low rate means treating the needs and interests of present and future generations on a more equal basis. In other words, short-term anthropocentrism applies a very high discount rate.

Now if Jeffrey's example holds, the higher the discount rate, the more self-defeating it is. Jeffrey's ideal is to indulge himself as much as he wants so long as someone else suffers the consequences. But we *do* experience the consequences of our recklessness. Neglect regarding flood defences during the 2005 New Orleans floods was a stark illustration of this. With extreme weather events increasing in frequency and severity, injustices committed against future generations may also be injustices we also impose on ourselves.

Yet we prefer a high discount rate because our economies are characterised by negative externalities (Stern, 2007, pp 27–8; and see Chapter Eight, this volume). An externality is that which is produced *through* an interaction but which is not factored *into* the interaction. If you wish to purchase my widgets, then I will charge you a competitive price based on the cost of the raw materials, production and transportation, plus a reasonable profit for myself. But these calculations do not take other costs into account. The van transporting the widgets contributes to the noise, congestion and pollution experienced by Bob, whose lives near my factory. The negative effects of my business thus produce social costs, for example, pollution causes ill health that entitles Bob to healthcare partly funded from my taxes. But since such social costs will be borne by everyone, while the profits of selling widgets accrue to me alone, I have no reason to factor such external costs into my business. GDP measurements are notoriously ineffective at distinguishing between activity that is and is not socially and ecologically destructive (Jackson, 2002, 2009, pp 32-4; also Stiglitz et al, 2010).

Thus, we seek a high discount rate because even when the consequences are visited on the present generation, an individual gambles that the costs of his activities will be spread across the entire community, particularly those – for example, the poorest – who lack the resources and political voice to do much about it.

Externalities extend across space, time and species. Negative spatial externalities occur when the global warming produced by wealthier nations has a most severe impact on the global poor (Osbahr, 2007, p 3). There are also negative temporal externalities in that present activities build up an ecological debt that may have immediate effects (such as New Orleans) but that also magnify across time (Purdy, 2008). And negative externalities are disproportionately visited on other species if even modest estimates of species extinction are correct. There is no rule demanding that negative externalities will have an impact across all sectors of space, time and species, but it seems reasonable to assume that the more we are governed by short-term self-interest, the more likely it is that they will.

So, in supporting a lower discount rate, environmentalists argue in favour of 'internalities' and positive externalities.[3] By an 'internality' is meant the process of factoring external costs into a transaction. A moral economy would treat Bob's wellbeing as important rather than as costs that can be ignored, deferred or borne by the community at large. Prices would need to reflect, or internalise, the full social and ecological costs involved in a market exchange. Typically, this would suggest that prices must rise. If you want to buy fruit from Argentina at your local supermarket, then you should bear the full costs of doing so. And if the prices of socionatural resources rise, then the implications for the poorest are obvious.

But not all external costs are negative. Bob may benefit by living near factories that make more employment opportunities available to him. This would suggest that prices should *fall* where the *positive* externalities of a relevant transaction outweigh the negative ones.

There are very large questions here, of course. What would an economy based on internalities and positive externalities look like (Stern, 2007, pp 352-3)? How low should the discount rate be? And how can we develop the political will to change when – given all the pressures we face in life – so many are reluctant to pay higher prices, to address climate change (although the costs of doing so mount the longer we delay) or to compensate those on lower incomes for those same price rises?[4]

Although there is no straightforward consensus on these matters among environmentalists, one key argument is that our short-term anthropocentrism is ultimately counterproductive. The more negative externalities there are, the more, in an interdependent world, they will interact and so create consequences that rebound on us sooner or later. Despite its apparent irrationality, short-term anthropocentrism persists because we are making a reckless gamble on those rebounds happening *much* later. Our children, grandchildren and great grandchildren may not thank us.

In sum, a green economy would frame itself across a longer timescale – Pinker (2011, pp 736-8) suggests that as societies evolve, they become more orientated towards the future. In the near future this is likely to involve some difficult conflicts and trade-offs. For instance, Rosnick (2013) estimates that reducing the US working week by 0.5 per cent per year would, by the end of the century, eliminate 25-50 per cent of the global warming that is not already locked in by reducing levels of consumption. However, this would entail the majority of US workers taking a pay cut unless there was significant redistribution from those – the top 1 per cent – who have acquired most of the income gains made since the 1970s (Stiglitz, 2012). In this and other respects, for example, rising energy and food prices, ensuring that measures to tackle climate change do not exacerbate poverty demands a commitment of economic resources and political will that few developed nations appear ready to offer.

Nonetheless, Schor (2010, pp 157-63) observes that trade-off economics must be eventually replaced by win–win approaches that yield double and even triple dividends. First, ecological regeneration restores the natural assets on which economic wealth depends. Resource depletion is, in the long term, more costly than regeneration (Stern, 2007, pp xv-xix). Second, when such regeneration is engineered by those who depend on natural assets, this not only benefits them monetarily, but also empowers communities and raises wellbeing. This requires personal and communal forms of shares in, and rights to, socionatural resources. Third, therefore, the political voice of the disenfranchised can be revitalised. Yielding these three dividends simultaneously suggests an economy of 'trade-ons' in which each becomes the condition for realising the others.

Ecosocial poverty revisited

How might the debates sketched above shape our understanding of poverty?

Take the taxonomy in Figure 4.2. Those in zone 1 have little by way of assets, although they possess large amounts of disposable time: they are asset-poor and time-rich. However, without the assets that can buy access to fulfilling, participative activities, that time is often 'empty time'. Those in zone 2 arguably have the worst of both worlds (Goodin et al, 2008, pp 16-18). They are both asset-*and* time-poor, having to spend large amounts of time in low-paid employment or other activities such as carework, without accumulating the socioeconomic assets to compensate. This represents 'treadmill time', digging holes and filling them

Figure 4.2: Social time zones

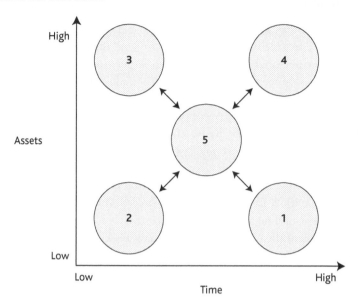

in again. Something similar happens to people in zone 3 but, while being time-poor, they are at least compensated through the possession of considerable assets; for example, this 'potential time' would describe the position of many well-paid, middle-class professionals (Bunting, 2004; Goodin et al, 2008, pp 77-80). Those in zone 4 have the best of both worlds, for example, those who have retired on large pensions and can experience 'sovereign time'. Many in zones 1-3 yearn for zone 4, although only some in zone 3 have a realistic chance of attaining it.

To what extent does this taxonomy correspond to social realities? Like any model we should be wary of editing the facts to fit the hypothesis. Rather than inhabiting one zone exclusively, it is likely that many people experience several during their lives. Someone on a low income may save so that once a year, during a foreign holiday, they temporarily experience 'sovereign time'. A male breadwinner household may include a zone 3 husband and a zone 2 wife. Nonetheless, to the extent that these zones capture social divisions, the research of Goodin et al (2008) suggests that social democratic countries possess few instances of zones 1 and 4 – because they are more economically, politically and culturally equal – and more social mobility (also OECD, 2010, Chapter 5). In many respects, then, the social democratic ideal is to make 5, where the possession of assets does not require the sacrifice of excessive amounts of time, as large and inclusive as possible.[5] This ideal of 'socialised time' has both socioeconomic and environmental dimensions. Let's examine these in turn (see also Chapter Eight, this volume).

Socialised time 1

First, zone 5 embodies the view that time is a social resource interwoven with other resources. The time we have available to us, and the use we make of it, is not simply a matter of personal determination but largely one of social opportunities and dis/advantages. Since zones 1 and 2 are more likely to be occupied by those on low incomes, the just distribution of time cannot be separated from other questions of distributive justice. A cooperatively organised economy is one that harmonises differing asset-time paths (that is, it clusters zones 1-4 towards 5), recognising that the quantity and quality of time available for individuals, families and communities is influenced by what we give to one another as fellow citizens. Time becomes an object of progressive government intervention.

This contrasts with a free market capitalism in which possession frequently implies dispossession. The acquisitive practices that have characterised the post-1980s were bought at the cost of greater inequality, relative deprivation and social exclusion. This applies not only to income and wealth, but also to time. Snider (1998) documents the extent to which employees are suspected of stealing time from their employers when, so often, it is the other way around. To possess time economic liberalism encourages you to dispossess others of theirs, forcing them to steal time from themselves to compensate.

As indicated earlier, over the last four decades growth has been diverted towards profits and capital to the disadvantage of both earnings (including many on middle incomes) and the social wage (there has been downward pressure on social expenditure) (Kumhof et al, 2012):

> ... while most countries have experienced a declining share of wages in national income over the last four decades, the decline in the wage share in the UK is particularly high by international standards. (Reed and Himmelweit, 2012, p 5)

And as the proportionate values of wages fall, so people must work longer hours or take more jobs (Ehrenreich, 2001; Toynbee 2003). As the value of the state pension tumbles, so people are required to extend their working lives, a burden that falls most heavily on those on low incomes. The household debts that came to characterise *laissez faire* capitalism – and which drove the 2008 financial crash – were accumulated not only in the form of credit cards and mortgages, but in a time-squeeze experienced by many millions (Schor, 1992, 2012), all of which contrasts with the more balanced welfare state capitalism of the 1950s and 1960s. Social policies have bowed to this shift by becoming more and more conditional.

The temporal interventions of the economic liberal state have two functions. First, they keep the relatively affluent tied to zone 3, envying the securities of zone 4 that remain out of reach. Zone 4 is so enticing, and zones 1 and 2 so undesirable, that many in zone 3 are compelled to sacrifice short-term wellbeing for the long-term hopes of entering zone 4. Second, those interventions seek to expand zone 2. Social insurance is eroded, trades unions are attacked, labour market regulations are dismantled, corporate and higher rates of taxation are lowered, benefits are reduced and conditionalities are increased. To put it crudely, the aim is to get as many of the disadvantaged into shit jobs for shit wages. Keep them busy and keep them underpaid.

Both the middle and poorer classes experience acute forms of insecurity, as a result, with the former encouraged to blame the latter and the latter encouraged to blame themselves – which means that each strata blames the one below it for its feelings of anxiety and fear. Insecurity then motivates people to support the kind of punitive social policies for which the US stands as an exemplar (Standing, 2011). We punish those less advantaged in order to increase the social and moral distances between them and us. We seek security by making others insecure. Keep them busy and underpaid and at each other's throats.

Socialised time 2

Second, one outcome of free market capitalism is that people are diverted away from other forms of value and wellbeing, particularly those centred on the natural environment. By chasing the zones above us, and by individualising our fate, we are seduced into a competitive, aspirational rat race. We are encouraged to seek individualised solutions to social problems, to jump from zone to zone rather than trying, collectively, to reshape the composition and position of the zones vis-à-vis one another.

The time devoted to earning and spending is not only time taken away from preserving and enriching the natural world; it is a time-use that may help to destroy that which needs preserving. Those in zones 1 and 2 may certainly care about ecological issues, but lack the time and/or the money to do much about it. Those in zone 3 can afford to care monetarily, but may have little time or energy for much else. You can tend a garden (it's therapeutic and good exercise) or clean rubbish away from a wood, but what meaningful contribution can you make beyond the local?

True, those in zone 3 can always choose to downsize but, in a world of rising prices, where being 'left behind' risks a fall into the zones below, this is a gamble that relatively few have the courage to take. To downsize is to 'downtime' but, fearful of being thrown off into those zones of impoverishment, constant struggle and surveillance by public and private agencies, we are driven to sacrifice the only time we have (our all-too brief lives) in order to avoid being on the wrong end of socioeconomic inequalities. We embrace a time-squeeze for fear that, if we don't, others will force us to do so on their terms.

Thus it feels easier to seek status by abiding with the norms of earning and consuming. Working for another, in paid employment, often exhausts our capacity and energy to work *for and with* others in a common enterprise; 'leisure time' often means recovering from paid employment and recharging the batteries in preparation for another bout. Environmental waste becomes an acceptable compensation for the effects of social and human waste.

Ecotemporal deprivation

We are now ready to revisit the categories and principles left at the end of Chapter Three.

Socionatural resources are spatial but also temporal in that they endure through time – perhaps the zones in Figure 4.2 should be reimagined as *space/time zones* (see Fitzpatrick, 2001). In addition:

- they are the means through which humans endure through time;
- human interventions affect the quantity, quality and longevity of socionatural resources.

Both of which are made harder by what I now call 'ecotemporal deprivation'.[6]

You can be deprived *within* time. Suspecting they face decades of empty time, some young people from impoverished backgrounds are more compelled to seek solace in gangs, violence, drugs or other self-destructive behaviour than their wealthier peers. They are lectured on the virtues of hard work and aspiration. Yet the treadmill time of zone 2 resembles the labours of Sisyphus; the hole you are filling in today is the one you dug yesterday. Your consolation is that at least you are thought of as more deserving than those anti-social scroungers in zone 1.

And you can be deprived *by* time. As argued earlier, the hierarchies of contemporary capitalism are immobilising, disconnecting individuals from one another and present selves from future selves. To be poor means being less able to endure through time because the lower your income, the lower your life expectancy and 'healthy life expectancy' is likely to be. This being the case, many are less able to preserve socionatural resources than they might wish. This is not necessarily because people lack the correct motivations, but is primarily due to social institutions and economic practices.

Ecotemporal deprivation thus means being controlled by time rather than being able to control it, with others, through possession of sufficient socioeconomic and socionatural resources. As in Chapter Three, this argument can be broken down:

(1) *Not possessing enough time.* Once a year, the UK Taxpayers' Alliance identifies the day on which, as they put it, people stop working for the government through their taxes and start working for themselves, their agenda being to lower the tax rate. The Trades Union Congress (TUC) similarly calculates how much unpaid work, including overtime, employees effectively perform for their employers. A comparable exercise can be performed in respect of socionatural resources (Simms et al, 2006). As these resources absorb a greater proportion of household income, how much time do people have to spend acquiring the money to afford them? How much time do we effectively give

to energy companies, for instance? And what effects on the quantity and quality of time does this have for low-income households? Thus, poverty implies restrictions in the quantities of available time.

(2) *Not having sufficient mobility across time.* If you possess a good wage – or shares, inheritances, rental property, and so forth – the easier it becomes to plan for the future, to protect yourself against contingencies and to respond to opportunities. What Giddens (1991, pp 7-8; see also Leisering and Leibfried, 1999, pp 240-3) calls the biographisation of the life course is easier for middle- than for low-income households. Should I retire a few years early and live modestly? Should I continue to work and enjoy a higher retirement income? These are questions that those on low incomes are less able to ask themselves. The higher the social wage, the more people on low incomes can approximate to that middle-class freedom of choice. Redistributions and measures to smooth out the life course are about more than readjustments to final income; they are about fostering a sense of mutual security in which we can all plan ahead. But with the erosion of the state pension, the evisceration of social insurance and the polarisation of labour markets, that sense of collective shelter goes too. And as socionatural resources become more expensive, so they contribute to this temporal immobilisation.

(3) *Not inhabiting valued times.* The social nature of time is something our common-sense intuitions easily miss. Surely a minute is no longer for you than it is for me! Yet the subjective experience of time belies that intuition. You inhabit a zone distinct to that inhabited by someone living a few miles away (Fitzpatrick, 2001). Eight hours at work *is not the same* as eight hours of enforced inactivity. Eight hours at a job you love *is not the same* as eight hours at a treadmill job you hate but must endure because it pays the bills. Those who in one sense inhabit the same society are, in another, living in different zones. Space and time therefore fragment. At the periphery of the labour market this usually means a rotation between no work and 'shit work' under the disciplinary tutelage of the workfare state. Devalued people are those who are more likely to inhabit and be trapped within the marginalised zones of 1 and 2 (in Figure 4.2).

(4) *Not being able to control time.* Restriction, immobilisation and devaluation combine to leave the disadvantaged without sufficient control of their time. Those who can afford to buy the time of others (nannies, cleaners, personal assistants, and so on) are not only saving their own time, they are using time as a currency to acquire a higher social status. By contrast, those who experience treadmill time are those who cannot afford *not* to sell their time, servicing the domestic needs of 'the middle' (zone 3) or the privileged (zone 4). The more someone is dependent on selling their labour, the more they are dependent on selling not only their physical industry and/or cognitive skills, but on

trading in a large proportion of the only time they will ever have. Control over time and control over space therefore converge. With rising house prices and the separation of affluent from non-affluent neighbourhoods, someone who works as a cleaner or a security guard (or in several jobs) may have to travel great distances, spending precious hours every week, just getting to and from their low-paid employment. Those on low incomes are kept on the move, tramping from low-wage job to low-wage job, training scheme to training scheme.

(5) *Not adequately recognising the extent to which time is shared.* Against this background of social dislocation, the sense that the natural rhythms of time are part of the public, common good risks vanishing. As the post-war bell-curve becomes more bipolar (see page 58), the sense that the availability and meaning of time to one group is entwined with the availability and meaning of time to others begins to erode. Poorer neighbourhoods are the sites of lives lived repetitively, inadequate refuges from the cycle of no work/shit work that are statistically likely to ensnare your children too. Affluent neighbourhoods are signs of self-worth and transports into a secure future: promises that the mortgage will be paid off and your children will inherit your privileges. Poverty increases the risk of mental and physical ill health, reducing the quality and duration of life. Seasonal change is more likely to be life-threatening to the vulnerable, whether because of inadequate heating during cold winters or inadequate cooling during increasingly oppressive summers. Leisure time is altered depending on whether you have a decent garden, or access to parks and the countryside.

(6) *Not caring for shared time.* Thus, the pooling of time becomes individualised: you borrow time from yourself rather than teaming with others to enhance the time available to all. The former ethos – mutual systems of security to protect against shared vulnerabilities – is replaced by a them-versus-us hardening of attitudes ('why should I donate my time, that is, taxable earnings, to undeserving strangers?'). The socialisation of time, the counter-lottery to the brute luck lotteries of birth and death, is weaker than before. And if our sense of shared social time has eroded, then what chance for an appreciation, sharing and protection of the natural world? Time devoted to wage-dependency and consumerism is time that could have been spent on 'internalities' and positive externalities. A time = money market society distracts us from the intrinsic value of nature (Adam, 1998, pp 65-9). Can possessive individualists establish effective normative and ethical connections to other species and future generations? Can those who interpret poverty as behavioural manage to lower the discount rate and internalise costs? Will the relatively affluent agree to pay the full ecological cost of socionatural resources while protecting those lower down the income and wealth ladder? Dislocated in time and space from nature we become desensitised to the temporary but

beautiful fragilities of our surroundings. Oblivious to our own mortalities we are disagreeably surprised at the speed with which our lives get away from us.

As in Chapter Three, I assume that an ecosocial approach to poverty implies that (1)–(4) are incomplete without reference to (5) and (6), and vice versa. I also assume that they correspond to the principles outlined in Chapter Two:

- 'Minimum entitlements' relate closely to items (1)-(3) in the above list, for example, being entitled to socionatural resources at a reasonable proportion of one's income in order to enhance the quantity and quality of time available.
- 'Property rights' relate closely to (3) and (4). Think of bulk purchasing schemes, begun in the Netherlands, where communities bargain collectively for lower energy deals than companies are otherwise willing to offer (Scott-Smith, 2011, pp 8-9).
- 'Political voice and democratic representation' relate closely to (4) and (5), that is, having a stake and voice in the firms and organisations that manage, sustain and distribute socionatural resources.
- 'Obligations of value' non-humans and future generations relate closely to items (5) and (6), since if we affect the quantity, quality and longevity of socionatural resources, and if they are the means through which humans endure, then there is an obligation to nurture, improve and bequeath what we have inherited.

As such:

> Poverty implies forms of temporal alienation and exclusion, for example, immobilisation within the residualised and devalued zones of the empty and treadmill times that characterise economic liberal capitalism.
>
> Those temporal deprivations affect and are affected by a relative lack of access to, and control of, the socionatural resources that influence the freedoms and capacities of individuals to endure through time.
>
> Ecosocial poverty therefore incorporates an ecotemporal deprivation that impedes individuals' power and opportunity to flourish and to fulfil their obligations to value and care for others (which includes enabling socionatural resources to endure through time).

Conclusion

Chapter Three explored the spatial dimensions of socionatural resources and proposed that these are highly relational. This chapter has extended that analysis to a further dimension, that of time, and argued that time is also relational. At its best, the classic welfare state enabled social groups to socialise and 'pool' their time, although its successes must in some respects be highly qualified. This is because capitalism's tendency is to immobilise and freeze time, which is why social radicals have long sought to unfreeze it through, for instance, systematic reductions in working hours. To this must be added the problems created by the short-term anthropocentrism that has dominated social and economic systems. Yet high discount rates and negative externalities are things we can no longer afford to indulge. An ecosocial understanding of poverty brings these ideas together. I defined ecotemporal deprivation in terms of the categories introduced in Chapter Three – quantity, mobility, value, control, sharing and caring. As before, these were related to the principles outlined in Chapter Two and the chapter ended with another iteration of ecosocial poverty.

We are now in a position to summarise and consolidate the analyses of Chapters One to Four, giving us a basic model that we will apply throughout Chapters Six to Ten.

Notes

[1] In theory, if less frequently in practice.

[2] In discussing social changes I am aware of the need to take other factors into account: new technologies (including the internet), globalisation in a post-communist era, newly industrialising countries (especially China), and so forth. Economic liberalism has driven some of this, but to some extent it is also a consequence of such broader changes.

[3] A lower rate but not a zero rate, which would value present and *all* future generations equally. Bizarrely, Skidelsky and Skidelsky (2012, pp 130-1) condemn environmentalists for supporting a zero rate, a crude and unsubstantiated generalisation.

[4] Environmentalists say that in order to lower the discount rate we should construct an economy of internalities and positive externalities. However, we could do the latter without lowering the rate to any great extent; for example, we could continue to prioritise the present, and we could continue to neglect the interests of non-humans. The 'counterproductive' argument being made here may supply an adequate response, but these 'large questions' illustrate why the debate is ultimately a moral one, that is, what we owe to others as well as ourselves. At some point over the last half-century, however, economics and moral philosophy parted company, a divorce for which Keynesian social democrats are as much to blame as economic liberals (more used to invoking Adam Smith than actually reading him).

[5] Economic liberalism pushes the zones away from 5 and from each other.

[6] Which is not to claim that spatial deprivation is perfectly conjoined with temporal deprivation. An elderly person with a disability may live in a beautiful neighbourhood while experiencing too much empty time. Someone may have a deeply fulfilling job and a good wage but live in run-down surroundings. The fact that poverty has always been complex and multifaceted need not prevent us from sketching a general picture.

FIVE

Summary

The purpose of this chapter is to summarise Chapters One to Four, and to offer a bridge to Chapters Six to Ten.

Chapter One welcomed the capabilities approach's recognition of complexity, pluralism and diversity, but proposed that it is flawed in several respects. First, it has failed to ground itself in a universalist frame of reference that is both sufficiently robust and flexible. And second, it unjustifiably downgrades the importance of income and wealth, material resources, economic power and the distributive paradigm, both to the capabilities approach itself and to any understanding of contemporary capitalism. The chapter then adapts the work of Holland in identifying a category of meta-capabilities (that which makes other capabilities possible), based on the premise that the interdependency of social and natural environments is both strong and fundamental. The chapter ended by suggesting that in so far as 'poverty' implies a multidimensional 'poverty of capabilities', we ought to focus on the socionatural conditions underpinning those multiple dimensions. Thus, an ecosocial understanding of poverty defines it as the deprivations resulting from an inadequate distribution of, and participative access to, those resources that are key to both natural and social environments.

The aim in Chapter Two was to formulate an appropriate conceptualisation of resources. It began by arguing that natural assets have not been given sufficient attention in a range of literatures. It then critiqued a principled justification for ecological modernisation by proposing that intrinsic value should be at the heart of social thinking and social reforms. We should look beyond ecological modernisation to more radical approaches, albeit ones still rooted in the pragmatic need to apply economic categories and ideas to the natural world. This then inspired the first elements of an ecosocial account via a discussion of decommodification, alienation and exclusion, domainship and ownership. This account argues that we lack sufficient control over socioeconomic resources and adequate synergies between socioeconomic and natural resources; it proposes both the socialisation of natural resources but also the 're-naturing' of economic and social relations through an ethic of 'qualified partial ownership'. This led to the idea that 'socionatural resources' should be subject to the principles of minimum entitlements, property rights, political voice and democratic representation, and obligations to value. The chapter closed by offering an initial definition of ecosocial poverty.

Since socionatural resources border, occupy, affect and are affected by space, Chapter Three reviewed several debates relating to social space. During the era of welfare capitalism, this understanding inspired policies that, while flawed, were motivated by a sense of egalitarian justice. Under the 'bipolar' economic liberalism of the last four decades, social spaces have fragmented and diverged. One consequence is that we have become less able and willing to recognise the solidarities that link, and the processes that influence, distant spaces and life courses. The interrelatedness of different spaces is now more likely to manifest itself as mutual estrangements, hostilities and antagonisms. Not surprisingly, social injustice has typically accompanied growing environmental injustices. The chapter then proposed that anti-poverty policies are needed to reattach spaces to one another, but such policies must take ecological imperatives into account. It concluded by defining and outlining the key elements of 'ecospatial deprivation'.

Since space relates to time, Chapter Four reviewed several literatures dealing with time in order to complete our theoretical account. It proposed that welfare systems sometimes socialise time, sometimes reflect broader socioeconomic and temporal inequalities, and sometimes exacerbate those inequalities. For decades now, a social conception of time has given way to 'absolutist time' in which our capacity to alter the collective rhythms of our everyday and communal lives has become institutionally restricted and defined in highly individualised terms. In addition to social dislocations, this encourages the short-term anthropocentrism that is ecologically damaging. Time is made to appear immutable rather than as something we may shape for and with one another as interactive social beings. The chapter offered a model of space/time zones, in which the socialised time of zone 5 represents an alternative ideal to the hierarchies and rigidities of economic liberal capitalism. It concluded by defining and outlining the key elements of 'ecotemporal deprivation'.

On this basis of these chapters, an ecosocial account of poverty:

(1) Is grounded in, but seeks to build on, existing relative (or more accurately, 'relational') understandings of poverty, exclusion and deprivation.

(2) Identifies a dual injustice, that is, in terms of both social *and* natural wealth.

(3) Proposes that we lack an equitable distribution of, sufficient control over and adequate synergies between socioeconomic and 'socionatural resources', such that addressing one type of resource is ineffective unless we address the other.

(4) Recommends a re-socialisation of the economy and a re-naturing of the social via a principle of 'qualified partial ownership'.

(5) Argues that ecosocial poverty implies falling below some decent minimum access to, ownership of and control over key socionatural resources due to malfunctioning social institutions and systems, involving inequalities in rights and obligations.

(6) Specifies the principles against which the distributions, and participative control, of those resources should be assessed:
   • minimum entitlements
   • property rights
   • political voice and democratic representation
   • obligations to value and care for the worth of other beings.

(7) Finds that defining ecosocial poverty as a deprivation of socionatural resources implies various spatial and temporal deprivations which can be broken down into several categories:
- *Quantity:* not possessing enough space and time due to systemic, institutional inequalities, for example, space/time zones, which allow some to flourish at the expense of others.
- *Mobility:* not possessing sufficient mobility across space (geographical segregations) and time (lacking the power to plan for the future and insure against uncertainties and vulnerabilities).
- *Value:* inhabiting space/time zones that devalue because they are widely devalued.
- *Control:* lacking the social and political voice needed to challenge and reverse the above disempowerments and disadvantages.
- *Sharing:* misjudging and underestimating the extent to which environments (social, natural and socionatural) are interdependent.
- *Caring:* lacking the capacities and opportunities (but not necessarily the motivations) to preserve, sustain and enhance the value of shared social spaces and natural habitats.

Chapter Two also noted that minimum entitlements, property rights, political voice and obligations to care are both distributive and procedural (recall Table 3.1).

In short, ecosocial poverty refers to,

> Ecospatial and ecotemporal deprivations due to socioeconomic disadvantages and a relative lack of access to, and control of, key socionatural resources.

We can also now assemble the main elements of this account and contrast it with other interpretations of poverty (see Table 5.1). So far as the ecosocial row is concerned, please note that this is a preliminary sketch only, and we elaborate on it in Chapters Six to Ten (for a summary, see the Conclusion).

I appreciate that breaking complex debates down in this way is a classic hostage to fortune. First, because when we mention 'causes' we are talking about what appear to be causes from within a particular explanatory framework. We hope that our framework is robust and reasonably accurate, but debates are clearly replete with ideological and methodological contestation. Second, even within a framework, what counts as what isn't always clear. You become unemployed, experience stress and develop a chronic illness that prevents you from getting a new job. Which is cause and which is symptom? The original act of being made unemployed? But that itself may need to be contextualised. Despite these difficulties, and at the risk of oversimplification, I propose to use the cause/symptoms/solutions categorisation in order to make sense of the data and debates in the chapters ahead.

That done, we can now construct a matrix by fitting together our four principles, six categories of deprivation and five socionatural resources: energy,

Table 5.1: Accounts of poverty

	Causes and explanations	Symptoms	Solutions
Economic liberal	– State intervention – Restricted freedom – High taxes and public spending – Moral hazard – Benefit dependency – Social egalitarianism	– Bloated public sector – Lack of, or malfunctioning, agency – Ailing economy – Dependency culture – Underclass	– Minimal state – Reduced social spending – Greater role for profit-making providers, eg private insurance – Incentives – Means-tested safety-nets – Workfare
Conservative	– Liberal relativism – Stress on rights rather than obligations – Moral hazard – State/public crowding out family, charity and community	– Moral deficits – Intergenerational transmission of 'cultures of poverty' – Erosion of civic values (eg laziness and criminality) – Underclass	– Enforceable obligations – Moral paternalism – Workfare – Stronger families and communities – Social 'remoralisation'
Social democratic	– Deregulated markets – Inequalities restricting opportunities and social mobility – Lack of affordable childcare – Lack of decent wages and jobs	– Public squalor vs private affluence – Social exclusion – Unmet needs and deprivation – Vulnerabilities – Debilitating inequalities, eg in health and longevity	– Labour market regulation – Economic growth – Social rights and fairer distributions – Public spending – Social insurance – Universal welfare services
Socialist	– Capitalist class structures – Exploitation – Systemic and undeserved dis/advantages – Capitalist state – Private ownership and control of key resources	– Social and moral distancing – Pathologisation of social problems – Class domination and bias – Profits valued more than people	– Economic democracy – Socialisation of capital – Cooperative forms of association – Use-value and decommodification – Planning – Equality of conditions

(continued)

Table 5.1: Accounts of poverty (continued)

	Causes and explanations	Symptoms	Solutions
Feminist	– Gender-bias in state welfare and public services – Labour market discrimination and disadvantage – Public/private divisions – Sexual division of labour – Male-dominated political systems	– Lack of affordable childcare – Gendered wage inequalities – Restricted employment and career opportunities – Lower benefit entitlements for women – Greater risk of poverty for women	– Extensive parental leave and childcare – Equal pay and removal of 'glass ceiling' – Improved access to occupational and state benefits – Cultural change in caring responsibilities – Greater recognition of value of unpaid work
Ecosocial	– Unsustainable economic growth – Growth-dependent social distributions – Climate change agenda separate from economic and social policies – Alienation and exclusion from social and natural wealth	– Corporate dominance of key socionatural resources – Profit-based exploitation of resources – Spatial and temporal deprivations – Increasing vulnerabilities related to climate change and relevant deprivations, eg fuel and food poverty	– Limits on carbon emissions – Green taxes and sustainable growth – Fairer distributions and democratic control of socionatural resources – Internalities and positive externalities

food, land, air and water. As Schuppert (2012) notes, there is a risk here. Resources are dissimilar in various ways. Water and air transcend property boundaries in ways that is not the case with land, for instance. To talk about rights to and the distribution of 'resources' might therefore overlook the extent to which resources differ from one another. I try to allow for key differences in what follows, but certain nuances and subtleties have been skated across.

What we end up with is Table 5.2, although note the resources row has been shaped to reflect the organisation of the chapters to come (hence the reference to Land I and Land II).

The task for the rest of the book is to fill in those empty cells. What makes things slightly more complicated is the need to ensure consistency between this

Table 5.2: An ecosocial matrix 2

Principles	Deprivation categories	Social and natural interdependencies				
		Socionatural resources				
		Energy	*Food*	*Land I*	*Land II*	*Air/water*
Minimum entitlements	Quantity					
	Mobility					
Property rights	Value					
	Control					
Voice and democracy	Sharing					
Obligations to value	Caring					

matrix and Table 5.1. Therefore, each of the following chapters reviews the causes, symptoms and possible solutions to poverty in light of the particular socionatural resource being discussed. The template around which the discussions are based is represented in Table 5.3. Completing this template within each chapter will then enable us to fill in the empty cells of Table 5.2 once we reach the concluding chapter.

The essential question for the following chapters is this: to what extent does an ecosocial approach allow us to understand existing literatures, critique recent developments and prescribe future courses of action?

Table 5.3: An ecosocial matrix 3

	Causes	Symptoms	Solutions
Quantity			
Mobility			
Value			
Control			
Sharing			
Caring			

ECOSOCIAL POLICIES

SIX

Energy and fuel poverty[1]

What do you do when you switch on a kettle? You trigger a flow of electrons that warm the filament and heat the water. Those electrons are transmitted down a distribution system (transformers, power lines and substations) from a plant in which turbines and generators are powered in any number of ways: by burning natural gas, oil or coal; nuclear energy; or alternative energy (such as hydropower, or geothermal and biomass sources).

What do you do when you switch on a boiler? The gas comes into your home from a low-pressure distribution zone, which is in turn fed by a national transmission system in which compressor stations push the gas through 173,000 miles of iron, steel and polyethylene mains pipeline. Gas enters the system from terminals attached to pipelines from the North Sea or from other countries – although liquefied, natural gas can be delivered by boat.

In short, the simplest act connects you to vast histories played out across immense distances. The engines of the last 250 years of social development and economic growth have been fossil fuels (coal, oil, natural gas), formed over hundreds of millions of years from the decomposition and compression of dead organisms.[2] Organic matter originates in turn from the heavier elements formed in the last stages of a star's life billions of years ago, before it ejected those elements violently into space. All energy is ultimately solar energy.

Energy prices have been rising dramatically for a number of years now (Boardman, 2010a, pp 73-5), and although we should be wary of predicting the future – much depending on the availability of oil and whether other energy sources can be found (Yergin, 2011, pp 242-3, 419-20) – the era of cheap energy may not return. In any event, ecological imperatives require us to reduce our use of fossil fuels, and develop cleaner energy sources, which is likely to further increase prices, at least in the short term.

This raises three questions for social and environmental policy-making (Diesendorf, 2011). First, how can we protect the incomes of the poorest as energy prices rise? Second, how do we ensure that all people are sufficiently warm while also achieving reductions in carbon emissions? Finally, how do we manage the climate change transition as the problem shifts from the need to keep homes warm during cold winters to the need to cool homes during excessively hot summers? (The nightmare scenario is one of colder winters *and* warmer summers.)

That final question is not one we discuss here.[3] So far as the first two questions are concerned, research into fuel poverty which also addresses climate change suggests that the answer to both depends on finding an effective policy synergy. In other words, with an intelligent application of energy-efficiency programmes, government subsidies and coordinated governance, low carbon technologies, tariffs and, yes, traditional transfer policies (living wages, generous pensions, benefits and tax credits) we can both protect the poorest, reducing and eventually eliminating fuel poverty, *and* decrease carbon emissions. Could such a convergence of policy agendas be managed? To what extent does the existing literature speak to the ecosocial approach? Does that approach identify any gaps in existing research and debates?

In setting out to explore those questions this chapter is concerned with gas and electricity, rather than oil (Heinberg, 2011, pp 106-18).[4] It is also largely concerned with the *consumption* of energy, although in one instance I suggest why research and commentary should be more concerned with production and delivery processes. We begin by outlining the basic facts about fuel poverty. Then we consider the synergies and possible trade-offs identified by the literature dealing with fuel poverty and climate change. Finally, I connect these debates to the ecosocial understanding of poverty, as summarised in the previous chapter.

Basic facts

Not surprisingly, buildings account for much of the energy we use and carbon we emit. Buildings are responsible for at least 36 per cent of all GHG emissions and 41 per cent of all CO_2 emissions (Committee on Climate Change, 2010, p 197). They account for 40 per cent of total energy consumption and two-thirds of all electricity consumption (DECC, 2011, pp 29, 136). Of the total amount of energy used in buildings, two-thirds is gas or oil and one-third is electricity. Around three-quarters of this energy is used by the residential sector and the remainder by businesses (not including industrial processes) (Boardman, 2012a, p 5). Changing the design and the use of buildings is therefore central to both the fuel poverty and climate change agendas.

In the UK, a household is defined as fuel-poor if it needs to spend more than 10 per cent of its income on fuel to maintain adequate warmth (21°C degrees for the main living area, 18°C degrees for other occupied rooms).[5] Those experiencing it habitually have to juggle heating costs against other basic needs, such as food. The figures for fuel poverty since calculations began (they have not been calculated every year) are as follows (DECC, 2013b, p 18): 'vulnerable households' are those that contain elderly members, children, people with disabilities or the long-term sick. For instance, Macmillan Cancer Support (2010) found that people who have undergone cancer treatment in the previous year are twice as likely to be in fuel poverty as the rest of the population, and are likely to remain there because of costs associated with the disease.

The trend since 2004 has been upwards, with a sharp peak in 2008-09 that has subsided again (see Table 6.1). According to the DECC (2012, pp 32-5), three-quarters of all fuel-poor households can be found in the lowest two income deciles and the highest rate is among the unemployed, where over 50 per cent of

Table 6.1: UK fuel poverty

Fuel poverty (millions of households)	1996	1998	2001	2002	2003	2004	2005	2006	2007	2008	2009	2010	2011
All UK households	6.5	4.75	2.5	2.25	2	2	2.5	3.5	4	4.5	5.5	4.75	4.5
Vulnerable households	5	3.5	2	1.75	1.5	1.5	2		2.75	3.25	3.75	4.5	4	3.5

households are in fuel poverty. Eighteen per cent of lone parents with dependent children are fuel-poor. And,

> In those households where the oldest person is aged between 65 and 84, over a quarter are in fuel poverty. Over a third of households where the oldest person is aged 85 or over are fuel poor. (DECC, 2012, p 35)

Although a sizable minority of the fuel-poor are owner-occupiers, the majority rent their homes from private or social landlords.

Fuel poverty is caused by rising prices, inadequate incomes and energy-inefficient homes. Government interventions can clearly be counterproductive (by depressing the incomes of the poorest) or helpful (energy-efficiency subsidies can be directed towards new boilers, insulation, double glazing, solar panelling, draught-proofing, and so on). The Labour government attributed the post-2004 increase mainly to rising energy prices that was only partly offset by income growth and greater energy efficiency (DECC, 2009). It should be observed, however, that Labour's record on reducing all forms of poverty began to stall around the same time.

Therefore, although income measures are incomplete (some households may need higher temperatures than those stated in the official definition), there is a close correlation between fuel and income poverty. Being fuel-poor is a good indicator that you are poor in other respects too.

The lower your income, the more difficult it is to provide for basic needs, and the less is available for non-essentials and for savings, thereby affecting individuals' quality of life and sense of security. Also, a low income typically raises opportunity costs, making someone less willing and able to take risks – such as changing jobs – and more likely to be trapped in deprived circumstances. Low-income households are also more likely to use pre-payment meters that disadvantage them compared to customers paying by direct debit.

Liddell and Morris (2010) reviewed a range of literatures and concluded that although reducing fuel poverty has only modest effects on the physical health of adults, there are significant impacts on the respiratory health of children and on the physical health of infants. The mental health effects on adults and adolescents are also encouraging. As Walker and Day (2012, p 70) observe: 'In Sen's terms fuel poverty can have impacts on the capability to achieve a range of valued functionings in everyday life.'

There are some obvious conflicts between some policies designed to reduce fuel poverty and those designed to reduce carbon emissions. On average, the richer the household, the higher the amount of carbon it emits. Roberts (2008, p 4471) observed that the 'poorest 10% of households produce only 45% as much carbon dioxide emissions from their homes as the richest 10%.' More recently, Hargreaves et al (2013, p 5) find that 'the richest 10% of households in Great Britain emit three times more than the poorest 10%.' The poorest are particularly vulnerable to energy prices rises, with a 1 per cent rise in fuel prices likely to result in another 40,000 households entering fuel poverty (Jenkins, 2010, p 832). Clearly, then, trying to suppress carbon use by raising prices – and/or introducing a carbon tax – would have a most severe impact on those least able to afford them and those least responsible for producing emissions in the first place.[6]

Political solutions and prospects

The last Labour government tried to address fuel poverty in several ways.

Economic instruments
- Increasing the incomes of the poorest, for example, through benefits (such as Winter Fuel Payments), and tax credits (such as pension credits).
- Reducing fuel bills through voluntary 'social tariffs' (where the government encourages energy companies to reduce fuel costs for vulnerable and low-income customers) and other 'social price supports' offering additional discounts.

Regulations
- Improved energy efficiencies. Some helped the poorest directly, for example, the Warm Front programme provided grants and reduced annual fuel bills by £360-400 on average; some were more indirect, for example, the boiler scrappage scheme.
- Parallel initiatives such as the Carbon Emissions Reduction Target programme and various Public Service Agreements.

Information
- Publicity campaigns (through helplines, advertising, leaflets and consumer advice networks) to encourage greater energy efficiency, including changes to lifestyles and daily habits, and to encourage low-income households to regularly switch suppliers.
- Improved advice about benefits and welfare rights, for example, some Warm Front recipients were entitled to a subsequent benefit entitlement check and data-sharing.

Since 2010 (for recent developments, see Snell and Thomson, 2014), the Coalition government has:

- introduced a Green Deal Finance and Energy Company Obligation (see below);
- reduced subsidies for solar panel installations;
- exhorted consumers to 'shop around for the best deals';
- indicated it wants to simplify energy bills, reduce the array of energy tariffs and make it easier for households to switch suppliers;
- indicated that Winter Fuel Payments could be withdrawn from affluent pensioners.

Having set ambitious targets for itself, for example, eliminating fuel poverty for all households by 2016, Labour was seduced by the falling energy prices of the late 1990s into believing that fuel poverty could be reduced without introducing substantial changes to energy markets. New Labour therefore wanted to reduce energy costs for low-income households, but was reluctant to challenge energy firms any further. It thought it could humanise markets by working *with* firms in partnerships inspired by a social conscience. The Coalition government has pretty much adopted the same stance.

Take the example of social tariffs. This approach derives from the widespread view that targeting is the most cost-efficient and effective way of assisting the poorest. Baker (2006, pp 28-30) reported that suppliers, regulatory bodies and government representatives all preferred targeting in order that limited resources could reach those most in need. This, despite a wealth of evidence that targeting – by raising administrative costs, complexity, feelings of stigma and so by lowering take-up – is usually less effective than its champions admit (Fitzpatrick, 2012, pp 221-3, 227-8). Thus, barely 25 per cent of the money allocated to relieve fuel poverty actually goes to the fuel-poor (Boardman, 2010b, p 53), since 'passport benefits', such as Income Support and Housing Benefits, do not necessarily identify the fuel-poor accurately.

The attraction for government in addressing fuel poverty lies in the triple dividend doing so might yield. Reductions in fuel poverty:

(1) assist low-income households with knock-on consequences for other social objectives;
(2) facilitate (with government assistance) energy-efficient technologies and firms;
(3) are capable of reducing carbon emissions and providing a potential shock absorber against future climate change, enabling environmental targets to be met.[7]

We have seen that (1) is undermined by rising energy costs and over-confidence in the efficacy of targeting. To these we might add the effects of energy markets in which competition is fairly minimal. In November 2012 the Financial Services

Authority started an investigation following allegations by a whistleblower that the £300 billion wholesale gas market had been frequently manipulated by some of the big energy companies; and even in the absence of such manipulation, the suspicion is wide that prices are quick to rise when wholesale costs increase but slow to fall when those costs come down again.

A combination of austerity economics and the Coalition government's reluctance to pursue an active investment strategy has paralysed (2). Not that Labour's approach was vastly superior. Consumer Focus (2009) found that a major energy-efficiency programme, costing £21 billion in 2009 prices across seven years, would reduce fuel poverty by 83 per cent, prevent the risk of fuel poverty re-occurring in the future and reduce the fuel bills of the fuel-poor by 52 per cent (and their carbon emissions by 59 per cent). This is three times more than the last government was spending.

And even were fuel poverty to be decreasing, the environmental improvements of (3) do not follow automatically, although as Pearce (2012) reports, UK local authorities have often been lazy in assuming otherwise. The 'rebound effect' describes what happens when savings made per unit of energy encourage *more* energy usage (Berners-Lee and Clark, 2013, Chapter 6). A 'direct rebound' happens when consumers use more of the same commodity; an 'indirect rebound' occurs when users switch from one commodity (warmth and household appliances, in this case) on to another which is also energy-intensive (Pett, 2009, p 1676). In short, as bills come down people may jack up the temperature, or spend some of the savings on other carbon-heavy goods, services or activities, so that overall carbon emissions do not decrease or decrease by less than is desirable. The rebound effect potentially makes energy-efficiency measures counterproductive. We review this issue below.

Therefore, triple dividends may or may not exist depending on whether national and local governments and energy firms make genuine, well-funded, coordinated and evidence-based attempts to realise them. Much of the difficulty lies in bringing together short- and long-term imperatives. A solution to fuel poverty that is effective in the short term but that makes it harder to reduce carbon emissions in the long term is no real solution at all. The following literature suggests ways of bringing these timelines together.

Ultimately, however, we have to be concerned not just with the retrofitting of buildings, but their spatial distribution.[8] Anne Power (2008, pp 4489-90) points out that population density falls as households become smaller, for example, more houses are needed as more people choose to live alone. This lower density then means that the housing stock occupies more space and has a greater environmental impact due to higher energy use (it takes more energy to supply two single-occupier houses than a single house occupied by two people).

> Aligning more progressive social policies with environmental limits
> and avoiding the expansion of average space and energy per person
> are critical to sustainability ... we have at least 18 million family-sized

homes, far more than the actual number of families. The distribution of space is highly unequal but we have more, larger homes in the UK than elsewhere in Europe. (Power, 2008, p 4490)

We therefore have to reconcile a series of objectives. First, the need for higher density communities to avoid the disadvantages of low density to which Power draws attention. Since it is the affluent who tend to spread out, occupying the most desirable rural and semi-rural areas, using space more efficiently and sustainably in the form of higher density housing may imply reducing sociospatial inequalities. We consider this issue in Chapters Eight and Nine later. Second, the poorest households often need more space (more and bigger rooms, gardens, and so on), but if this is not to propel an increased and unsustainable level of energy use, then there is a need for greater energy efficiency. This imperative is central to the following discussion.

From trade-offs to synergies?

Before examining specifics it is worth making the point – first raised in Chapter Three – that an ecosocial approach does not pretend that there can ever be a perfect, once-and-for-all solution. This is because a green society has to be constantly remaking itself. There may be ecological limits, but the scale of nature, the extent to which humans are woven within it, and so the intricacies and unintended consequences of our interventions into the natural environment, all mean that we should approach matters in a spirit of flexibility and reflexivity. We should act, plan and reform while leaving enough policy 'spare room' for those acts, plans and reforms to be adapted and revised. Such is implied by the very term 'adaptation'.

An ecosocial agenda therefore means (1) acknowledging the extent to which there are currently few synergies between social and environmental goals; (2) accepting that there can never be perfect synergies between those goals; and (3) working to promote synergies wherever possible. The contentious claim here is (2). Observing that there can never be perfect synergies is to concede that trade-offs will always have to be made because some priorities will override others.

This is because there are bound to be limits to our knowledge (what we should do) and limits to our capacity to achieve rapid and efficacious social organisation (how we should do it) – collective action problems, in other words. Thus, even if we can pinpoint a problem and its causes, knowing when, where and how to respond effectively to it is, more often than not, likely to be difficult. The very interdependency of social and environmental factors is also what makes the new realities we face extremely complicated and resistant to easy answers and swift interventions. We should not be paralysed by complexities but nor should we succumb to the ideological temptation to ignore them. There is an urgent need for ecosocial policies precisely because there is always a lag in the policy process and so a need to stress some priorities at the potential cost of others. We will often have to feel our way forward pragmatically, in a fog of uncertainties, of risks we cannot assess and potential outcomes we cannot fully anticipate or discern.

Yet even if there is no one-size-fits-all, the literature on fuel poverty and climate change suggests that much more can and must be done than is acknowledged by existing political orthodoxies.

Brenda Boardman

Relatively few sustained attempts to link fuel poverty debates to those about climate change have been made (see also Seymour, 2000, pp 76-8; Johnson et al, 2008, pp 10-15; Ekins et al, 2011; Gough, 2013, pp 197-201). Ekins and Lockwood (2011) argue that tackling climate change requires energy price rises over the long term. If these are not to hurt the poorest, then rebates on energy bills should be available, conditional on households adopting energy-efficiency measures.

Perhaps the most prominent author in the field has been Brenda Boardman (2010a, p 119), who states that:

> The strong correlation between levels of carbon emissions and prices for the different fuels means that most climate change policies are good for fuel poverty and most policies to improve the energy efficiency of low income homes are good for climate change.

(As such, Boardman supports the principle of PCAs.) She identifies three possible exceptions to this general rule, however.

First, there is the rebound effect, as described above. The effect is very difficult to measure, and no real consensus exists, but it seems reasonable to estimate that the direct effect amounts to no more than a third of the savings made through energy efficiency (Sorrell et al, 2009). In short, two-thirds of the reductions produced from greater efficiencies are consolidated as real emissions reductions. However, it is much harder to estimate other aspects of the rebound effect (Dimitropoulos, 2007), and wide variations in household behaviour cannot be ruled out (Druckman et al, 2011). The difficulty derives from the fact that the effect is not a constant, but alters according to a number of intersecting variables, including the income, composition, existing energy efficiency and other characteristics of a household. Boardman (2010a, pp 179, 207) observes that already-warm homes are more likely to direct savings towards non-necessities, for example, flights. In colder households – which typically have lower incomes – savings will enable temperatures to rise (which is surely a desirable result) since there will still be less money for that household to spend on other energy-using activities. Therefore, targeting efforts on the coldest, least energy-efficient households 'will limit the growth in discretionary energy consumption' and constitutes a sensible economic policy.

Second, since carbon taxes are regressive, they should be introduced carefully to ensure that the poorest households are protected. This might mean taking the emphasis away from certain forms of low-carbon electricity generation as:

> ... this could have the effect of pushing fuel prices to an uncomfortable level for the fuel poor. Reducing demand is almost always considerably cheaper than supplying it. (Boardman, 2012b, p 146)

The targeted energy-efficiency measures she supports vis-à-vis the rebound effect therefore apply here too and include: improved building insulation, low-carbon technologies, reverse tariffs (see below) and feed-in tariffs (in which households are paid for the energy they produce from renewable sources). Additionally, because the poorest are most likely to buy older, energy-efficiency appliances second-hand, scrappage schemes are needed for a range of goods (Boardman, 2010a, p 120).

Finally, Boardman (2010a, p 209) criticises governments' tendency to fund efficiency improvements through utility companies. This simply leads to higher utility bills, hitting the fuel-poor most severely. (Boardman bypasses the point that such regression will be exacerbated when those utilities are privately owned and answerable to shareholders in a competitive market rather than to customers. The idea that privatised, for-profit utilities fawn over their customers is a fairy tale that economic liberals must tell themselves before bedtime.) Yet UK governments prefer this approach because the alternative – government-directed and taxpayer-funded – is habitually judged to be old-fashioned tax-and-spend, and so politically unacceptable.

This is why measures to protect the poorest have been made through voluntary 'social tariffs', where the government encourages energy companies to reduce fuel costs for vulnerable and low-income customers. As we saw earlier, however, there are problems with this approach. As based on figures from the late 2000s, only 8 per cent of the fuel-poor benefit from those tariffs (Boardman, 2010a, pp 86-8).

Much of what Boardman (2010a, Chapter 9) says is consistent with the ecosocial approach to poverty. She makes room for both social and ecological concerns since she recommends aligning the timescales for meeting fuel poverty *and* climate change targets. She is concerned to ensure minimum entitlements to resources, not only in terms of income redistribution and improved minimum wages, but also the money needed to fund long-term energy efficiencies and so improvements to assets (building stock):

> ... every home is owned by someone and is worth a considerable sum of money. Unlocking this equity, even for the fuel poor, is the core of the following proposals.... If the value of the property becomes linked to its level of energy efficiency ... then not investing in energy efficiency improvements would lead to the value of the property declining. And investing in energy efficiency improvements is, literally, an investment in the value of the property. (Boardman, 2012b, p 146)

In other words, Boardman signals the importance that property and property values play in any discussion of fuel poverty. (We return to this below.) And although hers is technical, fairly a-political analysis, it is clear that she is critical of the existing arrangements between the state and utility companies.

Diana Ürge-Vorsatz and Tirado Herrero

A second attempt to link fuel poverty and climate change debates has been made by Diana Ürge-Vorsatz and Tirado Herrero. They first echo the view of the last four chapters that relative, or inter-relational, poverty:

> ... stresses the conditions that a *decent life* should fulfill and identifies a list of items (eg, diet, clothing, shelter, environment, etc) that define the necessities that are recognised as such in a society.... Thus enjoying an adequate provision of domestic energy services is one of those basic needs that a household is expected to meet. In that sense, energy poverty is one component of a multi-faceted deprivation notion that encompasses the various aspects of human life. (Ürge-Vorsatz and Herrero, 2012, p 84, emphasis in original)

Therefore, deprivations in access to energy (manifested as fuel poverty) should be understood as one element in a web of deprivations, such that addressing one part of the web is likely to be ineffective unless we address the rest too.

However, Ürge-Vorsatz and Herrero (2012, p 85) reject the idea that Income Support *per se* can be central:

> ... providing a long-term solution to the energy poverty problem via households' income (eg through subsidies to energy costs or fuel payments) is often difficult because extra income may not be used by households for covering their unmet energy service needs or for improving the energy efficiency of their dwellings.

Often poorly targeted and expensive, Income Support schemes are too dependent on the whims of policy-makers, and subsidies may be a temporary solution at best. At worst, they are counterproductive in the absence of energy-efficiency measures 'because lower-than-real energy prices provide wrong economic signals and thus result in a capital stock whose efficiency is lower than that justified by economic rationality considerations' (Ürge-Vorsatz and Herrero, 2012, p 85; see also Jenkins, 2010, p 838). This can lock households – potentially for decades – into higher energy expenditures than are desirable. Therefore, efforts should generally be targeted on improving housing stock:

> The energy performance of the dwelling is thus identified as the key factor to take or keep households permanently out of energy poverty

while contributing simultaneously to reducing GHG emissions. But other co-benefits can be accrued as well, as there is evidence of the significant net employment creation and energy dependency reduction effects of investing in buildings' energy efficiency. (Ürge-Vorsatz and Herrero, 2012, p 86)

In this context there are two potential conflicts, or trade-offs, involving the rebound effect and carbon pricing.

Ürge-Vorsatz and Herrero (2012, p 87) go further than Boardman, denying that the rebound explanation has much relevance:

> It may be argued that potential savings are estimated following the unrealistic assumption that households living in energy poverty will not increase their energy consumption following an improvement in the energy performance of their dwelling.

In other words, since we want poorer households to be warmer, why should we categorise this as a 'take-back' from efficiency savings? So far as carbon pricing is concerned, we can avoid trade-offs between social and environmental goals by targeting carbon taxes on affluent households and by ensuring that low-income households are well insulated and have access to low- or zero-carbon measures and to feed-in tariffs.

For long-term synergies to take effect (carbon-zero homes that are adequately warmed and cooled), state-of-the-art retrofits and technologies are required; otherwise buildings may be 'locked into' sub-optimal measures that are both ineffective and that need new retrofits before long anyway.[9] On the one hand, although expensive, the most effective retrofits will pay for themselves several times over in the long term; that said, initiating the comprehensive programme we need seems beyond the incremental, market-based obsessions of (most of) today's politicians. Avoiding 'lock-in' should be a priority since

> ... under certain circumstances (ie, demonstrated technical and economic feasibility of the state-of-the-art solution alternatives), the sustainable solution may be to wait out until a complex, deep retrofit can be performed on a building rather than force large-scale, superficial renovations. A negative effect of this strategy is that it lets current or increased emissions and energy poverty levels go on unabated for a number of years until the political decision for deep efficiency is taken. (Ürge-Vorsatz and Herrero, 2012, pp 88-9)

By aligning social and environmental goals, that is, the resources and potential savings that accrue to each, we may 'tip the expenditure-benefit balance in favour of action' (Ürge-Vorsatz and Herrero, 2012, p 89). We therefore need an integration of 'policy fields' that are currently separated. Walker and Day (2012, p 75; see also Boardman, 2012b, pp 144, 146) make the same point:

> Whilst fuel poverty is a problem of energy underconsumption, it is occurring within an overall climate of energy overconsumption and the two issues must be addressed in an interconnected way. Without this, the justice of reducing fuel poverty may be overshadowed by consequent exacerbation of global social and climate injustice.

Like Boardman, Ürge-Vorsatz and Herrero appeal to an ecosocial agenda. They are concerned with minimum entitlements ('enjoying an adequate provision of domestic energy services is one of those basic needs that a household is expected to meet' [Ürge-Vorsatz and Herrero, 2012, p 84]), which generates an emphasis less on income and Income Support than on improving housing stock over the long term. They are more dismissive than Boardman of the rebound effect and, so far as I am aware, do not discuss utility companies.

An ecosocial consensus?

We can therefore see that the debate about fuel poverty has both spatial and temporal implications. Spatially, it concerns the availability, use and efficiency of household space; temporally, fuel poverty is something that can help trap households in a cycle of deprivation. Energy, too, has a spatial dimension (the occupancy and accessibility of fossil fuels) and a temporal one (the longevity and sustainability of such fuels and the need to develop alternatives). These debates therefore speak to the framework outlined in Chapters Three and Four.

Let's try to sum all this up by filling in the cells of Table 5.3 in relation to energy. Based on the previous sections, Table 6.2 encapsulates much of what I imagine Boardman, Ürge-Vorsatz, Herrero and others would argue and propose.

How to ensure policy coherence across the solutions column needs careful consideration. For instance, if what the poorest lack is sufficient living space, then at least the space they do occupy is easier to heat. We want the poorest to have more space, as Chapter Three noted, so long as this does not compromise the need for carbon reductions. (We return to this issue in Chapter Eight.)

The italicised phrases in Table 6.2 indicate those places that I think warrant additional attention.

Green assets

First, take the reference to 'green assets' in the mobility row. Boardman argues that we should (1) tie the equity of a property more firmly to its energy efficiency and (2) enable the fuel-poor to benefit from that equity. Some reform in favour of (1) has already occurred. All homes going on the market are now required to have an energy performance certificate (EPC) (energy efficiency and environmental

Table 6.2: The ecosocial poverty of energy

	Fuel poverty		
	Causes	**Symptoms**	**Solutions**
Quantity	Energy inefficiency; low incomes; high energy prices	Household spaces inadequately warmed	Tax-funded retrofitting, targeted at low-income households, and other energy efficiencies, eg appliances
Mobility	Proportionately high energy expenditure reduces capacity to save	Fuel poverty trap – reduced capacity to escape vicious cycle of inefficiency, income and prices	Tax-funded retrofitting, targeted at low-income households, and other energy efficiencies. *Green assets*
Value	Fuel-poor given insufficient priority within energy markets and government policies	Fuel poverty trap. Inadequate assistance in the form of social tariffs	Tax-funded retrofitting, targeted at low-income households, and other energy efficiencies
Control	*Fuel-poor lack social and political power*	*Continued devaluation of fuel-poor households' needs and interests*	*Control of budgets; improved market regulation and socialised control of utilities*
Sharing	Lack of integration of fuel poverty and climate change objectives	Dual injustice: fuel poverty and high carbon emissions. *Rebound effect*	Synergies between social and environmental 'policy fields'. Non-regressive carbon taxes
Caring	Lack of integration of fuel poverty and climate change objectives	Continued dual injustice. Unsustainable energy consumption. *Rebound effect*	Reverse tariffs; shift to renewable technologies and zero-carbon energy systems; PCAs

impact ratings), which ranks houses from A-G, although most purchasers continue to overlook them in favour of traditional criteria (loft conversions, conservatories, etc) (Boardman, 2012a, pp 69-70). The Coalition government has made a move in favour of (2). The Green New Deal, introduced in 2013, allows people to borrow money from a private provider to improve boilers and insulation. The loan (at 7 per cent interest over 10-25 years) is fixed to the property, that is, it is taken over by a new tenant or owner, and repaid through energy bills, but if the improvements lower energy use, then (theoretically) savings should outweigh the costs. There are various assessment, set-up and operating charges. Boardman (2012a, p 79; Harvey, 2013) anticipates that,

> The introduction of mandatory minimum standards for private-sector landlords means that few tenants would be expected to agree to the green deal finance, as this would result in them subsidizing the landlord's obligation. Green deal finance will, therefore, be taken up primarily by owner occupiers....

As for the Energy Companies Obligation (ECO), where energy suppliers must spend £1.3 billion per year subsidising insulation for poorer consumers,

> As all households contribute equally to the ECO, through their fuel bills, it is a regressive measure unless almost all is used to fund improvements in low income homes. (Boardman, 2012a, p 80)

Although it is early days, at the time of writing – July 2013 – neither the Green New Deal nor the ECO have registered much success.

There is thus considerable scope for bringing (1) and (2) together more effectively. From 2018, it will already be illegal to rent out an F- or G-rated property on the EPC scale. The minimum could be raised further and integrated more effectively into the housing market. Boardman (2012a, p 78) suggests that EPCs could be issued for all homes. Those that do not meet a minimum efficiency standard would need additional work done on them before they could be sold or rented out, thus making them worth less in the market than more efficient buildings. Boardman (2012a, p 109) proposes a timescale:

- from 2018 onwards no F- and G- rated properties can be sold/let;
- from 2025 no E- or D-rated;
- from 2032 no C-rated;
- from 2039 no B-rated.

Thus, all properties would be in or near the zero-carbon A-band by 2050.[10]

Going even further, Boardman wonders whether *any* building with low standards could attract a higher Council Tax. It goes without saying that such reforms would meet with resistance and would need to protect low-income owner-occupiers and tenants.

But since carrots can be designed as well as sticks, those obstacles need not be insurmountable. For those who make substantial and early improvements, Boardman (2012a, pp 115-16) recommends: lifetime mortgages, 'green' mortgages, grants and loans from a government-backed Green Investment Bank (including low and even zero-interest rate loans), stamp duty rebates, Council Tax discounts, low VAT rates on retrofitting and energy-efficient appliances. The money could come from auctioning European Emissions Trading Scheme permits. (Note that Boardman does not imagine that financial signals alone will change behaviour in the required direction.)

Weighted towards low-income households, such measures could help the poorest to accumulate the stock of assets, which, as we saw earlier in Chapter Two, they frequently lack. Particular schemes to facilitate tenants' rights can be imagined. For instance, longer rights of tenure – perhaps even co-ownership – could be envisaged for tenants shouldering a higher burden when improving the property's rating. Some assets could even be mobile, carried by low-income individuals from property to property, and some could even be heritable.

All in all, these represent imaginative proposals that policy-makers should start to consider and pilot. But there is a very large elephant missing from the room. Where, we must ask, are the energy companies in all of this? Boardman imagines utilities funding scrappage schemes but, by and large, more radical proposals to regulate and re-socialise the energy market are missing from the literature on fuel poverty. Boardman (2012a, p 89) is well aware that,

> Policies that foster the relationship between local people, their community and local government are poorly understood, but are an important part of delivering the social ambience within which to achieve low-energy communities in practice.

It is difficult, however, to picture any 'social ambience' being formed unless individuals, communities and local government have a stake and a voice in the production and distribution of energy. Otherwise, what we are saying? That consumers and government should spend the next 30 years decarbonising themselves while companies continue to price-gouge with minimal expectations that they will foster ecosocial objectives?

Curiously, such a conclusion might be implicit within the following claims:

> Energy is an unusual commodity, as it can only be consumed in a piece of capital equipment. It is the efficiency of this capital equipment (a light bulb, refrigerator, boiler) that determines the value the household obtains from its energy purchases. (Boardman, 2012b, p 143)

> Concern over fuel poverty is about the distribution of access to energy services (rather than energy itself).... (Walker and Day, 2012, p 70)

But unless we are concerned with the justice and sustainability of the production process, then it is difficult to envisage end-of-the-pipe reforms as being efficacious. It seems short-sighted to focus on consumption without considering the umbilical connections between production and consumption (Teske, 2010, pp 56-7; Bloomberg New Energy Finance, 2012). Energy is a socionatural resource above and beyond its distribution in the form of an 'energy service'. Even electricity – a flow of electrons – still depends almost entirely on the utilisation of primary resources, mainly non-renewables (oil, natural gas, coal, uranium), but increasingly renewables too (water/wave, wind, geothermal, solar). And as previous chapters argued, we all have stake in what happens to socionatural resources.[11]

Social and political control

The second set of italicised phrases in Table 6.2 – the control row, referring to the principle of political voice and democratic representation – therefore suggests that the fuel-poor are deprived not simply because of price rises and energy inefficiency, but because they are denied the social and political voices to make a difference. They are disadvantaged as participants and citizens, not simply as consumers. In gas, electricity and coal markets, the shareholder is sovereign, and while all non-shareholders will thereby be disempowered to some extent, this will most adversely affect those without the resources to compensate.

As indicated in Chapter Four, the system of ownership is not my primary concern. Decades of globalisation and liberalisation in the energy sector make it unlikely that any single model can be recommended for all nations. In some countries a nationalisation of energy companies will be preferred while others will continue to prefer a heavily market-based system. That said, one major study anticipates that the conjunction of ecological imperatives with a need for greater energy security may well encourage greater decentralisation and localisation in an industry that has been highly centralised historically (Skea et al, 2011).

Without more engagement of the public in climate change policy it is unlikely that 'commitment to and understanding of the need for emissions reduction' can be delivered (Ekins et al, 2011, p 61). Engagement can imply nothing more than improved consumer information and education campaigns. A more ambitious approach (see Hawkes et al, 2011, pp 239-43) – particularly around micro-generation technologies – could facilitate a form of 'energy citizenship' in which people become co-producers, co-investors and therefore co-owners of energy systems, whether as individual households or as members of cooperatives and communal micro-grids. In an industry dominated by sales and profits, the real savings to be made by consumers may be too slender and/or too long term to attract people to the energy efficiencies that need to be made. More imaginative approaches can be envisaged, for example, reorganisation that favours not-for-profit suppliers, which breaks down the divisions between shareholders and stakeholders, implements market regulation around green imperatives and which opens up for-profit companies to civil society (deliberative parliaments that shape company policy?).

Walker and Day (2012, p 72) summarise the same point under the headings of information, representation and accountability:

> In terms of access to information, being able to know the scale of the problem of fuel poverty, its occurrence and patterning is fundamental to being able to address it, and also to enabling advocacy and campaigning groups to call policy bodies to account. Having ready access to information on energy prices and on ways of being more efficient in energy use is also important in informing the responses of vulnerable consumers and those that are supporting them. In terms of "meaningful participation in decision-making", the interests of those affected by fuel poverty need to be properly represented in a variety of relevant decision-making processes – in energy policy and strategy, energy pricing and market regulation, housing policy, energy efficiency policy and so on – if they are to be given some priority alongside

other concerns and addressed effectively. This involvement is an issue at different scales of governance – from international energy policy arenas, through to local community fora. In terms of access to legal processes this is important in providing mechanisms for challenging the decision-making and actions of both public bodies with responsibilities for vulnerable consumers, and private energy companies. Having laws and regulations in place in the first place which protect the interests of the fuel poor is a necessary prerequisite, but then enabling low income and other vulnerable people and their advocates to use the courts to enforce these laws and regulations is also important.

Yet this sits uneasily alongside their view that,

It seems clear that the focus of the next generation of policy will be on improving the energy efficiency of housing rather than addressing the other distributional inequalities of incomes and pricing. (Walker and Day, 2012, p 73)

Presumably, they mean that simple Income Support measures, for example, social tariffs, and so on, do not work effectively. This appears reasonable, as we saw above.

But since 'distributional inequalities' surely include unequal ownership of property, and because we should define property to include stakes in energy companies, then we should not equate 'incomes' with traditional Income Support transfers, and not confuse 'pricing' with the self-serving interests of energy monopolies. In other words, policies to improve information, representation and accountability require stakeholders to possess and exercise property rights. We could also imagine a social dividend system. Some of the wealth generated by carbon taxes and energy markets can be earmarked for sustainability projects and programmes; some could be distributed in the form of an unconditional income, as happens in Alaska with oil extracted from Prudhoe Bay (Widerquist and Sheahen, 2012, pp 11-15; Fitzpatrick, 1999, Chapter 7).

Ürge-Vorsatz and Herrero (2012, p 85) also tend to think of income simply as household expenditure and, to repeat, there are, indeed, limits to what Income Support schemes can achieve. But if we characterise income as 'assets' that include budgets that local communities derive as social dividends from the companies they co-own, and can invest in local energy-efficiency schemes, then we reimagine poverty not simply as a lack of income but as a lack of voice and of participative inclusion that can be addressed through more imaginative forms of redistribution. In short, radical reforms can be proposed by synergising the themes of income and assets, distributive inequalities and participative decision-making.

If nothing else, then, the ecosocial approach recommends that research into fuel poverty and climate change be concerned not only with buildings and energy demand, but also with the characteristics and social-environmental significance of the entire energy chain. Energy is not simply that which powers your kettle;

it is a resource that connects you to the rest of the matrix of socionatural interdependencies. Although his concern is with oil, Urry (2013, p 1) comes close to the truth:

> Energy systems are incredibly important. They 'generate' very varied and often highly unequal economic, social and political patterns.

If the future is indeed characterised by reduced energy demand, cleaner energy and decentralised systems, we might be led back to the view of Illich (1974, p 17) when he claimed that 'only a ceiling on energy use can lead to social relations that are characterised by high levels of equity'.

Rebound effect

The final italics in Table 6.2 concern the rebound effect. As we saw above, Boardman is more concerned with rebound than Ürge-Vorsatz and Herrero, although none believe this to be a major problem (see also Barker et al, 2007; Pett, 2008, 2009). Indeed, rebound is desirable when poor households 'take back' efficiency savings in the form of higher household warmth, although there is no guarantee that this will happen. The rebound effect is modest, at least for low-income households, precisely because, as Anderson et al (2012, p 51) find, they are often forced to divert the savings away from considerations of warmth (for instance, the heating versus eating dilemma many households experience). In short, in a continued trade-off between comfort and other necessities, it is often the latter which is preferred.

To these views I would simply add that although we want the coldest, low-income households to be warmer, we do not want any home to be so warm that efficiency savings are significantly counteracted by increased carbon emissions. In short, minimising the rebound effect without compromising on ecosocial objectives may imply giving a greater role to 'reverse tariffs' where the prices charged for the first tranche of energy units consumed is cheaper than for later tranches (Boardman, 2010a, pp 93-4). As a simple example, if we judged 21°C degrees to be reasonable, then anyone who uses more than a stipulated amount would need to pay an escalating surcharge.[12] In other words, some forms of rebound are more ecosocially desirable and acceptable than others, and such a realisation needs to be applied both to research into the rebound effect and into pricing policies.

The point is to emphasise the obligation to care and to recognise natural values – the sharing and caring rows in Table 6.2 – by making what Brunner et al (2012, p 57) call an 'environmental consciousness' more central to policies promoting energy saving. Brunner et al observe that the amount of energy people consume and waste often exceeds their estimates. A 'habitus of modesty' therefore implies a greater consciousness of the need to use space more effectively and less carelessly, including those with the most to lose from wasting energy (for a literature review of coping strategies, see Gibbons and Singler, 2008). But let me repeat what was said in previous chapters. This is not about singling out 'the poor' as somehow ecologically ignorant or immoral. Pett (2009, p 1686; see also 2008) found that low-income households 'seemed generally interested in their carbon footprints but were not likely to be able to do anything to reduce them further.' Further research into the rebound effect is undoubtedly needed.

Conclusion

This chapter has been largely concerned with two questions: how can we protect the incomes of the poorest, and how do we ensure that all people are sufficiently warm while also achieving reductions in carbon emissions? The burgeoning literature on fuel poverty and climate change suggests that realistic policy synergies between these imperatives can be found, although they are rarely in evidence in governmental policies today. There are double and even triple dividends to be fashioned, but these will not happen easily or automatically. This implies a whole series of measures to be implemented and maintained over the next few decades, including:

- major retrofitting programmes, with governmental coordination and taxpayer funding;
- dissemination of low-carbon technologies;
- reverse tariffs;
- feed-in tariffs;
- scrappage schemes;
- non-regressive carbon taxes;
- PCAs;
- equity schemes that tie social and ecological objectives together.

We saw that such initiatives are more than consistent with an ecosocial model and help us to understand what this approach could mean in practical terms. Table 6.2 drew attention to several areas that arguably require more debate: green assets, control and sharing of energy resources and the rebound effect.

We are left with two considerations. First, Roberts (2008, pp 4472-3) anticipates a shift in the problems associated with fuel poverty:

> Over the next 40 years, warmer winters and warmer summers with more extreme heat may shift the problem of fuel poverty from one principally of inadequate heating in winter to one which also features inadequate cooling in summer.... This need may be particularly acute in urban heat islands for vulnerable elderly living in thermally poor dwellings....

This means that when designing and implementing the above measures we need to ensure they are flexible, that is, appropriate for summer cooling as well as winter warming. We need reprogrammable buildings that can provide insurance against the uncertainties of the future. Without knowing exactly how much warmer winters and summers are likely to be, we need flexibility built into our reforms and reflexivity built into the policy-making process. The worst scenario is to act now and lock ourselves into approaches that only need to be reversed at unnecessary expense and effort in 20 or 30 years time. To repeat: this is why Chapter Three stressed the dynamic, resilient 'remaking' aspects of a green society and its ecosocial politics.

Second, if to be poor means being deprived of sufficient space, how can we increase the living space of the poorest in the context of the higher density communities that we need for greater energy efficiency and sustainability? We consider this question later, in Chapter Eight.

At the end of the Introduction I stated that the ecologically excessive, careless and destructive use of key socionatural resources is connected to the social deprivations that characterise that usage for millions of those on low incomes. In terms of energy, our fossil fuel dependency has been misplaced, locking our social and economic infrastructures into a reliance on non-renewables that we have only begun to reconfigure and that will take several decades more to alter. Combined with profligate and profit-driven energy markets, the poorest are bearing the brunt of this. If we are to make a successful and fair transition to an economy of renewables, then mitigation and adaptation policies must make their interests front and centre.

Notes

[1] Energy poverty refers not only to space heating needs, 'but also other energy service demands such as space cooling, lighting and powering appliances' (Ürge-Vorsatz and Herrero, 2012, p 84). However, for the sake of convention, this chapter refers to all these needs and demands as 'fuel poverty'.

[2] And 80 per cent of the world's energy still consists of those fuels.

[3] Since fans and air conditioning use energy, the alternative is 'passive cooling'. For instance, redesigning house interiors to enhance ventilation and shading, as well as altering and taking advantage of natural surroundings, for example, planting trees to improve shade, in order to increase air circulation and to decrease the solar radiation absorbed by buildings.

[4] Oil only accounts for a small proportion of UK domestic energy. Nonetheless, it does have an impact on poverty, in the form of high transport costs absorbing household income, for instance. Also, the more governmental and voluntary agencies have to spend on oil, the less may be available for anti-poverty policies (see Bridge and Le Billion, 2013, pp 216, note 7). We consider transport later, in Chapter Nine.

[5] I say 'is', but from 2014 a new definition of fuel poverty is being adopted, based on the work of John Hills (see DECC, 2013a).

[6] Adding investment costs to bills are likely in any event. Upgrading the UK's electricity connections to meet key climate change targets could cost up to £5 billion, requiring over 600 miles of cabling to connect to new energy sources. The transition should therefore be as non-regressive as possible.

[7] By upgrading its buildings and housing stock, the country helps to protect itself against at least some of the unforeseeable energy and climate change shocks that may hit us in decades to come.

[8] Some believe greater emphasis than at present should be given to demolition/new build (see, for example, Boardman et al, 2005; Preston et al, 2008). However, others advocate the retrofitting of existing stock with minimal demolition, believing that initial measures should be targeted on fuel-poor homes and cheap housing (Power, 2008, p 4489; cf Jenkins, 2010, p 832). This is not a debate we review here, although there appears to be no conclusive evidence one way or another.

[9] For a useful overview of retrofitting in practice, see Joseph Rowntree Foundation (2012); for data from a new build project, see Bell et al (2010).

[10] These dates could be adjusted, obviously, depending on considerations of what is feasible and necessary. For instance, Hansen (2009, pp 173-5) argues that coal emissions must be eliminated by 2030 if CO_2 is to peak at 400-425 parts per million and return to 350ppm by the end of the century.

[11] Renewable sources are not free either (Yergin, 2011, pp 596, 614-8). They still require an infrastructure for collection and distribution, and therefore decisions about priorities and the allocation of resources.

[12] This is a simple example. A reverse tariff system would need to allow for seasonal and household variations (to allow for age and ill health), increasing the complexity of such a system.

SEVEN

Food and food poverty

For most of human history, if you expended more energy in acquiring food than you derived from it, you would eventually starve. But in the fossil fuel era, the amount of energy we use in the production *of* food exceeds the energy we derive *from* food by a factor of 10 (Heinberg, 2011, p 130). By accessing hundreds of millions of years of stored sunlight we have evaded the old expenditure versus consumption equation, while swelling the population from 1 billion to 7 billion in less than two centuries.

Famines and starvation have not disappeared, obviously, because such profligacy has been bestowed by the affluent largely on themselves (Patel, 2007). Developed nations have devoured the earth's inheritance, leaving countless millions, both now and in the future, to rely on the scraps. But regardless of when oil, gas and coal peak, or whether new miracle technologies emerge, there must come a time when either it is no longer practicable to access those fuels, or we decide to limit the emissions they create, or both. In other words, the energy equation is on its way back.

None of this should be surprising since food has long occupied a central place in political and social policy conflicts (Vernon, 2007, Chapter 8). In the late 1970s the then Leader of the Opposition, Margaret Thatcher, pointed to shopping baskets that seemed to shrink year after year. 'Unlike inflation-happy socialists,' went the message, 'wives and mums know the real cost of living.'

Yet as is now clear, it is difficult for wives, mums or any of us to know what powerful market actors do not want us to know. Companies (and governments) depend on consumer passivity, complicity and ignorance about what goes into food and what consequences it has (Singer and Mason, 2006, pp 8-12). The industrialisation of farming alienates consumers everywhere from the food production process, but this blindness is especially virulent where corporations control the food chain. The consumer revolution took social contexts out of shopping, constructing food as nothing more than an economistic series of cost-benefit decisions made by 'active' customers in supermarkets humbly grateful for their business.

This was not always the case. Since food is a basic need, a lack of regular, good quality food summons at least two of Beveridge's five giants: want (poverty) and disease (ill health), each of which makes it difficult to work and affects the learning of children. Although it would be naive to imagine there was a magical moment 'after the 1940s when hunger vanished from Britain' (Vernon, 2007, p 273; see also Townsend, 1979, pp 167-9), memories of the 'Hungry Thirties' shaped the political conscience of post-war reformers – including middle-way conservatives – until the 1970s.

But if you disparage the principles of needs and rights, these 'giants' lose their salience as *social* problems requiring *collective* responses. Having first suffered from the politics of food (she achieved public recognition in 1971 when, as Minister for Education, she withdrew free milk from some classrooms, earning the appellation 'milk snatcher'), Thatcher's legacy was to individualise and de-socialise our understandings and practices. Her yearning for the restoration of soup kitchens was first laughed at by ministers normally submissive to her nostalgic dreams of a Golden Age destroyed by welfare state hedonism. But by tapping into an intolerance towards social explanations and solutions, Thatcher's judgemental populism eventually become normalised within everyday discourse. Many an exasperated politician has sighed that the poor would be less obese if only they ate better and exercised more (a message reiterated by much of the media).[1] By 2012, over half the respondents to a Demos poll wanted the government to stop claimants from spending their benefits on cigarettes or alcohol, and 38 per cent extended this to junk food (Wheeler, 2012). However, such polls rarely interrogate what drives people to cigarettes, alcohol and junk food in the first place.

Thus, in the wake of the 2007-08 financial crisis, with austerity the preferred response of the Coalition government, and with yet another reinvention of the vocabulary of 'the undeserving poor', the UK experienced an alarming rise in the number of food banks (which distribute emergency food parcels) and of children going to school or bed hungry.[2] The 'heating or eating' dilemma (see Chapter Six) is a daily one for many, and one in five mothers miss meals in order to prioritise their children.[3]

Conservative attacks on the concept of relative poverty were never going to lead us here, they once assured us. Avoiding absolute poverty would be sacrosanct, and this meant that, 'A family is poor if it cannot afford to eat' (Joseph and Sumption, 1979, p 27). If you judge that family to be hungry because they are undeserving, then they are not really poor, are they? So it's not really your responsibility, is it? Absolute poverty can be vanished too, it seems, once you learn the correct moral conjuring tricks.[4] Thus the food insecurity once associated with the 1930s has returned. The Golden Age is back.

Given this pathologisation, this de-socialisation, this non-political politics of food, have we the ethical resources needed to address food poverty? And since we now struggle to understand the social contexts of food production and consumption, can we successfully address the social politics of climate change? This chapter proceeds by presenting some recent facts and figures about food poverty before drawing on the most systematic attempt yet made to understand food as the intersection of social and ecological imperatives. It ends by mapping this notion of 'ecological public health' against the ecosocial matrix with which previous chapters have dealt.

Recent developments and prospects

UK food prices rose dramatically – 12 per cent in real terms – in the five years after 2007, so although they spent more *on* food, UK households purchased 4.2 per cent *less* food in 2011 than in 2007 (Defra, 2012a, p 54), all of which had particularly detrimental effects on the poorest fifth who spend 16.6 per cent of household income on food (Defra, 2012a, Chapter 5) compared to the average household's 11 per cent. Not surprisingly, many coped with rising prices by 'trading down' to cheaper, processed and thus less healthy food, but for low-income households, there wasn't much 'further down' they could go (Flaherty et al, 2004, pp 112-13). The poorest tenth spent 17 per cent more on food in 2011 compared to 2007, but purchased 29 per cent less fruit and 20 per cent less vegetables (fruit prices rose by 34 per cent over this period). Their intake of nutrients thus fell between 2007-12 for the simple reason that fresh fish, fresh meat, fruit and vegetables cost more, making them even less affordable for low-income households at a time when food price inflation exceeded wage and benefit rises. On average, every day the poorest tenth eat less than half the fruit consumed by the richest tenth, and those who eat high quantities of processed meat run a higher risk of developing cancer and heart disease (Campbell, 2013).

It is also no surprise, then, that charitable assistance has increased over this period (Lambie-Mumford, 2013). According to The Trussell Trust, in the spring of 2013 the UK had more than 320 food banks which had issued food parcels to over a quarter of a million people in the previous year, a fourfold increase since 2010.[5] The figures would be higher except that a maximum of three visits a year are allowed for people who must be referred by a GP, charity or other agency. Nor do these figures allow for similar actions by churches, housing associations and other charities. FareShare feeds over 35,000 people a day, distributing unsold or surplus food from the industry.[6] In February 2013 it was reported that the UK was close to violating its obligations to the UN's Economic and Social Rights Convention which sets out minimum standards of access to food, clothing and housing (Butler, 2013b).

For those facing desperate circumstances, any assistance is surely welcome. Yet Riches (2002) argues that food banks enable governments to 'look the other way', neglecting hunger and nutritional health in the expectation that others will take up the moral slack. Anti-state politicians effectively say 'Look, we told you charity works better than state hand-outs'. Food banks thus risk being institutionalised, that is, co-opted into the very political and economic strategy that created the problem in the first place, taken as evidence of the voluntary sector's success rather than of free market and corporate capitalism's failure. Poppendieck (1998, pp 269-83, 293-4, 300-8) calls this a 'two-for-one' bargain: (some of) the hungry are fed while volunteering motivations are fulfilled. And charity can also be disempowering, by taking the emphasis away from social rights, universal provision, jobs, wages and the organisational capacities of poor people themselves (who risk being constructed as the helpless, compliant, grateful recipients of the compassion of others) (Poppendieck, 1998, pp 155-9, 263-8).

Recent developments should also be understood in terms of the long-term evisceration of high streets and shopping boroughs, once much more diverse than they are today. The top four supermarkets now have a 62 per cent market share of food and non-alcoholic drink purchases in the UK. Food poverty thus intersects with the phenomenon of place poverty in the form of 'food deserts'. These were noticed in the 1980s and early 1990s. With large supermarkets opening on the edges of cities (under the benevolent gaze of the Thatcher government), smaller retailers were often unable to compete with their aggressive marketing, one-stop convenience and loss-leading practices. Nor could emasculated local authorities do much to stem the tide. Food deserts particularly afflicted low-income communities that were less likely to have access to those superstores, or good quality retailers, both because of restricted transport (especially car ownership) and because there were fewer profits to be made for shops locating in their communities (Wrigley, 2002).

The proliferation of local 'convenience superstores' since the late 1990s (for example, with mini-Tescos blanketing the country) has scattered oases across those deserts but not necessarily reduced the underlying problem, since they are dominated by processed food, and by capturing the market can keep prices at uncompetitive levels (Dowler et al, 2007, p 136). The debate about food deserts has subsided, if only because places differ and it is difficult to make straightforward generalisations (Macintyre et al, 2008): 'The geography of food poverty cannot be simply drawn on a map' (Hitchman et al, 2002, p 9). Nonetheless, it would be simplistic to deny a correlation between geography and access to, and choice of, food (Kneafsey et al, 2008, p 14; Caraher et al, 2010). And as Steel (2008: 147-52) observes, countries that have restricted and controlled supermarket expansion more effectively than the UK are less likely to experience food deserts and food poverty.

A new climate for food

Overall, then, few of the food practices across developed countries seem ready to deal with global warming. Take waste. Over 60 per cent of the waste produced by UK households is avoidable (Defra, 2012b, Chapter 5), while according to the European Commission, the European Union (EU) wastes 50 per cent of its edible food.[7] In addition to the obvious financial costs, such waste has adverse environmental impacts too, because of landfills and because of the energy, GHGs, water and soil embedded in food:

> ... food waste is equivalent to 15 million tonnes of CO_2 emissions, and the vast majority goes into landfill, where it generates methane. (Lang et al, 2009, p 200)

The higher the level of processing and calorific content, and the later in the supply chain food is wasted, the heavier the impacts. Globally, about one-third of edible food gets lost or wasted every year (1.3 billion tonnes) – enough to feed the world's hungry several times over (Stuart, 2009, p 83). Some of this is due to damage inflicted during harvesting, transport or storage, but some is due to retailers refusing to stock food that is blemished or aesthetically unappealing (Stuart, 2009, pp 102-8). And the more consumers waste, the more they purchase replacements, leaving supermarkets with little incentive (other than PR) to apply or encourage different practices. Yet nor do consumers have a particular reason to change their habits since, compared to developing nations, food prices are relatively low vis-à-vis average incomes.[8] Yet where concerted efforts are made with recycling schemes, immense improvements *have* been achieved (Steel, 2008, pp 278-81).

The social and ecological agendas are converging, then. If, as expected, prices continue to rise, without intervention levels of nutrient intake among poorer households are likely to remain inadequate. Oxfam (2012, p 5) estimates that between 2010-30, export prices for:

- maize could rise by 177 per cent, with up to half the increase due to climate change;
- wheat could rise by 120 per cent, with around one-third of the increase due to climate change;
- processed rice could rise by 107 per cent, with around one-third of the increase due to climate change.

These percentages may even be underestimates depending on what happens to oil prices, extreme weather events and panic buying.[9] And as prices rise and food insecurity grows, so ethical considerations drop down the list of shoppers' priorities.

All of which leaves us ill equipped to deal with the new challenges headed our way. According to Lang (2010, p 1821),

> A bedrock of some new and some old fundamentals will reshape food systems in the 21st century: climate change; a fuel/oil/energy squeeze; water stress; competition over land use; labour pressures; urbanisation; population increase; dietary change and the nutrition transition with accompanying healthcare costs; and social inequalities within and between countries.

A series of collisions has been anticipated (Harding, 2010). With world population expected to reach 8 billion by 2030, global food poverty can only decrease if affluent countries reduce their resource- and energy-heavy consumption of meat and dairy (Singer and Mason, 2006, Chapter 16):

> ... it takes an estimated 11 times as much grain to feed a man if it
> passes through a cow first.... It also takes a staggering *thousand* times
> more water to produce a kilo of beef than of wheat. (Steel, 2008, p 9)

And it takes 160 litres of oil to make a tonne of maize in the US, all of which
increases the risk of crop failure and soil exhaustion.

Let us now take a more considered look at these challenges, utilising the key
work that has been done by Tim Lang and various co-authors.

Food policy and poverty

Research into food poverty has recently gathered pace (Leather, 1996; Craig and
Dowler, 1997; Dowler and Turner, 2001; Dowler, 2002; Hitchman et al, 2002,
pp 23-51; Dowler and Tansey, 2003; Marmot and Wilkinson, 2005, Chapter 9;
Dowler and O'Connor, 2012). Lang et al (2009, p 255) define food poverty as
'persistent underconsumption' and food security as 'a state where everyone is fed
well, sustainably and healthily, and able to choose culturally appropriate food.'

For Lang et al (2009, p 257), food policy holds a mirror up to social policy
since 'poverty in general and food poverty particularly expose decisions about
the allocation of resources.' In the Victorian era food philanthropy was often
a means of social control, in which this basic need was made conditional on
recipients demonstrating ethical and behavioural improvements to their character.
In the post-Second World War era, a more societal emphasis took over, a 'never
again' ethos in which food became a material and public good. By the 1980s
an individualistic and moralistic emphasis had returned, albeit in a consumerist
context stressing the importance of customer empowerment, information and
choice. Although the social control aspects never faded entirely, they have returned
with a vengeance in recent political and public debate. The argument that tackling
poverty is more cost-effective in the long run is drowned out by a moralistic
discourse about the failures of 'the poor' who are always made to resemble a drain
on social resources. Therefore, an economic and moral revaluation is required.
We need a new mirror:

> Ultimately, food poverty is a matter of human concern and care, the
> recognition that one's fellow citizen – whether this word is defined
> in planetary, regional, national or local terms – is not too dissimilar
> to oneself. The need for food from a healthy, sustainable food supply
> is common.... (Lang et al, 2009, p 258)

Within food policy we therefore find a familiar tussle between absolutist and
relativist perspectives, with the former emphasising the amount of food essential
for physical survival and health, and the latter stressing that food is necessary for
personal wellbeing, self-respect and social interaction, because food is as much
about sociocultural positioning as it is about physiological needs. As such:

... both absolute and relative approaches are valuable. They show the absolute characteristics, such as lack of resources and physical health outcomes, alongside relative aspects of food poverty and inequality, such as feeling isolated, not being able to eat what you feel necessary ... studies have shown policy-makers that there are consistently large groups of people experiencing food deficits, even in developed countries. A study of Londoners may show different food problems to those experienced in sub-Saharan Africa but, for Londoners, that is their reality. (Lang et al, 2009, p 262)

Lang et al stress that the individualist discourse of recent welfare politics (the emphasis on lifestyle and habits) makes it hard to correct such deficits, however. What feeds this individualism are lingering images in the popular and media imagination of the Dickensian poor as thin and threadbare, where sedentary corpulence was associated with affluence – gout was the 'rich man's disease'. This contrasts conveniently with today's perception that low-income individuals are more likely to be overweight or obese – although the reality is more complex (Dowler et al, 2007, pp 129-30; Bennett, 2013). 'See, since they could spend their money wisely, but choose not to do so, why should I care about them?' The images of indigence have changed but the central message (poverty is due to deficiencies of character) has barely altered.

This may help explain why supermarket expansion has been so popular among policy-makers for decades now, including New Labour (Dowler et al, 2007, p 144). A market-dominated politics means it is easier for governments to make cheap food available than healthy food affordable. They are also more cost-effective for low-income shoppers (the late lamented corner shop lacked economies of scale), and since supermarkets can make it easier to purchase fruit and vegetables that, too, feeds the individualistic discourse ('they could spend their money wisely').

In other words, consuming the wrong kind or excessive amount of food is tantamount to a failure of agency. If what you are is what you eat, then the body becomes a screen for reading character and constructing a narrative either of personal worth or weakness, where weakness implies succumbing to appetites that responsible consumers are meant both to indulge (shops need shoppers, after all) *and* control (you need to keep yourself alive and healthy and shopping). Lurking within this economic liberal discourse, therefore, is a subtle moralistic tone, one applied to families, too, as part of a wider panic about social change that is particularly directed against poorer households (see Fitzpatrick, 2008a, pp 141-8).[10] Moral character requires strong families, it is claimed. If the characters of the poor are deficient, then their families and support networks must be too. An equation is therefore constructed in which unhealthy diet and nutrition is a sign of irresponsible agency, lack of respect for self and others, family breakdown and antisocial communities.

By contrast, a sociostructural analysis highlights the 'psychosocial' aspects of health in which relative low income matters because of the stress and anxiety it creates (Wilkinson, 1996, pp 156-65). Lack of income accompanies the need to make unenviable choices:

> It is not that families in poverty are unaware of the health benefits of eating certain types of foods; just that that these assume a lower priority than the immediate concern of filling stomachs. (Lang et al, 2009, p 260)

Social exclusion matters because food signifies the need to fit in, to be regarded (and regard oneself) as normal, as belonging to the social group:

> A family may be well-nourished from a calorific perspective but experience deprivation through lack of access to valued foods.... This can result in making decisions about food, not on the basis of cost or health but to meet social objectives, as when parents on low incomes buy more costly branded foods for their children in order not to let them feel at odds with their peers. (Lang et al, 2009, p 262)

An affluent society makes foods high in sugar, salt and fat more available *and*, because they are often cheap, dangles them in front of those who seek whatever escape or short-term stimulation they can in a society that they know devalues them. The 'new food poverty' is one dominated by processed, energy-dense and high-calorie foods, in the context of a seductive, airbrushed but also judgemental popular culture.

These kinds of relativist perspectives have been familiar for decades, going back at least to Peter Townsend and the Black Report. More recently, environmentalist critiques have contributed to the familiar structural-relativist challenge to individualism:

> Today, cheap food is under attack for externalizing environmental, as well as social, costs. Behind cheap food may lie uncosted or under-costed externalities in the form of threats to the environment, healthcare bills, distant workers on low wages and other social dislocations.... Rather than polarizing understanding – and therefore policy – between the general and specific, macro-economic and food policies, it is more sensible to accept that the two foci are related. (Lang et al, 2009, pp 262-3)

If – in my vocabulary – our political economics has to become more ecosocial, then what Lang et al are pointing to is an understanding of food policy and poverty which more directly and transparently incorporates social and ecological perspectives. The developed world manages to combine overconsumption (and so a high ecological footprint) with new forms of stratification in which those on low incomes are deprived, both in terms of nutrition and physiology, but also in terms of sociocultural belonging, that is, they are excluded and devalued.

What solutions to these problems can be envisaged? Despite my earlier caveats, charities remain important. As noted above in relation to FareShare schemes, food companies have begun to donate surplus food, at least partially filling a gap left by recent welfare state retrenchment. The other main solutions proposed to food poverty include: market regulations and taxes; education and information campaigns; technical innovations, for example, genetically modified (GM) foods (Singer and Mason, 2006, pp 202-12); and public welfare, for example, guaranteed Income Support and school meals (McMahon and Marsh, 1999, pp 6-11; Gustafsson, 2002). Yet Lang et al (2009, p 266) argue that it is difficult to generalise: 'The conclusion from this welter of important data is that single factors are unlikely to be the sum of the situation.'

What *is* clear is that the 'downstream' solutions favoured by economic liberalism, emphasising customer choice and responsibility at the point of purchase, have not worked. The assumption has been that consumers will act wisely (for themselves and others) with the addition of correct signals, such as labels, information and health campaigns. Poor individuals can be transformed from failed into responsible consumers by being alternately shamed about their habits and encouraged into new ones:

> The purpose of information and education strategies is to change behaviour. They fit psychological analyses locating the reasons for poor nutritional intake primarily at the level of behaviour and attitudes, rather than the societal or economic level. (Lang et al, 2009, p 171)

Yet market individualists fail to understand the structural and social contexts of individual behaviour. Steel (2008, pp 196-7) identifies a vicious cycle, for instance. As we have become used to ready meals and packaged vegetables – in which others effectively cook our food for us – so our cooking skills decline. New homes are built with smaller kitchens than older houses and this, in turn, encourages us to reduce our cooking skills still further. We travel further to purchase food that has often travelled thousands of miles to reach us, and that we then do little more than heat up in kitchens too small to do much else. This ever-shrinking circle of space and capabilities has an adverse affect on the poorest in particular.

More systematic solutions that focus on the 'upstream' are therefore needed, that is, what happens throughout the food chain before food reaches the shelf. This is an approach that the climate change agenda similarly enjoins.

Natural environments and food[11]

Despite its long history (see, for example, Schumacher, 1973, pp 87-96; Carson, 2000), let us continue with the synthesis attempted by Lang et al (2009; see also Leahy, 2004; Dowler, 2008; Agyeman, 2013, Chapter 2; Berners-Lee and Clark, 2013, Chapter 13). Human health and natural health are symbiotic and interwoven. They propose: (1) growing food has an impact on the environment and (2) the health of the environment affects the amount and quality of the food available to us. Let's review these in turn.

Food supply chains have an impact on the environment in a number of ways. Inputs on the production side include inorganic fertilisers, pesticides, machinery, ploughing, feed, deforestation and interventions into the water supply. These have many effects, including: loss of soil fertility, depletion of water systems, acidification and air pollution, loss of biodiversity and overgrazing. Once the food is grown it has to be processed, packaged, distributed, sold, refrigerated, cooked, excreted or discarded, all of which uses energy, creating carbon emissions and waste.

In the UK the agri-food sector (including manufacture, transport, retailing, and so on) accounts for 19 per cent of GHG emissions, which is, in fact, less than two-thirds of the EU average (Lang et al, 2009, p 197). Thus,

> Food transport's externalities are identified as including: GHGs, air and noise pollution, congestion, accidents and infrastructure impacts. Attempts to cost these externalities for the UK have been priced variously at £1.9 billion and £4 billion. (Lang et al, 2009, p 198)

In fact, estimating externalities is fiendishly complex since it is a matter of morals as much as economics (Thompson, 2012, pp 224-6). Negative externalities include 'food miles' as food now travels over vast distances, amplified by the desire for all types of food to be available to consumers during all seasons, in what Lawrence (2004, pp 87-98; see also Paxton, 1994) calls a 'permanent global summer time'. Yet driving 6½ miles to a food shop produces more carbon than air freighting a pack of green beans from Kenya. 'Local production' and 'low ecological footprint' do not always or necessarily coincide (Lang et al, 2009, pp 199, 298; see also Singer and Mason, 2006, pp 140-50). But food miles also bring some positive externalities, including supporting workers in other countries. Ballingall and Winchester (2010) find that some of the world's poorest nations, particularly in sub-Saharan Africa, could suffer considerably from European reductions in food miles.

Conversely, climate change affects, and is further expected to affect, food supply in ways that are equally diverse and multiple:

> The commonly presented scenarios include impacts such as an increase of extreme climate events and rising sea levels and shifting temperature zones. Agriculture and food impacts include some regionally specific advantages, such as increased rainfall or milder temperatures and longer growing seasons, but the overall picture is negative. There will be more extreme weather events from drought to flooding, and so harvest loss,

increased and wider spread of crop and livestock diseases (currently witnessed with blue tongue disease and avian flu), water loss, and shifts in optimum growing areas for particular crops. Particularly at risk are those parts of the world where populations and their agricultures are already highly vulnerable to disruption, notably in areas prone to flooding, such as estuarial zones. Along the supply chain there will be disruption to sourcing of foods, unexpected shortages, and transport and supply locations. (Lang et al, 2009, pp 196-7)

The growing recognition of this human–nature symbiosis has driven attempts by governments and industry – often in partnership – to manage the food–environment relationship more effectively.

Since the Second World War, agricultural policy has been mainly concerned with improving levels of production, largely in the form of agricultural subsidies, guaranteed minimum prices, tariff protection and the purchase of surplus production. But since the 1990s the emphasis has shifted, with subsidies decoupled from production and directed towards agreed public goods:

> ... the maintenance of agricultural land, including permanent pasture, in good agricultural and environmental condition ... cross-compliance with a range of regulations covering environmental protection, animal and plant health, animal welfare and food safety. (Lang et al, 2009, p 209)

However, an ecosystems approach to the management of fisheries has been mixed at best (see also Singer and Mason, 2006, pp 111-14). The need to conserve stocks has been difficult given the issue of overlapping and disputed territories – as well as a fair amount of politicking, corruption and non-enforcement of laws.[12] Changes have been industry-led, with consumers given little relevant information.

Overall, however, issues of biodiversity, environmental protection, pollution and GHGs *have* entered the policy process. So-called 'conservation agriculture' includes minimal soil disturbance, permanent soil cover and crop rotations. Thus, organic farming involves the abolition of inorganic fertilisers and most synthetic pesticides, although, according to Lang et al (2009, p 210), 'with reduced production levels, it does not necessarily make it more efficient in terms of land to energy input ratios or in terms of GHG emissions' (cf Singer and Mason, 2006, pp 197-202, 216-18). Despite its popularity with some consumers, organic farming occupies a fairly minor position within agricultural production overall. Within 'conventional agriculture', meanwhile, improvements in the use of nitrates and pesticides, protection for vulnerable areas, integrated farm management and integrated pest control techniques have been introduced. The principle of sustainability has therefore entered the production process:

> Natural capital (including soil, water, air, plants, animals and ecosystems) has to be integrated in agricultural systems in the form of regenerative technologies, such as: use of nitrogen-fixing plants for soil conservation, use of natural predators for pest control, integration of animals into cropped systems. Social capital entails utilizing: farmer and community labour, and knowledge and experience; and underpinning community cohesion. The aim is to achieve enhancement of both the quality and quantity of wildlife, water, landscape and other public goods of the countryside. (Lang et al, 2009, p 211)

Although we should also heed Kaufman's (2012, pp 49-56, 65-72) warning that corporations have adopted the sustainability principle to forestall a more stringent approach forced on them by governments or consumers. They seek, in other words, to set the terms of the debate, control relevant information and data, co-opt some green non-governmental organisations (NGOs), manage public opinion and so subtly 'regulate the regulators'. Sometimes the strategy is not so subtle. In 2010 the UK Coalition government was allowing major retailers to dominate a Whitehall project on health, smoking, alcohol and food policy – overseen by the Health Minister referred to in note 1 (Hickman, 2010). Clearly, the food supply chain in developed countries remains dominated by private corporate governance, the assumption being that, once standards, auditing regimes and labelling are in the place, consumers can be left to make appropriate choices.

Beyond the production process, steps to reduce adverse environmental impacts have been made in terms of water use, waste, recycling and packaging, and greater energy efficiencies. Since many initiatives emerge at the EU-level or higher, and given both the internationalisation of the supply chain and the dominance of big manufacturers and retailers, national states have adopted a horizontal form of 'mixed governance' (Fitzpatrick, 2011d, pp 164-8). The main instruments have included stronger regulatory standards, landfill taxes, target setting and voluntary agreements.

Lang et al (2009, p 213) identify some positives here, with retailers recognising the business case for more responsible action. They are less complementary about attempts to place the emphasis on consumers' capacity to make informed choices (through certification and labelling schemes) that will send the correct eco-friendly signals back down the supply chain. As noted earlier, they welcome attempts to more directly shape, edit and encourage consumers' ecological values and choices, with retailers and public sector institutions having a central role to play. These upstream solutions involve what is called 'choice-editing', and we explore an aspect of this below.

In sum, Lang et al's (2009, p 218) conclusion at the end of the 2000s was that,

> ... policy-makers have not found many of the answers yet; but some of the right questions are beginning to be asked. Step changes are needed to ensure the health of the environment and our ecosystems,

and the future quality of our food supply and human health; but these substantial step changes are still to be made.

Ecological public health

Clearly, then, for Lang et al (2009; see also Goodman et al, 2010, p 1783) the immediate task is to challenge the economic liberal orthodoxy of the last few decades with its emphasis on consumer choice and competences (or deficiencies) – where food is just another commodity – and its rejection of social rights and state welfare. Only in this way can we begin to reconcile social and environmental domains within what they call an 'ecological public health' (EPH) agenda (see also Barling et al, 2002; Lang et al, 2002):

> … the pursuit of public health requires the analysis of the composite interactions between the material, biological, social and cultural dimensions of existence. This demands a new mix of interventions and actions to alter and ameliorate the determinants of health; the better framing of public and private choices to achieve sustainable planetary, economic, societal and human health; and the active participation of movements to that end. (Rayner and Lang, 2012, p 353)

'Ecological' thus refers both to the natural environment and to these complex, mutually determinate relationships (Rayner and Lang, 2012, pp 62-5, 92-102). Obesity, for instance, is made possible by developed nations monopolising the world's resources, and should be understood, not as greedy people hoovering food into their mouths, but via the interactions of material, biological, cultural and social dimensions (Rayner and Lang, 2012, pp 316-21).

Lang (2010) summarises EPH's main elements:

- food quality (fresh food, sustainable sources, local production)
- social justice (animal welfare, fairtrade, good work conditions)
- environment (water, climate change, land use, soil, biodiversity, organic)
- health (safety, nutrition, cultural practices, for example, marketing and store checkouts; see Haigh and Durham, 2012)
- social determinants (access, affordability, socioeconomic status).

There is already some evidence of development in this respect, with UK healthcare beginning to emphasise prevention rather than simply treating conditions once they develop.

Yet such integrative, joined-up strategies have been fairly modest simply because they neglect a wider set of contexts. How effective are education and information campaigns likely to be against a background of energy-dense supermarket choices (rich in fat and sugar), sedentary workplaces and high carbon economies (oil- and car-dependent)? In short, no choice or institution is separable from the broader socioeconomic and cultural context. You can set up exercise classes for overweight people and you can reduce the footprint of the NHS, but such measures are of minor significance in the long term unless you attend to the entire system. Reducing the food chain's negative social and environmental implications implies broader and more radical socioeconomic and cultural changes.

The need for integration quickly bumps up against obstacles that resist it, therefore:

- *Market actors:* supermarkets are likely to oppose anything that challenges their dominance or to co-opt change that cannot be resisted ('greenwash').

- *Political inertia:* politicians focus on the short term (elections) and governments' policy processes are characterised by multiple layers of governance that engender policy drift without firm leadership.

- *Cultural non-compliance:* the needed political and social challenges conflict with the individualistic and consumerist assumptions of the last half-century.

- *Scientific and social uncertainties:*

    ... the need to work out a more subtle and complex way of judging what an adequate diet is, one that integrates not just nutrition and carbon but also issues such as place, time and mode of production.... This will be complex and suggests that future food policy will not be of a "one size fits all" variety. Different outcomes and approaches may be suitable for one policy issue but not for another. (Lang et al, 2009, p 299)

Overall, then, policy and strategic integration must accompany an admission of complexity (uncertainty, conflicts, competing imperatives and lack of clarity). But EPH also assumes that resolving this 'integration + complexity' dilemma requires a renewed emphasis on *food democracy* rather than the fetishisation of consumer choice. Rather than merely providing 'downstream' solutions, for example, food labelling, there is a need to reframe consumers' understandings of the social, health and environmental impacts of what they purchase:

    ... choice is too often presented as what consumers do, while down-playing the choice-editing made "upstream" in food-supply chains by contracts and specifications from farm to shop.... The ecological impact of consumerism might be great, but that is not the same thing as building policy process on a myth that consumers are in charge. (Lang et al, 2009, pp 304-5)

In short, we can see EPH as corresponding to the ecosocial understandings I have been formulating and categorising throughout this book. Table 7.1 summarises and highlights the conjunctions without much need for further commentary.

Table 7.1: The ecosocial poverty of food

	Food poverty		
	Causes	**Symptoms**	**Solutions**
Quantity	High food prices, especially relative to the lowest incomes	Malnourishment; poor nutrition; debt and heat-or-eat trade-offs; greater risk of ill health	Higher wages, benefits, tax credits, etc. Price caps
Mobility	Prevalence of supermarkets; restricted choice and diversity. Food deserts	Food insecurity. Limited availability of and access to good quality food. Impoverished social interaction	Market regulation. Revitalisation of high streets and other shopping boroughs
Value	Individualisation of social problems; assumption of consumer freedom and market sovereignty	Psychosocial risks and anxieties; reliance on processed foods. Cultural disrespect. Reliance on charity	EPH. Renewed emphasis on social determinants. *Upstream/choice-editing*
Control	Alienation and exclusion from the food production process. Emphasis on consumers' responsibilities	Dominance of big four chains. Poor households judged as 'failed agents and consumers'	*Food democracy. Upstream/ choice-editing*
Sharing	Domination by food corporations; consumer passivity. Over-consumption of meat and dairy	Negative externalities, eg loss of soil and water capacity, and biodiversity. Avoidable waste contributing to carbon emissions, eg landfill	EPH; new producer–consumer relationships. New taxes, eg on waste
Caring	Energy imbalance due to reliance on fossil fuels. Separation of social and ecological imperatives	Negative externalities, eg loss of soil and water capacity, and biodiversity. Avoidable waste contributing to carbon emissions, eg landfill	EPH. *Scaling-up sustainable, conservation forms of agriculture and aquaculture.* Low carbon food chains – including local sourcing and fewer food miles. New taxes, eg on waste

Two critical reflections

Free markets are comforting for many because they easily become our adjudicator not only of what is possible or impossible, but also of what is right and wrong; the attractiveness of at-a-distance corporate governance is that it allows others to make our decisions for us. But if what we need is to recognise market relations as a sub-set of morally informed social, public and environmental policies (Sandel, 2012), then our task becomes one of reconciling a plurality of moral perspectives, methods and judgements. 'Food ethics'[13] has become a popular and alluring phrase (our food reveals what and who we care about), but it carries with it a weight of social expectations and ethical diversity (Kaplan, 2012, pp 9-13). In short, there is an openness about both EPH and our ecosocial model which, while offered as a virtue (a society is only an 'open society' if it remains open), contradicts the 2 + 2 = 4 certainties that so often characterise political debate.

I make this point because, in addition to many issues we cannot discuss here due to lack of space (see Lang, 2010, p 1819), Table 7.1 suggests two key questions (indicated by the italics in the table).

First, how can we 'scale up' from farm shops, farmers' markets and organic box schemes while simultaneously 'scaling down' from supermarkets when food corporations and agri-business are so powerful? Lang et al (2009, p 286) stress the importance of social movements:

> ... the pursuit of food democracy is a ceaseless task, involving many interest groups, professions, trade unions, faith groups, voluntary organizations and community groups. The new language is of food citizenship, with rights and responsibilities. Citizens have capacities beyond those of consuming goods and services, they are active in society, which is more than simply a marketplace.

Indeed, we have already been here before – it's simply that so many of us have forgotten. 'Food democracy' movements were a characteristic feature of early campaigns for welfare reform:

> ... in the early 20th century, for instance, the dietary consequences of poverty brought together an alliance of women campaigners, medical interests and unemployed workers. They worked hard to build a political consensus around the value of welfare reforms, food safety nets and the need to give ordinary people more dignified lives. The indignity suffered by poor people due to cash shortages and poor quality diets was a persistent theme.... (Lang et al, 2009, p 284)

This emphasis chimes with that of many others. Riches (1997, p 175: cf Hitchman et al, 2002, p 11) talks of empowerment strategies and reasserting ownership over the production and distribution system. Kneafsey et al (2008, p 170) say that alternative food schemes critique and resist structures of power, and propose new forms of reconnection between food producers and consumers, including partnerships and direct sell schemes. And for an overview of cooperatives (the UK movement is dominated by food co-ops), see Scott Cato and Bickle (2010).

The concept of food democracy taps into the growing realisation on the part of western publics that democracy and 'free' corporate-dominated markets often conflict. But this being the case, are social movements and so on enough? The problem is that without coordinated and cross-national efforts, the effectiveness of social movements and local initiatives may well be modest. Welfare campaigns did indeed prepare the ground for later social policy reforms, but a majority of people only said 'never again' after a Great Depression and a world war gave them and politicians the impetus to propel social developments forward. Additionally, state welfare then often displaced community action in a centralising strategy which delivered universalism but which also suppressed 'bottom-up' initiatives, stifling social democracy's capacity to renew itself and eventually leaving it vulnerable to Thatcherite conservatism. For democracy to prevail the countervailing weight of states is required, but states that will not thereby undermine the democratic gains achieved. A 'food democracy' – and an ecosocial system more generally – faces the same dilemma of how to centralise and coordinate without surrendering its democratising energies (Connelly et al, 2011).

Second, how can we address climate change while protecting, and preferably *enhancing*, personal and political freedoms? We have become used to the 'choice = market choice' and 'freedom = market freedom' equations of economic liberalism. The danger is that in opposing the latter we may continue to accept its premise and believe that regulated markets equate to regulated people. Compare the following:

> If you enjoy unhealthy food so much that you are prepared to accept the risk of disease and premature death, then ... that is primarily your own business. Our focus is on the impact of your food choices on others. (Singer and Mason, 2006, p 4)

> ... [some people] just eat too much and should show more restraint.... the idea that it is wrong to be a glutton is in urgent need of revival. (Singer and Mason, 2006, p 278)

The first quote draws the self/other distinction that is central to Mill's utilitarianism, one with which many non-utilitarians concur. Yet although it is prefaced with a discussion of healthcare costs, the second quote is taken from a passage about Christian sin. Since something is sinful even if no one else is affected, the authors risk abandoning a self/other distinction and sliding into a moralistic discourse.

This would be a minor quibble except that a similar slippage occurs within EPH:

> ... what some call paternalism, be it the improvement of school meals or the banning of tobacco advertising, may accord with the informed collective will. It is there to enhance the conditions of life confronting the individual. (Rayner and Lang, 2012, p 38)

> The pursuit of public health continues J.S. Mill's call for liberty to be the antidote to paternalism. (Rayner and Lang, 2012, p 303)

In both cases, Rayner and Lang are supporting individual wellbeing and democracy against smothering forms of state and corporate dominance. But in the second quote, liberty is presented as an antidote to something (paternalism) approved of in the first quote.

The confusion may derive from the fact that they neither unpack the different kinds of paternalism that exist nor the diverse justifications for them (see Fitzpatrick, 2011a). For instance, in identifying a key problem with nudge economics and libertarian paternalism, that is, that it ignores corporate power, Rayner and Lang (2012, pp 272-5) appear to support a 'soft paternalism' (although without using that terminology). They support the Norwegian breastfeeding campaign of the 1970s, saying it succeeded because rather than seeing women's behaviour as the problem, and hectoring them to change, it *removed* pressure – the commercial interests selling breast milk substitutes.

But here is the challenge. Where harm-to-others is at stake, soft paternalism has no problem with prohibition, regulation and hectoring. The test for soft paternalists arises when appropriate 'structural' reforms are made and some individuals still indulge in harm-to-self. Do soft paternalists have the courage to permit this?

All of which relates to the agenda of upstreaming and choice-editing, by which is meant,

> ... the use of product and process specifications to frame consumer choice by introducing tougher standards, before the consumer selects between items. In effect, this is using conventional business practice for socially and environmentally benign ends. (Lang, 2010, p 1825)

But what kind of upstream interventions are appropriate? The nudge paternalist might be content to place unhealthy foods on the 'fat shelves', hoping that this will dissuade some customers from purchasing them, without actually preventing them from doing so. Rayner and Lang (2012, p 328) would regard this as inadequate. All foods should conform to minimum health standards, they say, implying before-the-shelf interventions which confront those commercial interests reinforcing 'anti-health behaviour'. Fine. But once market and social structures have been suitably altered, surely the soft paternalist has to leave individuals to make their own decisions. If some people want to quaff bags of sugar, then so be it.

We can therefore contemplate minimum prices for alcohol, tobacco and fatty foods. In Fitzpatrick (2008a, pp 103-8) I argue that the government has a right to protect its present and future citizens from the healthcare costs that such indulgences might impose on them. Similarly, when prohibiting harm to others we should often include non-humans as 'others'. But if the self/other distinction is to be maintained, the government does not have a right to say 'this is bad for *you*, therefore we are banning it', nor to raise health taxes beyond what is needed to protect others. I am therefore nervous of Lang et al's (2009, p 301; also Rayner and Lang, 2012, p 318) assertion that 'Obesity is to health what climate change is to the environment.' Where obesity harms others this may be the case. But in so far as obesity is merely harmful to the obese person, the assertion derives from the kind of paternalism from which we do indeed require an antidote.

All of which reflects back on the kind of food democracy we want. Rolling back the free market, without creating a new space for the top-heavy, nanny-knows-best state, implies some kind of deliberative democracy with greater participative inclusion in the policy process (Fitzpatrick, 2002) – including the food chain. Soft paternalism allows you to try and change someone's preferences so long as you respect the rational agency of those with whom you are debating.

In any event, my main point is that these are difficult, intransigent questions. Both EPH and my own ecosocial model offer an agenda and set of aspirations through which they can be discussed and worked through. But allowing ethics to contextualise markets means accepting an openness far broader, less certain and more unnerving than the prescriptions that come from allowing markets to dictate our ethical compass. Those who deny this, or expect a fully elaborated blueprint of policy reforms for the 21st century, may have to look elsewhere.

Conclusion

I began by arguing that food has been de-socialised by economic liberalism and by the domination of food corporations within the food chain. We then sketched recent developments and priorities, concluding that we are ill equipped to deal with the challenges of the 21st century. We reviewed the extent to which an individualistic politics locates the causes of food poverty in poor people themselves, and we saw that the principle of sustainability has (if only marginally) begun to influence policy concerning food and natural environments. The following section then outlined the EPH approach developed by Tim Lang and others, and Table 7.1 mapped this against the ecosocial themes developed in previous chapters. We concluded by raising two issues – concerning democracy and paternalism – that identify issues that will be central to the ecosocial politics of the 21st century.

Once more, we have seen that the destructive use of socionatural resources is connected to the social deprivations of that usage. In terms of food, the gluttony of developed countries has had obvious consequences for developing ones. Yet within affluent nations, too, the poorest have suffered. Economic liberalism has created both the corporatisation of the food chain and a culture in which ill health (especially when related to obesity) is blamed on consumption habits rather than on what happens before food reaches the shelves. Countries which have adopted a regulatory approach, focusing on public goods and public health, and concepts that must make increasing room for ecological objectives, do not demonstrate the same tendency to blame the victim.

Notes
[1] Including a future Secretary of State for Health (Little, 2008).

[2] Based on a survey by the Children's Food Trust – see www.childrensfoodtrust.org.uk/news-and-events/news/cold-chips

[3] See www.netmums.com/home/netmums-campaigns/support-your-food-banks

[4] As Townsend (1979, pp 33-9; see also Dowler and Turner, 2001, pp 16-18) observed, even good faith attempts to define absolute needs in terms of nutritional subsistence have failed, from Rowntree in the UK to Orshansky in the US, since what people need varies according to what their society expects and enables them to do.

[5] See www.trusselltrust.org – between April-June 2013, 150,000 people were referred to food banks, a threefold increase on the same period in 2012. This followed benefit changes including the Bedroom Tax mentioned in Chapter Three earlier (Butler, 2013a).

[6] See www.fareshare.org.uk

[7] See the UN's Food and Agricultural Organization at www.fao.org/index_en.htm

[8] Until 2007, the relative price of food had been falling for decades.

[9] As well as the phenomenon noted by Kaufman (2012), where food prices are spiked by speculators in the global futures and derivatives markets. Or more simply, those with money try to make more money from those who have little or no money.

[10] See the comments by MP Anna Soubry (Quinn, 2013).

[11] Note that I will not be discussing animal welfare here.

[12] See the 2009 documentary, *The End of the Line.*

[13] See also the work of the Food Ethics Council at www.foodethicscouncil.org

EIGHT

Land: housing and urban densities

Since buildings sit on it and food is grown in it, the last two chapters lead us towards another socionatural resource: land. Five topics seem relevant here. We deal with housing and urban density in this chapter, transport, flooding and waste in the next.

Britain has a higher population density than most European countries. If you took its 60 million acres and divided them between 40 million adults, the resulting 1.5 acres per person is equivalent to a box with sides that are 255 feet long. In fact, as noted in Chapter Two, Britons are packed into a space narrower than this for three reasons.

First, large parts of the country are owned by very few, whether corporations, such as the National Trust or the Crown, or family estates (since the Norman Conquest, in some cases). One-third of UK land is owned by just 1,200 families (Cahill, K., 2006, pp 308-9; 2010). Second, the countryside has been relatively protected from development. Third, as the rest of us make do with the leftovers, pressure on space obviously builds up. The domestic residences we occupy are distributed either via housing markets (private residences and rented accommodation) or assessments of need (social housing). Over the last four decades the balance – including planning and regulatory frameworks (Luhde-Thompson and Ellis, 2008, p 47) – has shifted in favour of housing markets, permitting those with the financial resources and political voice to occupy greater space and more desirable locations.

We have encountered housing already in Chapter Three (place poverty) and Chapter Six (energy efficiency). How does housing relate to land? More houses obviously means more of the country is carpeted not just with buildings but also with the public and private infrastructures needed to support them. Furthermore, the number of single-occupier UK households looks set to grow. The question of urban density therefore arises, and we explore this shortly.

In this chapter we look at the social and environmental impacts of the housing market. What effects do those markets have on the rates and nature of UK poverty? Do housing markets contribute to unsustainable urban densities? How should we explain these effects, and what solutions might be proposed?

Housing and poverty

The British obsession with property has deep foundations. Asa Briggs (1990) records how industrialisation and urbanisation first created slums and then a sense of revulsion against squalor on the part of social philanthropists, enlightened employers, charities, civic reformers, revolutionaries (such as Friedrich Engels), trade unionists, political campaigners and even, it seems, Queen Victoria. The dream of living somewhere better than what Nye Bevan condemned as 'rabbit-warren accommodation' (Foot, 1975, p 56) motivated the post-Second World War social housing programme that he initiated. Unfortunately, Bevan's emphasis on housing quality would be overtaken by a quantity-led approach, epitomised by stack-them-high tower blocks promoted by local governments too often mesmerised by modernist images of 'cities in the sky'. What Thatcher skilfully did after 1979 was to rearticulate those historical desires, turning them against the legacies of a social democratic politics that had grown lethargic, by exploiting disaffection with social housing and uniting individuals' aspirations to new visions of Britain as a post-industrial economy whose wealth would come from financial services and speculation. Share ownership and home ownership would be the New Jerusalem, delivered through the private sector.

The long-term consequences of this drove, and reflected, the shift in social values associated with economic liberalism.

Desert is now less a question of *being* than of displaying the outward manifestations of personal worth – conspicuous consumption, jobs, holidays and 'location, location, location'. You are what you are perceived to be by others in a marketplace. In previous, less affluent eras, you could be in need and still be judged as deserving. The respectable poor were valued, or at least patronised. But with the merger of 'worth' and 'wealth', to be in need increasingly became a sign of personal failings. If you need help, then clearly you are not working, or not working hard enough, and so, by definition, you don't deserve any help. Even belonging to groups formally exempt from disapproval is no longer a guarantee of immunity. A child from a deprived neighbourhood might be feral. A person with a disability might just be 'pulling a sickie'. The causes of, and barriers inhibiting solutions to, poverty barely register with two-thirds of the public (Hanley, 2009).[1] Poverty is regarded not as a series of awful – although often temporary – episodes that afflict millions periodically, but as a demon which, stalking our free market utopia, has to be exorcised again and again and again. The wealthiest have accelerated away, and if you cannot follow them financially at least you can assert your status by mimicking a widespread moral and cultural disdain for the disadvantaged. The poorest are punched and then blamed for their bruises.

That the welfare state has struggled to keep pace with these economic and cultural injustices can be seen in the area of housing. By 2013 the Housing Benefits bill stood at £23 billion,[2] with over five million claimants, making it a frequent source of moral panic and inspiring the benefit caps and 'Bedroom Tax' mentioned earlier in Chapter Three. Stripped of context, those statistics lead easily to salivating headlines in a popular press that also stamps its foot menacingly when the obvious alternatives (such as rent control) are proposed. The fact that Housing Benefit goes into landlords' pockets matters little, not when it is easier to rage at the (very rare) family living in mansions at taxpayers' expense.[3]

That context goes unmentioned for the simple reason that it consists of the property boom from which millions have benefited. Development land is now 200 times more valuable than agricultural land (Evans and Unsworth, 2012, p 1166). This is not to view people as selfish, necessarily. With the state pension withering, it is understandable that so many have sought to finance their retirement through housing. You climb the housing ladder – buying low, selling high – before retiring, releasing the equity, enjoying the proceeds and bequeathing some to the children. With millions playing the same game, this propels house prices upwards. And the more people play the game, the more the game is worth playing. No wonder that housing markets are sometimes described as pyramid schemes (Mulheirn, 2011). You might even become a buy-to-let landlord; with rising prices come rising deposits, meaning millions are forced to rent. The buy-to-let market takes properties off the market, demand outstrips supply even more, fuelling ever higher prices and deposits and rents. It's a win-win merry-go-round.[4]

Except for those on low incomes and no 'Bank of Mum and Dad' to help. Before the 1980s housing subsidies were directed at bricks and mortar (Webb, 2012, p 9). Since then, it is demand that has been subsidised to help tenants keep pace with soaring costs. Even with low take-up (up to a million people do not claim Housing Benefit), such entitlements led to the benefits bill that conservatives condemn (Fitzpatrick, 2012, pp 226-8), poverty traps being due not to low wages, but to 'lazy people staying in bed while the rest of us leave for work at 4.30am', etc, etc. Yet there is only so much that benefits can do to compensate for housing markets that powered the fantasy economy which crashed in 2007–09.

Overall, then:

- 43 per cent of social renters are living in poverty after housing costs;
- 38 per cent in the private rented sector are living in poverty after housing costs;
- 37 per cent of homeowners are in poverty if their imputed rent (see below) is not included in measures of household income. If it is included, few homeowners are in poverty (Tunstall et al, 2013).

Bramley (2012, pp 141-4) finds that, like poverty in general, there is quite a lot of 'churn' when it comes to housing needs. Most housing problems tend to be temporary because people:

- trade down to cheaper housing;
- adapt their spending to their income and/or housing needs;
- accumulate debt or run down savings;
- accumulate arrears on mortgage payments or rent;
- apply for state assistance;
- dissolve and/or become reliant on family support.

Yet these strategies may have adverse, knock-on consequences and, even if they are successful, problems can recur in later years:

> ... households with a current affordability problem ... are five times
> more likely to find hire purchase repayments a heavy burden, four times
> more likely to spend more than 40% of their net weekly income on
> food, and 1.7 times more likely to have no car. They are also slightly
> more likely to say that they have not bought any of a list of consumer
> durables over the last year. (Bramley, 2012, p 142)

Not surprisingly, problems are correlated with low income, few assets, high
rents and lower security of tenure: 'Private renting has the highest incidence
of problems, and owner occupation the lowest, with social renting occupying
an intermediate position' (Bramley, 2012, p 144). Lone parents, single-person
households and younger people are particularly disadvantaged.

In addition to benefits, other aspects of the post-war system remain. Good
quality, low-cost housing still exists with the social housing sector, accounting for
18 per cent of all households, having a fairly redistributive effect. Through area-
based initiatives and urban regeneration, New Labour sought a 'neighbourhood
renewal' (Cole and Goodchild, 2001). It also required builders to include affordable
housing in their development plans in order to receive planning permission (Monk
et al, 2006).[5] This was not simply about ensuring a supply of good, low-cost
housing, but about trying to facilitate social integration through a mix of tenures.

One effect of the 1980s sale of council housing was that it helped to disperse
different housing types into separate social spaces (Lee, 1994), although this
point about social distancing should not be overstated. Clarke and Monk (2011,
p 422) warn against making simplistic associations between spatial deprivation
and concentrations of tenure. The vast majority of social housing residents
'live in areas with between 10 and 60 per cent social housing.' Although areas
with high proportions of social rented housing suffer disproportionate levels of
poverty, tenure is only part of the problem, and we should not equate 'poor
neighbourhoods' with 'socially rented housing'. Targeting residualised areas makes
no sense when there are few such areas to be found.

That said, there is little to challenge the thesis, evidenced in earlier chapters,
that Britain is a more disconnected country than it once was, with housing
reforms adding to the cumulative effects of low wage employment, education
reforms and rising inequalities. For several decades after the Second World War
there was much less disconnection:

> ... 55% of British people born in 1946, and 48% of those born in
> 1958, spent at least some time in social housing in their childhood.
> (Lupton et al, 2009, p 3)

But the explosion in home ownership and the evisceration of local authority
housing reversed this trend (Beaumont, 2006; Lee et al, 2006), aided by changes to
labour markets (Hills, 2007). The North–South divide is largely due to property
prices, with low-skilled and public sector workers in the South increasingly

disadvantaged (Strelitz and Darton, 2003, pp 91-4). This divide should not blind us to intra-regional variations yet, overall, there are fewer in-between neighbourhoods than was once the case.

That bifurcation then becomes a source of the simplistic and highly politicised associations that Clarke and Monk warn against. New Labour's attempt at neighbourhood renewal was a worthy but tricky undertaking (Bretherton and Pleace, 2011; see also Darcy, 2010). Researchers disagree about its accomplishment, with some calling it a qualified success (Shaw and Robinson, 2010) and others more sceptical, arguing that, despite welcome extra finance, New Labour fuelled the demonisation of those seen to have excluded themselves from social norms (Mathews, 2010).

According to the Conservative-led Coalition government, most social problems are due to 120,000 'troubled families' (Casey, 2012).[6] Thus social housing has become associated with 'sink estates', antisocial behaviour and benefit dependency. When political parties talk about *troubled* families we all hear the dog whistle and know who, *and where*, they mean (Hanley, 2007).

Housing and the natural environment

In addition to its social effects, housing has implications for the natural environment, as we saw in Chapter Six. Those impacts can be direct (housing developments) or indirect (resources diverted away from ecological sustainability). Ten buildings do not necessarily have a worse impact than five buildings. Quantity matters, but what matters more is the geographical distribution of those buildings.

There is disagreement about how much sprawl exists in the UK. Officially, about 9 per cent of England's land area is urbanised (Stratton, 2012), but the Campaign to Protect Rural England contests this: 'the UK National Ecosystem Assessment shows that 14.6% of England's land area is already classed as urban – the third highest figure in Europe after Belgium and Holland.'[7] It depends on where you perceive sprawl as ending. A road takes up a fixed area, but the noise and pollution it generates spreads farther. The trend everywhere, however, is towards more sprawl. Since the 1950s,

> European cities have expanded on average by 78%, whereas the population has grown by only 33%. (EEA, 2006, p 11)

Even so, 14.6 per cent hardly seems like much. Due to restrictions on development, builders economise on plots: '... the average size of new homes has got smaller, so that the smallest new homes in western Europe now appear to be being built in England' (Evans and Unsworth, 2012, p 1166). If what counts as 'high' or 'low' density varies from place to place (Cheng, 2010, pp 13-16), perhaps Britain is already dense enough. So why be concerned?

The consensus is that, beyond a certain threshold, lower density housing is worse for the environment than higher density housing (Bulkeley, 2013, pp 64-5,

119-21).[8] This challenges the 'garden cities' approach of Ebenezer Howard (1985, p 11, emphasis in original): 'Town and country *must be married*, and out of this joyous union will spring a new hope, a new life, a new civilization.' But by and large, most regard higher densities as desirable:

> With low population density there are simply not enough people to make public transport a viable alternative to cars. We need to achieve a density of 50 homes per hectare as a minimum sustainable density to support a regular bus service.... Existing areas of terraced housing and low- and medium-rise blocks of flats normally far exceed this density, reducing energy use in transport, encouraging local shopping and offering easier conditions for high-efficiency renovation. Higher density also helps social integration and reduces isolation by supporting mixed uses and better services. Existing suburbs in cities and towns have an average density of 35 homes per hectare or less. They could be made more environmentally sustainable through subdivision of property and infill building, creating enough density to support local services and public transport within walking distance. (Power, 2008, pp 4489-90; see also Power and Houghton, 2007, pp 108-9)

If Power's minimum threshold is correct, then parts of the UK need to achieve higher densities.[9] Even central London is nowhere near the 'superdensities' of central Paris and Barcelona, for instance (Kohn, 2010, pp 50-7; see also Wyatt, 2008). In short, higher densities involve:

- lower consumptions of fossil fuels as people travel across shorter distances, often on public transport;
- more efficient heating and cooling systems (shared walls and floors/ceilings, urban heat islands; see Kohn, 2010, pp 37-41) (combined heat and power systems become more viable, as do district cooling networks);
- fewer cars, as well as more walking and cycling, often in shared public spaces that can facilitate social capital, communal integration and cultural diversity.

Higher densities can yield ecological, health and social benefits. I say *can* because we should be wary of making casual generalisations. As Mitrany's (2005) research in Haifa suggests, much depends on planning and design; high density in residential areas alone was widely perceived as negative, but in public and social areas, the response was more positive. Inputs from users and residents also matter. Forsyth et al (2010) draw on evidence from the Corridor Development Initiative, in Minneapolis-St Paul (Minnesota), to show that with community participation and control in the planning process, support for high-density housing can be built (see also Bulkeley and Mol, 2003). But the nature and efficacy of the planning system will itself depend on broader socioeconomic structures and political processes (Winston, 2010). Quastel et al (2012) show how 'densification' in Vancouver has a distinct class dimension, benefiting homeowners much more than renters. Poor, working-class and ethnic communities have been displaced from inner-city neighbourhoods (the process known as 'gentrification'). Thus, densification has been separated from environmental concerns (reductions in emissions) and social concerns (social housing needs) (see also Rachel Lombardi et al, 2011, p 292). Unsworth (2007, pp 741-2) found similar limitations in Leed's 'city living' apartment schemes.

Therefore, higher density *per se* is not a magic bullet.[10] As we saw in the last chapter, there is a need to reconnect people to the food chain, something that is central to the garden cities vision (Vale and Vale, 2010, p 24). And all cities require a degree of unplanned spontaneity, of chaos and excitement, where people encounter unknown others, and the identities of communities are open and organic (Heng and Malone-Lee, 2010). The needs for privacy, for contact with nature and to control spatial boundaries must be part of any higher density aspiration (Lawson, 2010). Nor should higher densities compromise the need, discussed in Chapter Three, to allow the poorest more domestic space than many of them currently have. Resentment, anxiety and social conflict can be the result of forcing people together. And while public spaces and parks are vital, Stenner et al (2012) and Coolen and Meesters (2012, p 65) suggest that private domestic gardens are both desired and desirable.

This more rounded appreciation of what urban reform could mean often motivates the drive for 'transition towns' in which all parts of a community work together to address climate change (Lockyer, 2010, pp 208-14; Bulkeley, 2013, pp 217-23). This means supporting local economies, for example, local food chains, energy generation and local currencies, building self-sufficiency and resilience, and experimenting with new communal and civic projects.

Similarly, many search for an ideal that combines features of both compact cities and garden cities. Holden (2004, p 106) refers to this as the 'decentralised concentration' of small, high-density cities with short distances between housing and services. Such 'polycentric cities' imply either dense centres within large cities, or groups of compact towns, although that is not our concern in this chapter.

If housing density lower than a sustainable minimal threshold is ecologically damaging, what should our response be? What creates low densities exactly?

Let's first dispel the opinion that we are powerless to do anything about sprawl. Gordon and Cox (2012, pp 567-8) argue that urban planning policies have relatively little impact given the workings of market forces, the inertia created by political-legal systems (based on private property rights) and the importance of cultural norms and standards; for example, it is easier to get Europeans into cars than to get Americans out of them. Increasing sprawl has been a feature of European and American cities for generations, they observe. Cities sprawl because that's what a capitalist economy requires. Gordon and Cox therefore salute the free market, anti-government bias that has characterised much (but not all) of the US experience.

But where other socioeconomic principles prevail, planning *does* make a difference (Bulkeley and Betsill, 2003, pp 142-3). According to Evans and Unsworth (2012), after 2001 housing density increased in England compared to Scotland due to planning guidance issued in the former but not the latter. Standards, taste and choice are important but are always shaped by differing social contexts into which policy interventions can be made (Evans and Unsworth, 2012, p 1175).

If we *can* re-engineer housing densities, therefore, what *should* we do? What should our policies target? There are many causes of urban expansion, suburban growth, commuter belts and edge towns (cf EEA, 2006, p 17), but key factors include:

- *Demographic change:* higher birth rates; more post-divorce households; more single-person households as people delay or avoid marriage; more single-person elderly households as people live longer and women typically outlive men.
- *Rising affluence and consumerism:* as more people can afford cars, more people buy them and more roads are then built (see Chapter Nine).
- *Technological change:* for instance, as cars become more fuel-efficient so they become easier and cheaper to run.
- *Policy priorities:* planners and policy-makers have been fairly conservative. Seen as a solution to congestion, road building frequently just fuels more congestion. Public transport has also suffered in the UK (we also review this in Chapter Nine).
- *Path dependency:* the past is sticky. Although planning can make a difference, it is often easier to prefer the line of least resistance. A common illustration of this is the rebuilding of London after the 1666 Great Fire when proposals to widen London's streets were rejected in favour of following the old layouts (Inwood, 2002, pp 95-6).
- *Unintended consequences:* Owen (2009, p 25) quotes an unnamed environmentalist: 'Sprawl is created by people escaping sprawl.'

The housing markets of the last three or four decades must be added to this list, if only because they haunt the items above. Demographic change boosts increased demand; increased wealth and consumer expectations drive housing aspirations upward; policy-makers seek the votes of homeowners as the latter become a powerful lobby; and people spread out in search of privatised forms of security as social rights are dismantled, social inequalities grow and notions of the common, public good erode.

There is an additional characteristic of housing markets, however, one that Brueckner and Helsley identify. Where the literature has normally regarded blight as causing sprawl – affluent families escaping inner-city conditions that attract low-income households – Brueckner and Helsley (2011, p 212) view both as being,

... responses to fundamental market failures affecting urban land markets. The analysis shows that distortions commonly identified as causes of inefficient spatial expansion of urban areas (unpriced traffic congestion, uninternalized open-space externalities, and underpriced suburban infrastructure) also cause an inefficient shortfall in housing reinvestment and maintenance in the central city.

In other words, private benefits to commuters and builders are higher than the social costs of, respectively, commuting and land development, because those costs are distributed throughout the community as a whole. This leads to excessive suburban development, depressing city centre housing prices and undermining incentives to invest in inner cities. Raising the private cost of sprawl – Brueckner and Helsley recommend congestion pricing and an open-space amenity tax – will rebalance those incentives and reduce urban blight (see also Bednar-Friedl et al, 2011).

Given the emphasis on externalities in Chapter Four, my endorsement of this argument will come as no surprise. Markets involve more than failures in the price mechanism, however. In theory, these are easily correctable. But at a more fundamental level, there is something irrational about the behaviour of market agents that price corrections may not address. In short, what also matters is the 'positional racing' of which housing markets are a key manifestation. To understand this and its social impacts, for example, poverty, and its ecological impacts, that is, low urban densities, we first have to understand the relevance of rent-seeking.

Rent-seeking

Rent is payment for the consumption of a resource made to that resource's owner. I own the home that I rent to you for £500 per month. I maximise my income by keeping your rent high, although not so high that I price myself out of the market.

Renters try to lower their rents by:

- moving from place to place, seeking the lowest viable rents;
- entering the social housing sector, in which rents are protected;
- saving, so that they can eventually become owners.

Where the user and the owner are the same, the 'imputed rent' is an opportunity cost: the owner-occupier foregoes the income to be derived by renting their house to others. When housing demand exceeds supply, my home's resource value may well increase above the standard rate of inflation, meaning that the imputed rent falls relative to the increasing wealth stored in the resource.[11]

In other words, rising house prices means that renters typically face rent *increases* while owner-occupiers face *decreases* in the relative imputed rent. (When supply exceeds demand the reverse happens.) Non-owners seek low rents in competition both with landlords seeking high rents and with owner-occupiers seeking lower imputed rents. This is why social democrats stress the importance of social housing, capital gains tax, rent control and tenants' entitlements – each offers some protection for non-owners from markets in which owners seek the highest possible returns. In a system where the sheer ownership of something confers such returns, it is therefore no surprise that people seek them, especially when government subsidies are attached. Until house prices dipped at the end of the 2000s the housing ladder was really a housing escalator where all you had to do was stand still while the laws of supply and demand carried you upwards.

But there is more. Some resources are 'absolutely scarce'. Absolute natural scarcity occurs when, for example, only so many people can experience a view of a particular landscape. The more people crowd in to enjoy the view, the less of a view there is to enjoy. Absolute social scarcity occurs because, for example, only so many people can occupy leadership positions. The more leaders there are, the less of a leader any one of them can be.

There are also relative scarcities. A relative natural scarcity retains some of its value regardless of crowding. A millionaire may choose the most expensive dish but the actual taste of the food does not alter even if everyone else in the restaurant buys the same item. A relative social scarcity also retains value. Leadership roles must be limited in number, but those roles can be rotated periodically.

A taxonomy of scarcities is represented in Figure 8.1.

But there's a catch. Those who occupy privileged positions will typically try to defend them. I don't want my view to be ruined by others; I don't want others undermining my leadership. Privilege extends to relative scarcities, too. I order the most expensive dish not just because of its taste but because I want to consume other diners' envy of my worth. If everyone else is eating the same food, much of its value *is* reduced. In short, what does and does not count as an absolute or relative scarcity depends not just on the thing itself, but also on the conflicts between those trying to use or own the thing. Scarcities are partly *manufactured scarcities*, matters of interpersonal and political conflict.[12]

How are scarcities manufactured? First, by restricting access: those who possess resources wield considerable power over how and how far those resources are distributed.[13] Second, by managing perceptions: I try to convince you that absolute scarcities cannot be made relative, or that what you think of as relative scarcities are really absolute ones. Manufactured scarcities are resources that are *made to be*, and/or *made to seem*, scarce. Inegalitarian societies are characterised by manufactured scarcities. Some are right-wing, for example, where the unequal distribution of wealth is represented, not in terms of power, inheritance or luck, but as the product of merit and fair competition. Some are left-wing, for example, where a communist party controls the distribution of offices. Genuinely egalitarian societies – by making natural resources, social resources and public goods available to everyone – are characterised by fewer manufactured scarcities.[14]

Rent-seeking behaviour should be understood in these terms. Owners raise the value of their resources by manufacturing the scarcity of those resources.

Figure 8.1: A taxonomy of scarcities

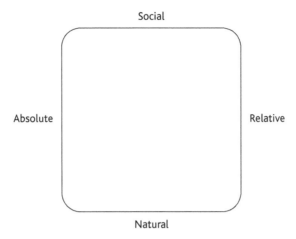

They restrict access to them and represent that restriction as desirable and/ or inevitable. Think of land. In one sense land has absolute limits, there being only so much habitable land on the planet's surface. But land is also subject to manufactured scarcity, as we saw in the 'Housing and poverty' section on page 143. The property boom of the last few decades, and the shift away from social housing, first kicks low-income individuals down the housing ladder and then blames them for being too lazy to climb. The rent-seeking of owners therefore involves not just acquiring a resource with rentable value, but the acquisition of a privileged position that allows them to control the opportunities for others to acquire resources.

As such, my rent-seeking as an owner is socially insensitive. Anything that reduces demand (or increases supply) is detrimental to my interests. If a government institutes a massive housebuilding programme, then the equity in my house falls and my stock of wealth tumbles. I am therefore going to kick up a political stink. Although the fact that the programme may be designed to help the poorest appeals to my social conscience, I cannot help but be conscious that my wealth is under threat.

My rent-seeking is also ecologically insensitive. If cutting down a tree to make room for a conservatory increases my house's equity, then so be it. In truth, since people seem to like trees, I have to bear this in mind too. But the point is that the intrinsic value of the environment is subordinated to marketable values. If people were happy to pay for conservatories and holographic trees, then owners would be incentivised accordingly.

Governments committed to social and environmental justice therefore have to address rent-seeking. Marxists propose to abolish the class of private owners so that productive property is owned collectively; social democrats prefer to increase social (and ecological) sensitivity while preserving private property. Both strategies are problematic. Abolition in the former Soviet Union just created different forms of privilege and rent-seeking. For social democrats the obstacles are also considerable. Spreading assets sounds attractive but, as noted in Chapter Two, since genuine asset distribution threatens the privileges of existing asset-owners, you fairly soon bump up against the limits of economic and political power. That is precisely why, seeking to expand the size of what the Left historically derided as the 'rentier class', conservative governments did so with smoke and mirrors. The privatisations of the 1980s and 1990s spread some wealth thinly while also allowing lots of wealth to be concentrated in the hands of the already wealthy.

In short, land is a socionatural resource, which, partly through housing markets, is manufactured into a scarcity by rent-seeking practices that encourage insensitivity to desirable social and ecological goals. Therefore, what Brueckner and Helsley view as a 'fundamental market failure' is only part of the story. A negative externality is not simply about the price mechanism failing to internalise costs, it is also about the social values and practices of individuals, in competitive pursuit of goods that ultimately bring less satisfaction than they expect (see below). In the conflicting, rent-seeking behaviour of competing groups, capitalism *depends on market failures* in which some are systemically disadvantaged.

None of this would have sounded particularly original in the 19th century to a pro-capitalist such as David Ricardo, a communist such as Karl Marx or a radical liberal such as Henry George. But the return of economic liberalism, the decline of labour movements, the timidity of social democratic parties, the collusion of the media, the corrosive effects of social inequalities and the evisceration of our political vocabulary has left us without the power to translate such understanding into real social change.

Positional racing

Some academic debates try to keep the flame alive. A positional good is a good whose value depends on its scarcity and whose value would therefore be reduced – and perhaps destroyed – if that scarcity was compromised. My house is expensive because its countryside view adds a value that a similarly sized house in a city street cannot have. If others build new houses so that they can enjoy the view, then pretty soon there would be no view to enjoy and no added value to be derived (Hirsch, 1977, pp 36-41). Let me adapt a common example.

In a stadium there are only so many seats that can occupy row 1, nearest the pitch. I pay the highest price because I want a good view *and* because it confers on me a higher status than those in the cheaper seats. If people from rows 2-50 were to crowd into row 1, no one would have a decent view. But this is unlikely to happen since each row has a positional advantage or status compared to those behind (row 2 compared to rows 3-50, row 3 compared to rows 4-50, and so on). Therefore, while envying those in front of them, the inhabitants of each row defend their territory from those behind. Radical social change is unlikely because everyone has a positional advantage to defend and because we often fear losses (from those behind us) more than we desire gains (from those ahead of us)

(Kahneman et al, 1999). This affects even those with little to defend; the less you have, the more small advantages become a source of self-respect in a system that devalues you. So, the very inequality that makes economic reform necessary also makes it psychologically and politically difficult.

The stadium example is stationary, of course. In reality, the members of each row try to keep up as those in front risk pulling away and those behind risk catching up. Positional advantages are maintained through competitive, *positional racing*.

Positional goods, then, are always socially exclusive in that they depend on others *not* having them. Economic growth can improve the comfort of everyone's seat, but there will always be a distinction between the better and the cheaper seats which rising prosperity does not alter. In Hirsch's (1977) famous phrase, there are *social limits to growth*.

The Right often denigrate this analysis, of course. In their attack on Robert Frank, Kashdan and Klein (2006) assume that,

(1) people desire consumption goods due to inherent characteristics of human nature;
(2) markets are always self-correcting (they 'spontaneously adjust');
(3) government action makes problems worse; and
(4) we should not exaggerate the damage positional competition causes.

As they say in relation to an example of Frank's, 'Buying expensive gas grills is a relatively harmless way for people to flatter the will to eminence' (Kashdan and Klein, 2006, p 431).

Points (2) and (3) have, of course, been vindicated in 2007–09 by one of the worst economic crashes in history. Or not. I forget.[15] Points (1) and (4) treat goods as static. They assume that conflicts are resolved by markets for the benefit of all, ignoring the extent to which markets are dominated by actors defending their advantages to the detriment of those below, for example, through manufacturing scarcities. The desire for position drives competition; in turn, the outcomes of competition socially construct positional desires and capacities. Point (4) further downplays social and environmental costs. Too many grills may tip the environment beyond a point that can be corrected.

Kashdan and Klein therefore ignore the realities of socioeconomic conflict, for example, *positional externalities* (see also Hirsch, 1977, p 53). A positional externality is created when, because of inequalities in resources, opportunities and powers, the quantity and severity of the negative externalities I impose on you exceeds the quantity and severity of the negative externalities you impose on me. To put it crudely, I maintain my position by getting those in the rows behind me to swallow my rubbish. Take three examples.

First, food poverty can be interpreted in this way. Greenhalgh (2005, p 1101) traces how the time-saving demands of the rich drove innovations such as prepared food, the cheapest versions of which now dominate the diets of the poorest. Second, the labour market is thought by some to constitute an insider-outsider system (van Parijs, 1995, pp 211-14). The monopolisation of jobs and wages by some creates the systemic low wages and unemployment experienced by others (the 'reserve army'). Finally, positional advantages are often intergenerational. The implications of poverty and class for educational attainment have long been understood (Reay, 2006). Bramley and Karley (2007) find that housing tenure provides an additional, independent factor. Your choices disadvantage other people's children.

In short, we cannot simply offer a bit of market tinkering as a solution to the problem of negative externalities when the competitive, positional racing which characterises market societies, and which market societies encourage, depends on the proliferation of those very externalities. Something more fundamental is required.

To sum up: to maintain positional advantage you must engage in a competitive race that involves avoiding the negative externalities of others and trying to impose your negative externalities on them. Positionality therefore adjoins the earlier discussion about rent-seeking.

To own a house is to occupy the front rows. This confers a positional advantage vis-à-vis renters – especially in the absence of state intervention – who lose (in higher rents) from the rising house prices that benefit landlords (via higher rents) and owner-occupiers (lower relative imputed rents). Furthermore, positional advantage denotes a power to manufacture scarcities and thereby to impose negative externalities on those less advantaged. I can lower supply by, for instance, campaigning against proposed housing developments, or against the social expenditure needed for social housing, or against Council Tax revaluation and property taxes, or indeed any scheme that threatens my advantages. Otherwise my positional status risks slipping, with all the emotional-psychological trauma that can create in a society characterised by competitive racing (Frank, 1999, pp 187-93).

As noted earlier, the housing market in one sense can be a win-win game I gain from people stepping on to the housing ladder *so long as they do so below me*, pushing the ladder higher and allowing me to rise accordingly. But the debate about positional goods highlights the extent to which this improvement is a comforting illusion (Frank, 1999, p 159). The same rising prices which privilege me relative to those on the lower rungs also make it hard for me to climb the rungs above. Leaving the race would therefore be better, yet it is somehow easier to cling to comforting illusions, no matter how irrational this may be.

Positionality and rent-seeking through housing markets therefore have drastic consequences.

Greenhalgh (2005, pp 1100-2) argues that markets are largely geared to satisfying the demands of the wealthy for positional goods that are time-saving and resource-heavy. This has two effects. First, the needs of the poorest are neglected. Second and third homes proliferate, with holiday homes typically under-utilised, even as homelessness persists. Second, with labour being diverted into delivering positional goods, the relative price of skilled labour rises, labour-intensive services become more expensive and so further labour-saving innovations are devised. Resources that could serve ecological ends are therefore directed towards satisfying lucrative but wasteful desires.

Such effects are variously malign and benign so far as the natural environment is concerned. Positional advantage encourages sprawl (I and those like me seek desirable locations far from the madding crowd) but may also limit it (my location is only desirable if it remains exclusive). Sprawl creates the low densities that add carbon emissions to the atmosphere due to the increased use of transport and domestic energy, but positionality can also contain sprawl as the wealthiest try to inhibit nearby housing developments.[16]

In terms of social justice the effects are less ambivalent. As everyone runs in order to stand still, runaway housing markets, as well as the shift away from social housing and 'bricks and mortar' subsidies, create the poverty detailed above. But the effects are also generational, affecting the middle classes too, the irony of which would taste delicious if it weren't so bitter:

> Owner-occupiers … approved the increase in the value of their homes…. [Yet] The same person will object to new homes being built in their area while regretting that their graduate son or daughter is still living at home or has to be subsidised to be able to afford "decent" living space. (Evans and Unsworth, 2012, p 1167)

What solutions can be imagined (see Hirsch, 1977, pp 182-90)? Are we on the positional treadmill forever?

The Marxist's solution is to abolish the rows, but the disadvantages of this are noted above. A compensatory alternative, one commensurate with existing practices, comes via the tax system. Through redistribution we might reduce the number of rows by pushing them closer together. However, when advocating taxation Robert Frank argues that one further consequence might be to slow the treadmill down and provide people with greater opportunities to jump off it. Frank (1999, p 222; 2011, pp 76-81) advocates increasing taxes on positional goods in order to encourage consumption of those goods such as time which are not subject, or less likely to be subject, to positional racing and manufactured scarcity. By limiting the consumption expenditures of the wealthiest we reduce the 'expenditure cascade' where, in order to keep up, the middle class must spend more, work more hours and save less (Frank, 2011, pp 61-2). Frank believes that economic instruments can effect changes to our social values and practices:

> … the fact that people at the top save more and spend less on [housing] will shift the frame of reference that influences the housing expenditures of those just below the top. So they, too, will spend less on housing, and so on all the way down the income ladder. (Frank, 2006, p 442)

Redistribution is not simply about compensating the least advantaged, but about redirecting resources and social priorities towards social and environmental ends (Frank, 1999, pp 207-10).

From an ecosocial perspective the objective must be not simply to slow the treadmill and provide people with non-positional alternatives, but to do so in ways that serve social and ecological principles directly. A general expenditure tax on luxuries may or may not do this. A specific proposal that many favour is that of a Land Value Tax (LVT).

Land value taxation

Dolphin (2013, p 14) says that LVT '... would be progressive, as richer people are more likely to own expensive land.... And it would be impossible to avoid. In many respects, an LVT is the ideal tax.' Similarly, the Mirrlees Review says that since land does not move, and its ownership is generally visible, it is relatively easy to levy taxation on land (Mirrlees et al, 2011, p 368).[17]

The Mirrlees Review offers two main justifications for a LVT (Mirrlees et al, 2011, pp 371-2). First, it would not distort behaviour nor discourage economic activity. Second, the rental value of land is socially determined rather than being due to landowners' efforts.[18] Since land which benefits from good infrastructure (such as transport links), property booms or proximity to community facilities rises in marketable value, a LVT returns some of those benefits to the social community.

The Mirrlees Review was concerned with market values and did not consider issues of ecological sustainability, or the intrinsic values defended in Chapter Two. This obviously adds another layer of complication to any efforts to determine the site value of land. Those activities which contribute to sustainability, benefit further 'external developments' and/or recognise and preserve a piece of a land's intrinsic value could be rewarded with a LVT rebate (see below). Those activities that do none of these things might be subject to higher rates of LVT. (This would introduce complexity into a LVT system, but the practicalities of determining and organising this we leave to one side here.) In short, there is a third, environmentalist argument for LVT.[19]

In terms of housing, these arguments for LVT mean that it would need to satisfy three objectives.

(1) Generate revenue that can be directed towards the poorest. If you want to live in an exclusive, low-density part of the country, you should pay the full social and environmental costs of doing so. Those not prepared to do so can reduce their tax burden by relocating.[20] The revenue generated can be distributed either directly (to low-income households) or indirectly (by increasing the supply of housing), or both. In short, rather than actually giving everyone a box of land whose sides are 255 feet long, LVT is the nearest equivalent, connecting individuals to a key socionatural resource that could generate a dependable stream of income. And if one further effect (as Frank alleges) is

to restrain the property bubbles that disadvantage the poorest, drive positional competition and stifle the development of non-positional goods, then great.

(2) Contain sprawl and facilitate higher density housing. If additional taxation encouraged large estates to be broken up and sold for development, so generating sprawl, then that might conflict with the need for higher density housing. So the design of LVT would need to be ecologically sensitive. Since the most valuable real estate is often found in city centres, a proper restructuring and revaluation could help to encourage the more efficient use of land.

(3) Assist other ecological objectives. The revenue generated by LVT could assist the energy efficiencies and building retrofits reviewed in Chapter Six. Such revenue might assist other reforms. Take one example. A lot of resistance to sustainability projects such as wind farms is a NIMBYist defence of property values.[21] Yet not all of that opposition is necessarily antisocial. The profits from wind farms typically flow away from the community that has to live near them. Since affluent areas are more successful at resisting developments, developers target poorer ones:

> ... areas less likely to oppose wind energy development tended to have populations with lower life expectancies, a lower propensity to vote in elections, and higher crime. (Cowell et al, 2011, p 7)

Therefore, development that diverts benefits to the local community can build support, redistribute resources, enable local ownership and control and improve the long-term social and environmental resilience of poorer areas:

> One exciting vision is that benefits flowing to communities from large, commercial wind farms could, over a 25-year period, leave the communities with a more sustainable, autonomous, locally embedded energy system, which retains more local employment and generates funds for other goals. (Cowell et al, 2011, p 4)

Arguably, then, LVT could be designed to further recognise and reward the contribution of those areas to increasing the availability of clean, renewable energy. In wealthier areas this could offset some of the surcharge levied on low-density communities and help to build the political support noted earlier in note 17.

Conclusion

This chapter has discussed land, focusing on housing markets and urban densities. It argued that housing-related poverty has risen due to a property boom, the decline in social housing and a shift in state subsidies towards Income Support. We saw that recent housing can also affect the natural environment adversely through the urban sprawl that creates densities lower than are ecologically sustainable. One key driver of urban sprawl is the housing markets of the last few decades. Poverty and sprawl therefore have a common denominator: the rent-seeking behaviour that typically favours owners above non-owners. This behaviour involves the manufacture of scarcities so that those enjoying a positional advantage can maintain their advantages despite the social and environmental harms such behaviour often creates. The solution is to rebalance priorities so that non-positional goods come to the fore. One way of assisting this is through LVT, although much depends on its design. See Table 8.1 for a summary.

This analysis suggests that, for all their good intentions, even the most progressive social policies have contributed to an enduring problem: a disenfranchisement from a key socionatural resource that affects the poorest most adversely. As Davy (2009, p 253) observes:

> ... the fiscal supremacy of tax-based or contribution-based social security prevented land reform in most Western countries.... The

Table 8.1: The ecosocial poverty of land 1

| | Land poverty 1 | | |
	Causes	Symptoms	Solutions
Quantity	Property booms. Emphasis shifted away from bricks and mortar; inadequate Income Support	Millions locked out of the housing market; high rents. Residualisation of social housing	Revenue from LVT diverted to social and ecological ends
Mobility	Demand exceeding supply. Rising cost of housing and development land	Inability to save; rising housing costs as proportion of income	New rights and powers regarding housing and land
Value	Sociostructural and political factors (including the effects of economic liberalism) effaced	Moral panics about benefit costs, sink estates, etc. Housing-related poverty treated as a sign of personal, moral failure	Shift in social, economic and political priorities towards social and environmental needs and new forms of citizenship
Control	Dominance of market values. Empowerment of homeowners and developers at expense of non-owners	Spatial and social distancing. Displacement and gentrification	Communal participation in housing reform and new urban redevelopments
Sharing	Sprawl and exclusivity	Housing densities at lower than sustainable levels	Higher density housing
Caring	Individualised rent-seeking behaviour	Low densities affecting energy use, eg transport and domestic heating	Revenue from LVT diverted to social and ecological ends

payment of housing benefits is supposed to satisfy the need for housing, either by the market or the social housing sector. In exchange, land policy and planning in Western countries take little notice of "secure land rights for all" ... and effectively keep the poor from the ownership of land....

In short, the socially careless and ecologically destructive use of land is closely connected to the housing deprivations experienced by millions. Overuse accompanies misuse. The UK welfare state has adopted *ex-post* compensations that leave the unequal ownership and control of a socionatural resource such as land more or less intact. The task ahead therefore requires us to be much more ambitious than simply raising benefits, altering tax thresholds or even subsidising new housing or deposits for first-time buyers. Will we shift our priorities and practices? Or will be continue to use the bruises we inflict merely as targets for the next punch?

We have not finished with land, however. Do the disadvantages accruing from positional, rent-seeking behaviour attach to housing alone? In Chapter Nine we turn our attention to three further issues: transport, flooding and waste.

Notes

[1] And with many policy-makers, although their ignorance is either deliberate or feigned; see 'DWP adds to confusion over consultation on child poverty' by Nick Bailey and Mike Tomlinson at *www.poverty.ac.uk*

[2] See Department for Work and Pensions, Benefit expenditure tables, at www.dwp.gov.uk

[3] The Coalition government looks set to change this, despite evidence that when the benefit is paid to tenants they often go into arrears, having to juggle other needs and costs on a limited budget. But that's fine. If you give money to claimants and they default, that can't be anyone else's fault but theirs, can it?

[4] Nor is there any sign yet of the financial crisis during 2007-09 altering Britain's love affair with property markets, although a future slump in prices cannot be ruled out.

[5] Based on Section 106 of the Town and Country Planning Act 1990. The requirement was suspended in 2012.

[6] For a rebuttal by Ruth Levitas, see www.poverty.ac.uk/articles-families/still-not-listening

[7] See www.cpre.org.uk/what-we-do/countryside/tranquil-places/in-depth/item/3159-the-industrialisation-of-the-countryside?highlight=YTozOntpOjA7czo1OiJ1cmJhbiI7a ToxO3M6Njoic3ByYXdsIjtpOjI7czoxMjoidXJiYW4gc3ByYXdsIjt9

[8] And a neighbourhood with greater density and a wide variety of housing types is likely to have a greater quantity of affordable rental units than a low-density neighbourhood (Aurand, 2010, p 1032).

[9] On my calculations, Howard's (1985, pp 13-17) ideal (30,000 people per 6,000 acres) works out at 12.35 individuals per hectare; 6,000 acres represents the entire estate, but even with housing confined to 1,000 acres, that still results in 74 individuals per hectare, which is lower than Power and Houghton's threshold of 120.

[10] Nor should 'higher density housing' be confused with high-rise tower blocks; the two are not synonymous.

[11] In 2013, UK houses were still overvalued by 20-30 per cent (see www.planetpropertyblog. co.uk/2012/09/19/uk-house-prices-set-to-collapse). Between 2001-11 average house prices rose 94 per cent compared to 29 per cent increases in average wages. It now takes first-time buyers an average of eight years to save a deposit, compared with one year in 1995 (see www.thisismoney.co.uk/money/mortgageshome/article-2262064/First-time-buyers-times-longer-save-home-deposit-did-1995.html). Imagine a standard inflation rate of 5 per cent and house price inflation of 10 per cent. The rent I charge you for occupying my £100,000 house rises from £500pm to £525pm. If I remain an owner-occupier, my imputed rent also rises to £525pm but this is a *fall* relative to the new value of my house (£110,000) − 100,000 ÷ 500 = 0.5; 110,000 ÷ 525 = 0.477 per cent.

[12] A point ignored by Mullainathan and Shafir (2013) in their otherwise interesting book on scarcity. I cope with my scarcities by exporting some of them to you. My row exports scarcities to your row. And the group of rows to which I belong exports scarcities to your group. We can call these groups 'social classes'.

[13] Wealthy homeowners have successfully resisted a revaluation and restructuring of UK Council Tax bands since 1991, although the 1991 valuation was inadequate even at the time. The tax bands were concentrated at the lower end of the property scale, meaning that relatively modest rises in the price of lower cost housing was met with a series of tax increases, but these tail off with the second highest and the highest bands, beginning at £160,000 and £320,000 respectively (in 1991 prices). Effectively, with two-thirds of households valued within the bottom three bands, the majority were paying to reduce the tax liability of the wealthiest, making Council Tax regressive even in 1991 (let alone following the explosion in house prices between 1995-2007).

[14] We do not have the space here to discuss the tragedy of the commons. The tragedy is in part due to fixed natural limits, but also due to collective action problems. Inegalitarian societies try to avert tragedy by effectively excluding many from the commons, for example, through privatising its resources and operating inequalities in private property; egalitarian ones try to find inclusive forms of organisation, for example, through cooperative control over and use of common resources (Ostrom, 1990).

[15] A quick scan of their recent publications suggests their faith is alive and well. Call this 'Matt Ridley syndrome'. Despite being chair of Northern Rock when it was bailed out by the UK taxpayer, Ridley's faith in free markets remains undimmed. This is because his is a genetic deterministic justification (see Fitzpatrick, 2005b, pp 117-21).

[16] This is my hypothesis at least. It would take more time than we have here to test it.

[17] So far as domestic housing is concerned, the Mirrlees Review does not advocate a tax on land separate from that of the building(s) sitting on it, although it leaves open the possibility of a full-blown LVT being introduced at a later date. In the short term, land taxation principles could at least justify tax restructuring, for example, the long-overdue revaluation of UK properties for Council Tax purposes, or a 'Mansion Tax'. If these are targeted on the super-rich – those whom economic liberalism has benefited the most and who have barely been affected by recent economic difficulties – then political support for more ambitious ecosocial reforms could be built.

[18] This has been argued by many, from anarchist communists like Kropotkin (2007, pp 118-19) to social conservatives like Winston Churchill (Brittan, 2012).

[19] Many will identify an oxymoron here. If value is intrinsic, then surely it has to be appreciated for its own sake; inserting monetary devises into the picture feels like a contradiction. However, recall that Chapter Two rejected an ethos of non-domainship on the grounds that the power we possess over nature can and should be wielded responsibly. Monetary instruments and incentives should certainly not exhaust our politics, but if they can assist the defence of intrinsic values, then they ought to be considered.

[20] This raises the problem of rural poverty, that is, those occupying low-density regions because of limited choice. A redistribution of LVT revenue would have to assist such households rather than penalise them.

[21] NIMBY = not in my back yard.

NINE

Land: transport, flooding, waste

In this chapter we tear through three more land-related themes. We discuss transport because in addition to the carbon emissions it produces, land is something we travel across, around, over and occasionally beneath to reach the places that matter to us. We discuss flood risks because as the world warms, land is increasingly subject to coastal, fluvial and pluvial flooding. How we adapt to those risks clearly affects the wellbeing of people who live and work in flood-prone areas, particularly the poorest. And we discuss waste because ours is a throwaway society that burns or buries its detritus on or within the land, affecting the health of those who live near incinerators, landfills and similar facilities.

Our dash through these themes will probably deny the topics the full attention each deserves, but it will enable our understanding of how and why climate change and poverty are increasingly interrelated to expand. The following sections review some recent debates, presenting and discussing the most relevant research. We then return to the thesis of rent-seeking and positional racing, pondering whether and to what extent the issues of transport, flooding and waste disposal can and should be understood in those terms.

Transport, poverty and social exclusion

Our principal concepts are as interrelated as ever (Cahill, M., 2010). Lucas and Currie (2012, p 155; cf Lucas, 2011) define 'transport-related social exclusion' as affecting people,

> ... on or below the poverty line, who do not usually have access to a car and many of whom will also be too old or too young to drive. Affected individuals therefore mainly rely on walking, public transport or lifts from others in order to participate in everyday economic and social activities.

Not everyone who experiences 'transport social exclusion' will be socially excluded in other respects, and it is possible to be socially excluded while suffering no or few transport problems. Overall, however, transport-related exclusion will significantly reduce one's ability to access jobs, healthcare, education and crucial social activities, and that reduced participation will, in turn, affect one's transport experiences.

For Hine, 'transport poverty' implies a deprivation in accessibility and mobility that reinforces, and is reinforced by, other key deprivations. Mobility implies the 'ability to get around' while accessibility is more about the 'get-at-able properties of a place' (Hine, 2008, p 50). A bus route may take you from work to your GP, but if you cannot afford to miss work, it is not accessible. If the surgery is open 12 hours every day then it may be accessible, but if you need to take two buses (or a taxi, or a very long walk) to get there, then your mobility is restricted. Three processes interact in relation to transport poverty, Hine concludes: the ways in which households organise themselves, the nature of the transportation system and the time-space organisation of the facilities people are trying to access.

This interaction between multiple deprivations implies various types of exclusion (Hine, 2008, pp 51-2):[1]

- physical – the barriers inhibiting access to services;
- geographical – poor transport provision (especially in rural and urban fringe areas);
- facilities – considerable distances between residence and important facilities;
- economic – high travel costs constraining access to facilities and jobs;
- time – demands on time restricting the time available for travel;
- psychocultural – perceptions of certain places and times (especially late-night travelling) as dangerous and so restricting access (also OFT, 2010, p 71);
- space – the management strategies of public and private systems.

Let's break transport poverty and social exclusion down into four headings: costs, mode, convenience and effects.

Costs

According to the Campaign for Better Transport (2008, p 1), from the late 1980s to the late 2000s, a period when the overall costs of motoring fell, UK public transport fares increased significantly to more than 20 per cent above the European average. Bus fares in England rose by 51 per cent between 1985 and 2009; in London, where fares have been regulated, the increase was slightly less severe (46 per cent).[2] Average rail fare prices increased by 60 per cent from 2002–12 alone. However, recent spending on transport *shrank* as a proportion of total household expenditure (from 14.5 per cent in 2001–02 to 13.4 per cent in 2009–11), although the percentages for rail, bus and coach spending remained the same. One possible reason is that some people changed their behaviour, that is, travelled less as a response to rising fares (O'Leary, 2013).

Low-income households:

- need to spend a higher proportion of their income on bus travel;
- struggle to access the best deals, for example, season tickets;
- experience added costs when paying for children's travel.[3]

Since low-income households are those most burdened by transport costs, the behavioural changes made in response to rising fares may involve even less access than before to the activities central to social participation and personal wellbeing.

Overall, then, the highest costs for accessing even the most basic public and private services are experienced by those least able to afford them (Clifton and Lucas, 2004, pp 25-6).

Mode

Those on low incomes rely more on bus services. Compared to people in the highest income quintile, those in the lowest make 58 per cent fewer trips as car drivers, 75 per cent fewer by rail, 50 per cent more trips on foot and 206 per cent more by bus or coach.[4] Just over half of the poorest fifth do not own a car, compared to 26 per cent of the total population, rising to more than two-thirds of unemployed people.[5] And the lower your income, the more likely your car will be an older, second-hand vehicle which is less fuel-efficient, more expensive to maintain (adding to financial burdens and stress) and more polluting (Clifton and Lucas, 2004, p 22). The working poor are also more likely to work non-traditional hours (shift work) when public transport services are less frequent (OFT, 2010, p 70).

Convenience

Docherty et al (2008, pp 85, 88-93) summarise the malign cycle at work in a car-dependent society. As cars enable and encourage sprawl, public transport becomes harder to organise and so less popular, that is, unless a bus takes forever winding its way down every other road, many rural and urban fringe areas will be under-serviced. To compensate for this, more people buy cars, more roads and car parks are built, land use becomes characterised by even more sprawl, public transport appears even less popular and flexible, and so it goes on.

Car dependency therefore becomes self-reinforcing and – in a Top Gear culture – one of those 'good dependencies' that is politically and culturally sanctioned.[6] This dependency is thus represented as symbolic of personal choice and freedom (Docherty and Shaw, 2012, pp 136-8). Indeed, Thatcher dreamed of Britain as a 'great car economy' and observed that anyone over the age of 26 using a bus was a failure.[7] Her deregulation of buses in the 1980s (outside London and Northern Ireland) reduced local authority control over bus operators, making corporate profit rather than social need the priority (Hine, 2008, pp 56-8).

Public transport (whether subject to public, private or not-for-profit ownership) then becomes a symbol of inflexibility, inefficiency, congestion, price gouging or (travel on a British train if you are puzzled by the next four words) all of the above. It is possible to have public schemes that are flexible, convenient *and* driven by social priorities, for example, community-based transport (Lucas, 2004, *passim*), but they require long-term dedication and funding.

The irony of all this is that car dependency leads to congestion and gridlock (see Chapter Three and below).

Effects

There are several key effects of all this.

First, the lower your income, the more likely you are to be killed or seriously injured on the roads (Clifton and Lucas, 2004, p 27), face worse air quality and have higher exposure to other negative impacts of transport.[8] The World Health Organization (WHO) (2004, pp 14-15) confirms that the least well-off socioeconomic groups are at greatest risk of injury and death from road accidents.

Second, for lower-income groups transport costs present significant barriers.[9] Lacking a car means that some jobs, salaries and promotion opportunities are outside their reach. Hine (2008, p 54) analyses income in terms of the time it takes to do certain things. The poorest individuals are disadvantaged when it comes to accessing local shops, post offices, supermarkets, doctors and hospitals, chemists, cinemas, pubs, libraries and council offices. The picture is more variable when it comes to banks, leisure centres, railway/bus stations and primary/secondary schools. Only in the case of one service – the dentist – were the wealthiest most disadvantaged. There are consequences for family life, too. Since a car uses as much petrol for one person as for four, those relying on public transport face higher relative costs when it comes to family holidays and outings.

Third, those experiencing transport poverty are also more likely to suffer disproportionately from environmental degradation (Kennedy, 2004, pp 157-61). We look at the principal instance of what Potter and Bailey (2008, pp 32-5) call direct, 'first-order impacts' in the next chapter: air pollution. 'Second-order impacts' refer to social and economic adaptations. For instance, as humans became dependent on fossil fuels and cars, so lifestyles become more sedentary, leading to less physical exercise, more obesity and rising levels of heart disease and type-2 diabetes (in conjunction with the food-related processes explored earlier in Chapter Seven). Local areas are hollowed out, with deprived households effectively forced to travel elsewhere for services, particularly healthcare, shopping and leisure (Clifton and Lucas, 2004, pp 15-19, 29-32; Power and Houghton, 2007, pp 191-4). The amount of walking and cycling in the UK has declined significantly since the 1950s (Tight and Givoni, 2010). The average time spent travelling on foot or bicycle decreased in England from 12.9 minutes per day in 1995-97 to 11 minutes in 2007.[10] Those on low incomes tend to walk more and walk further, but this fails to offset their greater overall risk of experiencing ill health and reduced longevity.

In sum, there is every reason to suppose that Lucas's (2004, p 291) depiction still applies:

> ... people living on the lowest incomes ... spend a far greater (and often punitively high) proportion of their income to travel less often

and over shorter distances than the average population. They also disproportionately suffer the disutility of our car-dominant transport systems. This is not only in terms of their over-exposure to noise, air pollution and accidents, but because of diminishing and increasingly unaffordable public transport services combined with a decline in local shops and amenities in the areas where they live. The effect of this 'travel poverty' is to significantly reduce their life chances because of a reduced opportunity to access a decent education, gainful employment, healthcare services and other amenities. In this way, the inequalities that are already evident within this sector of the population are reinforced.

Transport and climate change

According to the Department for Transport (2011, pp 2-4; see also DECC, 2013c, pp 16-17), in 2010 transport was responsible for 21 per cent of the UK's carbon emissions (it was 16 per cent in 1990 and 19 per cent in 1999), cars and taxis alone being responsible for 12 per cent (compared to 11.5 per cent in 1999).[11] Not only are we emitting more carbon (especially due to growth in international air travel), but the transport sector has not matched improvements found in other sectors. Furthermore:

- if emissions from the processing of transport fuels (for example, petrol or electricity) are included, transport accounts for 24 per cent of domestic GHG emissions;
- yet in terms of domestic transport emissions per person, the UK had the third best record of the EU15 in 2009 (behind Portugal and Germany).

Within the domestic sector as a whole,

> … emissions from passenger cars … account for 58% of domestic transport emissions (ie excluding international aviation and shipping). Lorries and vans account for a further 31% of emissions, and public transport (including both rail and buses) for 4%. (Sloman et al, 2010, p 606)

In order to reverse the direction in which we have been travelling, the Department for Transport's (2009) priorities include:

- a shift to cleaner technologies and fuels (ultra low emission vehicles, rail electrification, sustainable biofuels);
- promoting lower carbon choices (public transport, integrating travel modes, better information);

- market mechanisms (trading systems, price incentives, affordable public transport).

Sloman et al (2010) found that systematic efforts to reduce travel by car and to increase the use of other modes can be highly successful. However, unless transport reforms are attached to broader initiatives related to housing and land use, they are unlikely to be effective (Newman et al, 2009). This is because we are still suffering from the poor decisions made in previous decades. The Campaign for Better Transport (2012, p 7) underscores the points made in the last chapter:

> Since the 1980s, many cities have allowed large retail developments with swathes of free car parking to spring up on greenfield land far from the centre and poorly served by public transport. Large, low-density housing estates have added to this problem and helped to damage the prospects of city centre shops and businesses. In recent years we have also seen the centralisation of many essential local services, for example with large new hospitals being built on greenfield sites far away from where people live.

Ideally, then, new developments should be (Campaign for Better Transport, 2012, p 8):

- located around existing centres and public transport hubs;
- close to jobs, services and facilities that can be reached by foot, bike or local public transport;
- designed so that walking and cycling are safer, faster and more convenient than driving;
- built with lower levels of parking provision, which mainly serves to encourage car use and is a use of land that helps to reduce urban density.

Fortunately, such initiatives also assist efforts to reduce poverty and social exclusion. Families living in neighbourhoods with greater residential density, a greater diversity of land uses and transit services spend just 9 per cent of their income on transport as compared with 19 per cent spent by the average family (Aurand, 2010, p 1034). Also note that,

> ... emissions from transport show the largest variation across the income spectrum, with the highest income decile emitting seven to eight times as much as the lowest income decile for private road travel, and ten times as much for international aviation. (Hargreaves et al, 2013, p 5; see also Brand and Boardman, 2008)

There is thus more of a direct link between introducing carbon taxes in order to reduce emissions, on the one hand, and progressive redistribution, on the other.

Fuel duty escalators, congestion charging, parking charges, aviation taxes, and so on should reduce transport emissions *and* generate revenue that can help the least well-off but also help those on higher incomes, for example, by reducing congestion and travel time (Docherty et al, 2008, pp 97-9).[12]

Any regressive effects of carbon taxes can be reduced through investments in public transport that enable low-income households to abandon their cars. The Campaign for Better Transport (2008, p 2) estimated that a 20 per cent reduction in public transport fares would increase bus travel by 13 per cent and rail travel by 17 per cent, reducing carbon emissions in the process. All of this has long been appreciated by many local authorities, of course, the best of which try to unite housing, urban planning and transport policies systematically (Campaign for Better Transport, 2012). Although since national government, still wedded to free market ideals, has frequently hampered such initiatives, Docherty and Shaw (2012, pp 144-6) are not alone in believing that a genuine devolution and revitalisation of local government is essential if a 'public value' ethos is to revive.

Other measures would also pay multiple dividends. Proper speed enforcement has social benefits (the higher the speed, the greater the risk of severe injuries and death). If added to other transport measures, carbon savings would increase by 15 per cent if the 70mph motorway speed limit was more rigorously enforced, and 29 per cent if a new 60mph limit was introduced.[13] Brand et al (2012) find that electric vehicles would be the single most effective strategy for reducing emissions over the next 35 years. In addition to rail electrification, Sentence (2009, pp 404-5) also recommends the widespread use of a new generation of electric road vehicles, supported by an expanded supply of decarbonised electricity, in order to improve energy efficiency.

Flooding

According to the Association of British Insurers (ABI):[14]

- One in six homes is at flood risk – as many as one in four in London (Carrington and Salvidge, 2013).
- Over 2.4 million properties are at risk of flooding from rivers and seas, with 500,000 at 'significant' risk. A further 2.8 million properties are at risk of surface water flooding.
- Over 5 million people live or work in flood-risk areas.
- Fifty-five per cent of water treatment and pumping plants, 14 per cent of the electricity infrastructure and 2,358 schools are in flood-risk areas.
- Domestic flood damage claims typically range from £20,000 to £40,000.

Flooding has become associated with climate change in the public mind since the brutal floods of 2007, many people now recognising that it will become more frequent and severe in the decades ahead. For instance, pluvial flood risk (surface water flooding caused by intense rainfall overwhelming drainage systems) already accounts for one-third of all UK flood risk, and may leave 3.2 million people vulnerable by 2050 (Houston et al, 2011). According to Hammond (2009), 10 million people will be at risk from flooding by 2030.

Such predictions must be approached tentatively, if only because much depends on the strategies and policies we adopt. The obvious solution is to build and improve flood defences but, since it increasingly seems that climate change involves an oscillation in extreme events which, while occurring more frequently than in the past, will still be characterised by infrequency and uncertainty, knowing exactly how to juggle priorities and target resources is not easy. The Environment Agency reports that in 2012 the UK experienced flooding one in every five days and drought one day in every four![15] Personal and social costs are therefore likely to escalate in ways that are difficult to anticipate. The cost of the 2007 floods in England, about £3.2 billion (Brisley et al, 2012, p 36), may become a more regular occurrence, but the precise consequences are difficult to predict.

That said, few doubt that the poorest and most disadvantaged will be adversely affected. There is a firm correlation between social deprivation and flood risk, although exactly how firm is disputed and requires further research (Houston et al, 2011). It is undoubtedly the case that groups are vulnerable to differing degrees and in differing ways, according to gender, age, dis/ability and ethnicity, but by and large, the lower your income,

- the greater your risk of being flooded. For instance, low-cost housing has often been built on low-lying flood plains where construction costs are cheaper, while expensive houses may occupy more elevated positions due to the better views (Houston et al, 2011, p 19; Walker and Burningham, 2011, pp 228-9);
- the less able you are to afford insurance (see below);
- the more severe the consequences will be for your finances and health. Low-income households are generally more vulnerable to stress and trauma (Walker and Burningham, 2011, p 224), and those with pre-existing health problems are worst affected by flooding (Zsamboky et al, 2011, pp 30-1).

Walker and Burningham (2011, p 232) conclude that, 'this form of "triple injustice" does not at all equate with the global-scale rifts between those producing and suffering the consequences of climate change…but does mirror them to some degree.'[16] Additionally, low-income households are those least likely to demonstrate an awareness of flood risk (Burningham et al, 2008) which, in addition to the widespread perception that climate change is not an immediate problem, may be due to a fear that, once an area is identified as being at risk, insurance premiums could go up and house prices tumble (Zsamboky et al, 2011, p 46).

In the future we are therefore likely to experience flooding that is more frequent and severe, with the probability that those least able to bear the brunt will pay the highest price.

In his summary of recent research, Walker (2012, pp 133-5; cf Lindley et al, 2011) adds another interesting dimension. The risk of 'fluvial' (river) flooding according to income decile is very flat. This means that the risk to the most deprived from being flooded is more or less the same as that to the most affluent. River flooding is egalitarian! By contrast, the most deprived deciles are at significantly greater risk from sea flooding: 750,000 from the poorest two deciles are at risk compared to 80,000 from the richest two. Not everyone agrees with these findings, however. Fielding (2007) concludes that poorer social groups and the unemployed are at greater risk from *both* fluvial and sea flooding. Much depends on the methods used and further research is needed. But if Walker is correct, how might the discrepancy be explained?

Walker suggests that historic settlements with high property values are often located on river flood plains. Not only is housing in Oxford expensive, but it also buys you no protection from flooding. But in coastal regions things are different. First, many industrial ports have large working-class populations. Second, within coastal cities and towns cheaper housing has often been built on lower lying land, for example, reclaimed marshland. Finally, having declined in popularity with the increase in people taking foreign holidays, seaside resorts have experienced rising deprivation.

Location data only tells us so much, of course. Even if rivers are egalitarian, the distribution of social and economic resources and rights is not. Some have a greater capacity to cope with risks than others in two senses. 'Resistance' means the capacity to withstand the impact of a hazard and 'resilience' implies the ability to cope with or adapt to the stress caused by hazards. Once these factors are introduced, inequalities in river flood risks are more evident and inequalities in coastal flood risks are more pronounced (Walker, 2012, pp 135-9, 150-4).[17]

Ideally, flood defences should be so secure that community-wide resistance is guaranteed. Yet effective defences are expensive. Who is to shoulder the cost? How can we guard against affluent communities grabbing a disproportionate share of public resources? And defences can always be breached. The Thames Barrier may only be ineffective against a once-a-millennium tidal surge, yet this is still an appreciable risk. Vulnerabilities can be reduced but never eliminated entirely; those defences that are effective today may not protect against the rising sea levels and increased rainfall expected in the future.

In terms of resilience, having already noted the links between flood risk and social deprivation, let's examine the issue of flood insurance.

Flood risk and insurance

In the decade before 2013 flood insurance in the UK was provided under a Statement of Principles (SoP) that set out the insurance industry's commitment to providing flood insurance as a standard feature of home insurance for properties at some risk of flooding, and to continue to offer flood insurance to properties at significant flood risk (Defra, 2011). In return, the government promised to build flood defences and improve planning and management systems.[18] Even with the SoP in place, the UK's flood insurance system was still highly indebted to free market principles, in contrast to those nations where the state plays a greater role (the Netherlands, Denmark, Germany, Iceland, France, USA and Spain) whether in the form of market intervention or by taking full responsibility for flood damage (O'Neill and O'Neill, 2012, p 4).

With the SoP ending in 2013, industry and government have spent years locking horns over how to replace it. The conflict has concerned where the financial liability for future risks should fall, but the public debate played out in the media has usually been an unedifying game of chicken, with each side ramping up anxieties and daring the other to blink first. In truth, neither side is in favour of abandoning the UK's markets-first approach. The ABI is more interventionist, acknowledging that,

> No country in the world has a free market for flood insurance which successfully preserves widely available and affordable flood insurance for those at high flood risk without some form of government involvement.[19]

They are still committed to a fully competitive market for 98 per cent of properties, as well as a not-for-profit insurance fund to cover the 2 per cent (200,000 properties) at significant flood risk and for whom an open market would therefore be problematic. Those properties would pay a set price, varying according to Council Tax band, and the fund would reimburse insurers in the event of claims (with the government offering a reimbursable overdraft facility to cover major flooding). The fund would be financed by the high-risk premiums but also by a levy raised from *all* insurance premiums.

The problem with a competitive market system that largely passes the risk to individual householders is that it makes them bear the costs of something for which they are not responsible. They are obviously not responsible for acts of nature, nor for the adequacy (or otherwise) of the social, technological and managerial systems, procedures and practices that have accumulated over many decades and that either raise or lower the risks associated with acts of nature. Since deprived households are already more vulnerable to the social deprivations associated with flooding, making them bear all or most of the actuarial costs perpetuates the social injustices of poverty. We could introduce some redistributive mechanism, but this is not what the ABI proposal does – Council Tax bands are regressive, as noted in the last chapter, and the 98 per cent cross-subsidise the 2 per cent, regardless of income levels.

Whatever the scheme adopted after 2013, if insurance reforms lead to a more risk-sensitive differentiation in insurance coverage, housing in floodplains will become less insurable. Hammond (2009, pp 17-18) anticipates that uninsurable houses could fall in value by as much as 80 per cent, a prospect that could face 800,000 by 2035. Middle-income households would be hit by rising premiums and a slump in property values, but at least they will have the resources to cope and adapt. The greater damage would be done to those on lower incomes who can neither afford higher premiums nor sell their homes. There is thus a real danger that new forms of social blight will emerge, with the concentration of the poor in areas of higher flood risk (Lindley et al, 2011, p 24).

As O'Neill and O'Neill (2012, pp 8-15) observe, this is ultimately a question of social ethics. If there are many circumstances for which individuals are not responsible and over which they have little or no control, then an ethic based entirely on individual choice and obligation not only misunderstands the nature of human agency but also risks imperilling those who are most disadvantaged by those circumstances (Fitzpatrick, 2008a, pp 74-80). O'Neill and O'Neill therefore recommend a *solidaristic, risk-insensitive* insurance scheme, in which the basic requirements of social justice would be provided independently of individuals' choices. This would take the UK closer to those nations where the state plays a greater role, and dovetails with the public's opinion that the main responsibility for flood protection lies with government (Bichard and Kazmierczak, 2012).[20] The operational details of any such scheme must address a series of difficult questions.

How should flood insurance relate to other forms of insurance? How can we design a system that accommodates all of the imponderables we face over the coming decades? Should state assistance apply to all those at risk of flooding, including middle-income households, or only those disadvantaged due to income, dis/ability, age, and so on? Should someone who chooses to live in a flood plain be eligible for state-subsidised flood insurance? And if it's also the case that higher density neighbourhoods are more prone to pluvial flooding because they have fewer porous surfaces (Houston et al, 2011, p 19), how can the higher density developments advocated in Chapter Eight take this into account?

Nonetheless, O'Neill and O'Neill highlight the basic choice facing this country between insurance systems that pass most of the risks for social events (unemployment, accident, illness, old age) and natural events (flooding, droughts, heat waves, pollution) to consumers and those that, stressing our mutualities and interdependencies, are closer to the collective, social insurance principles to which the UK at least used to aspire.

Waste

Chapter Seven established that the food sector alone creates immense amounts of avoidable waste (Steel, 2007, pp 278-81). Stuart (2009, p 91) estimates that at least 18 million tonnes of carbon emissions (including 2 million from landfill) derive from wasted food, equivalent to 21 per cent of UK cars. Indeed, the true figure could be at least twice as high, meaning, on his figures, that 10 per cent of total GHG emissions come from producing, transporting, storing and preparing food *that is never eaten* (Stuart, 2009, pp 92-3). Once we take other social practices into account – paper and packaging, disposable electronic items and components, other business and household consumables – it becomes clear that waste accounts for an immense amount of the resource depletion and pollution that drives ecological degradation.

The social effects are also likely to be acute, although some of the details are hazy and the social determinants still poorly understood.

In their review of American and European research conducted since 1983, Martuzzi et al (2010) show that waste facilities (incinerators, landfill, hazardous waste sites) are disproportionally located in areas characterised by deprivation and/or minority ethnic households (see also Stephens et al, 2007; Richardson et al, 2013). It is likely that there are some geographical variations, however. Macintyre et al (2008, p 910) found that in Glasgow, 'Waste disposal sites were closer to more affluent quintiles.' And Fairburn et al (2005, p 79) found less evidence of a correlation between landfills and deprived areas in Scotland than Fairburn and Smith (2008, p 5) found in South Yorkshire, where the most deprived populations are:

- two to three times more likely to be living near a waste or landfill site than the rest of the population;
- most likely to be living next to multiple waste sites;
- most likely to be living near to non-active landfill sites.

Adverse health conditions deriving from such proximity (such as congenital anomalies, cancers, low birth weight and stillbirths) then compound the health effects of broader social disadvantages (Walker et al, 2005; Martuzzi et al, 2010, pp 23-5). Note, however, that some research suggests that the health risks from landfills are minimal (Jarup et al, 2002). Briggs et al (2008, p 1627) confirm the existence of environmental inequities associated with socioeconomic deprivation, particularly with regard to air pollution, but conclude that proximity to emissions sources was not significant, and that associations were in any event generally weak, subtle, variable and complex: 'there is no universally consistent system of environmental inequity.' Thus, even according to Martuzzi et al, because of the considerable methodological and data-gathering hurdles that exist, we still lack the evidence needed to address some key questions:[21]

- Are disadvantaged people, besides being disproportionally exposed to waste-related environmental risk, also more vulnerable to its impacts?
- Do risks vary in different social groups living in the same exposed place and, if so, to what extent?
- Is there a synergistic relationship between the adverse health effects of waste exposure and of the disadvantaged social environment, or do health risks associated with socioeconomic conditions act as multipliers for environmental factors?
- How preventable are the observed inequalities?

Nonetheless, they propose that given the broad picture, there is no reason not to act. The ecosystem needs to absorb less waste, and the poorest individuals need less of whatever waste remains to be located near them:

> Exposure inequalities can and must be reduced by appropriate measures of mitigation and abatement of emissions from potential sources. This includes not only established noxious agents (for example, particulate matters, persistent organic pollutants, heavy metals) but also emissions interfering with residents' quality of life (for example, odours, noise). (Martuzzi et al, 2010, p 25)

Such has been the agenda of social and environmental campaigners for many years, of course. It is because of controversies over waste management and location that the environmental justice movement emerged in the US (Cutter and Solecki, 2006). Whether it was living near the pollution coming from sewage outflows, being unable to stop the nearby construction of landfills and incinerators, or experiencing the noise and health-impairing fumes from freeways, the accusation was that rich white Americans were forcing their toxins and waste on, predominately, poor black Americans. The concept of environmental injustice quickly spread to activists and practitioners across many other countries. Governments and businesses have been forced to respond, to some extent, at least (Wheeler, 2011, pp 221-2).

To what extent is the basic accusation accurate, however? Walker (2012, pp 88-93) distinguishes between two processes: (1) waste facilities being located near disadvantaged residential communities, and (2) disadvantaged households being attracted to the low-income housing found near waste facilities, that is, because affluent individuals have the resources to locate elsewhere ('vote with their feet'). Point (1) resembles the place poverty introduced on page 59, such that due to existing disadvantages (in terms of jobs, housing, income, and so on) impoverished communities have little power to resist the siting of such facilities, adding to already-existing disadvantages. Point (2) corresponds more with the concentration, segregation and polarisation that we associated with 'people poverty'.

In his review of US research Walker concludes that evidence for both can be found, but with different 'patterns and dynamics at work' (for an opposing conclusion, see Oakes et al, 1996). There is no straightforward answer, in other words, at least not on the basis of existing data, and it may be that (1) and (2) are knotted together in ways that are inherently difficult to disentangle. Similarly, Richardson et al (2010, p 223) found that deprived areas are disproportionately exposed to municipal landfills in Scotland:

> ... area deprivation may have preceded disproportionate landfill siting to some extent, particularly in the 1980s, but landfill siting also preceded a relative increase in deprivation in exposed areas. Areas that became exposed to a municipal landfill in the 1980s were subsequently

1.65 times more likely to be classified as deprived by 2001 than areas that remained unexposed.

None of this necessarily proposes deliberate bias. Offering an analysis of institutional processes and dynamics, Stephens et al (2007, p 22) argue that waste disposal policies are not designed to hurt poorer communities but can do so as the outcome of a series of long-term, unintended consequences. In the absence of a countervailing force, policy processes and legal systems will disadvantage those who already lack political voice, legal expertise, economic power and social capital.

Let me cite a recent example from my region, the East Midlands. In 2009 Derby City Council considered a proposal for a waste incinerator to be located in Sinfin. The council rejected the plan because of health and environmental concerns, and in 2010 the UK's Planning Inspectorate also turned the scheme down. In 2011 the High Court overturned this decision after an appeal by the incinerator's proposers, Resource Recovery Solutions. In 2012 a second public inquiry approved the incinerator, a decision campaigners failed to overturn in the High Court in 2013.[22] The firm's assumption that the plant could be built and operated without 'significant risk' to public health was accepted. The decision to proceed also assumes that recent improvements in waste recycling will stall and that Derbyshire will continue to burn up to 50 per cent of its waste rather than reusing, recycling or composting it.

These background assumptions therefore drive a proposal that will have an impact on a ward, which, according to Derby City Council (2011, pp 12, 16, 28, 41), contains the city's highest proportion of:

- vulnerable children
- children with special educational needs
- lone parents
- Income Support claimants.

Sinfin, one of England's 10 per cent most deprived wards, also has large numbers of non-white residents and low levels of affordable childcare (Derby City Council, 2011, pp 23, 30, 46, 51).

Therefore, while we cannot rule out a narrative populated by evil corporations, supine politicians, deaf-blind judges and heroic activists, human perceptions, motivations and practices tend to be more mundane and less dramatic than this. Places like Sinfin are more likely to be targeted for incinerators than those like Kensington and Chelsea because injustice is sedimented. The flawed assumptions and decisions made yesterday become the context (the unexamined norms, frames and structures of institutional decision-making) driving forward today's equally flawed assumptions and decisions – and so the stage for tomorrow's too. Injustice does not always have to be present in any one act or decision for injustice to have accumulated, usually across many decades and generations, through the accretion of multiple layers of individual acts and decisions deposited on top of one another.

Thus I can find no evidence that Resource Recovery Solutions' assessment of 'no significant risk' takes the existing deprivation profile of Sinfin into account (see Resource Recovery Solutions Limited and Derby City Council, 2009), that is, the greater risks of ill health to which its residents are already prone according to every piece of credible research into health inequalities ever conducted.

Overall, we can conclude that waste is a major source of GHG emissions and that, while the details and lines of causation are still somewhat hazy, dealing with that excessive and often avoidable waste leaves the poorest to carry the greatest burdens to their health and general wellbeing.

Positional racing revisited

Let's summarise the preceding sections.

- Low-income households need to spend a high proportion of their income on transport, including the public transport modes on which they are more likely to be reliant. As society's car dependency has become self-amplifying, the least well-off have been further disadvantaged in terms of mobility, income and jobs, access to essential services and other participative activities. Transport is, meanwhile, responsible for 21-24 per cent of the UK's carbon emissions. Better planning and fuel-efficient technology can help, but ultimately what matters is the integration of transport policy with higher-density housing and land use policies. Given the large variation in transport emissions between the highest and lowest deciles, it is reasonable to posit that appropriate taxes and charges could not only reduce carbon emissions but, if the revenue is invested in public transport, also be fairly redistributive.

- The risk of flooding is likely to become more acute over the coming decades. There is every chance this will most adversely affect the poorest given the correlation between social deprivation and flood risk that already prevails. The lower your income, the greater your risk of being flooded, the less able you are to afford flood insurance, and the more severe the consequences for your finances and health. Adapting to increased flood risks requires both resistance (improved defences) and resilience, especially a sustainable and more progressive insurance system. Unfortunately, the UK remains attached to market-based principles of insurance, which pass much of the risk to individuals rather than to progressive solidaristic principles that spread the risks of social and natural hazards across the community.

- Much of the UK's carbon emissions is due to food that is never eaten. Furthermore, there appears to be a correlation between the siting of waste facilities and areas of high social deprivation, although regional variations exist. Whether and to what extent such proximity compounds the health problems of communities already at greater risk of ill health remains contested. It is also difficult to disentangle (1) the siting of waste facilities near disadvantaged communities from (2) disadvantaged households being attracted to the low-income housing found near such facilities; each process may accompany the other, if only because of the legacy of historical injustices that continue to accumulate.

Thus transport and avoidable food waste alone account for somewhere between one-fifth and one-third of UK emissions.

Now, to what extent have the above sections presented evidence for the critique advanced in Chapter Eight?

Chapter Eight proposed that owners seek the highest possible rents in the form of above-inflation price rises that disadvantage non-owners. Through the operation of economic and political power, including the monopolisation of key markets, manufactured scarcities and inequalities are created which allow owners to maximise their returns. Via urban sprawl and by shifting the political emphasis away from social housing, for example, owners have benefited from the resulting property boom to the detriment of those on lower incomes. Rent-seeking is therefore insensitive to desirable social and ecological goals.

Such rent-seeking can be understood as an attempt to maintain one's relative, competitive advantage in a race. But there are social limits to that race such that maintaining your advantage often involves running ever faster just to stand still. The competitors power a process that locks them into ever more competition. This race to nowhere demands that I impose more negative externalities on you than you can impose on me. The positional race involves illusions that are comforting (I stay ahead of you in the race) but irrational (the race can never offer real satisfaction and the negative externalities generated will resurface and hit the advantaged sooner or later – we might call this the 'return of the externalised').

For instance, sprawl and low urban densities are created in part by people seeking desirable locations. In turn, this sprawl produces negative natural externalities by increasing the pollution that doesn't care how expensive your house is and the emissions that drive global warming for which you (and your children and grandchildren) will pay a price. Negative social externalities are also created. Poverty and unjust inequalities also disadvantage the affluent, if the 'spirit level' thesis holds. And recall page 157 where we noted how some of those excluded from the housing market by rising values are the children of those same homeowners who then have to be subsidised through the Bank of Mum and Dad.

There are thus three processes:

(1) Racing and rent-seeking
(2) Negative, positional externalities
(3) Return of the externalised

Do the sections above provide evidence for these?

Transport

As both cause and effect of urban sprawl, car dependency has enabled the housing-based rent-seeking of the last half century. But perversely, as Docherty et al (2008, pp 93-4) highlight, for many journeys the marginal benefit to each driver is less than the marginal costs to society, thereby wasting resources and lowering productivity in ways that harm us all. As has often been observed, building roads doesn't relieve congestion; it just creates more (Goodwin and Noland, 2003). Supply creates demand and so more vehicles and more emissions. Congestion involves a battle between liberty and the common good where neither wins, the outcome of a comforting but irrational illusion.

There are thus many negative externalities that come back to haunt us all. For example:

- We are not free to enjoy the romance of the open road when others, seeking the same freedoms, are squashed into the same space.
- What was at first the convenience of driving to supermarkets became a necessity as those corporations squeezed local shops and small retailers out of business.
- We drive to the gym or pool to burn off the fat accumulated, in part, by sitting behind a wheel for so long.
- Designed to help solve the problems of excessive local authority rates, bus deregulation led to more buses from more bus firms competing on the same profitable routes and taking up more road space than before – and neglecting the unprofitable routes unless subsidised by local authorities.

In short, to live, work and shop in desirable locations we may have to use more fuel and energy (and therefore money), spend more hours every week in transit, often have to stand because of a lack of seating, spend more on maintenance, repairs and insurance (in the case of car owners), cope with the anxieties of inevitable delays, diversions and missed connections and, in general, *crowd on top of one another and then complain about crowding!*

Perversely, however, it is the comfort of the illusions which habitually prevails – or perhaps it's fear of the discomforts that abandoning illusions can bring. We may well regard an expensive home in an exclusive location as a well-earned reward for the time, effort and money expended in journeying there. The problem of exclusivity becomes its own solution, especially once we have scapegoated those who occupy non-exclusive space/time zones. We thrust roads through communities and complain about soulless neighbourhoods that lack communal identities and social loyalties. We come to equate mobility with virtue and condemn as undeserving those whom our positional competitiveness has rendered immobile (the unemployed, the low paid). We privatise ourselves, complain about the shabbiness of public spaces and so withdraw into private enclaves still further.

This is a classic collective action problem, which uncoordinated agents create and are then powerless to resolve. What makes sense for individuals in terms of their own personal needs and interests leads to a state of affairs from which we benefit less than we imagine. We may at some level recognise the sheer irrationality of excessive travelling, but what can any of us do? Instead, we keep pushing the same buttons as before, hoping for better results next time, despite the higher fares, oil price rises and longer jams that chip away at earnings and free time. And as transport emissions rise, so we rack up a carbon debt that future generations will be left to pay.

This is why for sociologists such as Urry (2007, pp 120-2) transportation technologies, processes and systems represent the intersection of competing tendencies within modernity. Cars signify a democratisation of mobility, an enablement of personal freedoms and the elongation of social relations across a diverse globe; yet they also bring the privatisation of experience, the retreat from shared publics, the conquest of otherness, an accelerated sameness, a distancing from a world rushing by that is projected onto screens which reveal and yet conceal that world. Cars intern their owners in the very act of liberation. You speed up because the others around you are speeding up, just as in a crowded room everyone must speak louder in order to be heard. The need-for-speed invests our social cultures, our consciousness and habits, our interior narratives.

In short, added to Chapter Eight's analysis of housing and urban density, I propose we can reasonably associate transport with our three processes (rent-seeking, positional externalities and return of the externalised).

Flooding

What of flooding? If Walker's distinction between coastal and fluvial risks is correct, then rent-seeking applies here too. River flooding is in part more egalitarian because flood plains have offered more exclusive locations than coastal resorts. True, many villages and towns located on flood plains will have grown from historic settlements, but this may just signify earlier forms of rent-seeking behaviour. If you could afford to own a country retreat to escape from the perils of London – its plagues, its violence, its overpowering stench – then yes, why not escape to St Albans or Stratford or Oxford?

It is perhaps more tenuous to draw a line from such rent-seeking to positional externalities and the return of the externalised. In the case of transport there is a firmer connection between the perverse incentives to travel and the consequences (congestion, carbon emissions, and so on). We *might* construct such a link in the case of flooding. Perhaps the economic liberal willingness to sacrifice public squalor for private affluence has undermined society's motivation and ability to build adequate defences or to respond effectively when disaster strikes. Such was the case in New Orleans. The resulting catastrophe then affects all Americans, not just the poorest and not just those living in the affected region. Furthermore, a profit-based, market-driven insurance system may over-burden individuals' finances, propelling the race up the housing ladder and so leading to the kind of financial bubbles that burst so spectacularly in 2007-09.

Nonetheless, scientists warn us against making too casual an association between climate change and this or that flood. The storm surge that hit the Netherlands, Belgium and Britain in 1953, killing 2,500, was one of countless catastrophes that have affected fragile and all-too-mortal humans throughout history. We don't need an elaborate theory to count the cost, mourn the dead or prepare for the future. The corpses floating in the water in New Orleans was a simple outrage regardless of the knock-on effects for the national economy, insurance premiums or the country's international reputation.

Waste

Similarly, until waste facilities start springing up in Kensington and Chelsea we can propose that rent-seeking applies here too. We do not have to find evidence that the Mayor of Richtown passed bags of cash to PolluteThePoor plc. All we need is an analysis of institutionalised bias, legacy and inertia. The resulting negative externalities are obvious. The food we never eat contributes to the emissions driving global warming. And if proximity does generate health problems, then the options involve either leaving the affected communities to cope for themselves or providing the services – including but not limited to healthcare – to treat the resulting conditions. There is thus either a moral or a financial cost to our throwaway economies and cultures.

That said, since some of those who suspect a strong link between ill health and proximity to landfills argue that more research and data is required, here, too, we might doubt the need to over-conceptualise the causal relationships.

In sum, the critique of rent-seeking and positional racing applies most directly to housing, urban densities and transport. In the case of flooding and waste we can see evidence of rent-seeking although the overall critique is perhaps more tentative and requires more research.

Conclusion

Our two chapters on land are now complete and, summarising the key points from the above discussion, Table 9.1 supplements Table 8.1.

The general conclusion advanced at the end of Chapter Eight holds and so does not need to be restated at length: the socially careless and ecologically destructive use of land is intimately connected to the deprivations experienced by millions of the least advantaged, particularly regarding housing and transport, but also in terms of flooding and waste facilities. Yet by neglecting the importance of land to questions of social and ecological justice we have deprived ourselves of the means to address the biggest problem we face in the 21st century. Social policy reforms, research and debates have long concerned themselves with housing and sanitation (it was such public health concerns that often inspired early campaigners), and has more recently acknowledged the importance of transport, but the tools needed

Table 9.1: The ecosocial poverty of land 2

	Land poverty 2		
	Causes	**Symptoms**	**Solutions**
Quantity	Emphasis shifted to profit-based services, with subsidies for particular groups. Inadequate flood defences and waste recycling	Residualisation of publicly funded public transport	Investment in public transport, flood defences, sustainable waste solutions. Improved opportunities for walking and cycling
Mobility	Expensive fares and costs. High premiums. Impoverished locations	Lack of accessibility and mobility. Inconvenience regarding shops, workplaces and services. Behavioural changes in response to higher fares	Higher urban densities. Cheaper fares. Shift away from car dependency and privatised insurance
Value	Deregulation and profit-based services rather than social needs	Disparagement of public values and social needs. Health vulnerabilities from flooding and waste facilities	Socially inclusive policies regarding transport and social insurance, so risks are shared communally
Control	Dominance of market values. Emphasis on private control and choice regarding transport and insurance	Reduced local government control and oversight of key services. Collective action problems	Revitalised local and regional democracy; spatial and temporal coordinations. More effective and participative political and legal processes
Sharing	Sprawl and exclusivity	Lack of participative inclusion in key social activities. Detachment between spatially distant places	Recentralisation. Higher density housing, private and public services. Integrated housing, land use and transport policies. Socialisation of risks and hazards
Caring	Individualised rent-seeking behaviour	High carbon emissions. Negative externalities pushed towards vulnerable groups and future generations	Cleaner technologies and fuels. Flexible, community-based transport; smart technologies. Enhanced sense of responsibility; development of coordinated, collective solutions

to integrate those issues into the correct ecosocial context have been lacking. This is a neglect that we need urgently to repair.

Notes

[1] Hine acknowledges his debt to the work of Andrew Church.

[2] See 'The effect of bus fare increases on low income families' at the webpage of the Passenger Transport Executive Group, www.pteg.net

[3] See note 2.

[4] See note 2.

[5] See www.poverty.ac.uk/report-social-exclusion-transport-necessities/lack-affordable-transport-hitting-low-income

[6] Good dependencies include car dependency, wage dependency, house price dependency and consumption dependency (overspending and debt). Completely different to benefit dependency, you understand, because that's a matter of personal moral failure.

[7] Two phrases certainly attributed to her (see www.parliament.the-stationery-office.co.uk/pa/cm200203/cmhansrd/vo030702/debtext/30702-10.htm). There is thus a parallel here between transport and housing. Instead of keeping fares (or rents) low, the emphasis shifted to targeting subsidies and concessions for rising fares on needy groups (just as Housing Benefit was meant to compensate for rising rents). Transport has not produced the same moral panic about costs and dependency, but similar elements are detectable. For example, 'why should everyone over 65 receive a bus pass when some don't need it?' The more welfare expenditure is used to compensate for a deregulated system, the more expensive it becomes and the more it offers a target for those wishing to dismantle universal benefits and services.

[8] See note 5.

[9] See note 2.

[10] 'No time for physical activity? The answer's on your doorstep, says NICE', www.nice.org.uk

[11] See also 'The problem with aviation', www.greenpeace.org.uk/climate/aviation

[12] The London Congestion Charge was introduced precisely because traffic through large parts of central London had slowed to a 19th-century crawl.

[13] UK Energy Research Centre, *Quick Hits: 2 Limiting speed*, www.ukerc.ac.uk

[14] See www.abi.org.uk

[15] See www.environment-agency.gov.uk/news/146242.aspx

[16] The least developed countries have a higher share of their population living in low elevation coastal zones (14 per cent) than OECD countries (10 per cent), with even greater disparities in urban distribution (21 per cent compared to 11 per cent) (McGranahan et al, 2007; cf Few, 2007).

[17] The 2005 New Orleans flood illustrates this (Walker, 2010, pp 139-48), and obviously many examples from developing countries could also be cited.

[18] See note 14.

[19] See note 14. For Defra's analysis, see O'Neill and O'Neill (2012, p 6).

[20] My quibble is that O'Neill and O'Neill (2012, pp 10-12) somewhat misrepresent luck egalitarianism by relying on Rakowski's free market version. For an analysis of Rakowski and others, see the draft paper 'Modified luck egalitarianism and entitlements to a social minimum', available from the author.

[21] For instance, see the work on the health effects of landfill sites by the Small Area Health Statistics Unit at www.sahsu.org/content/sahsu-research-and-policy

[22] 'Sinfin and Spondon Against Incineration'. Spondon is a wealthier area about 6 miles from Sinfin.

TEN

Air and water

Introduction

The 350-400 cubic feet of air an adult breathes every day has already been exhaled by countless others, including non-humans. Air is therefore a tangible reminder of our delicate interdependencies. What we breathe depends intimately on what others do and do not do. Much the same is true of water. People have been able to survive for two weeks without food, but without water you will probably die within days. And all water is recycled, passing through organic systems (and certain organs, let's admit it) that we tend not to think about closely.

Air pollutants are different to carbon emissions, that is, GHGs such as CO_2. The five main air pollutants are 'particulate matter' (also called 'particulates', which can be up to 30 times thinner than the width of a human hair), carbon monoxide, nitrogen dioxide, ground-level ozone and sulphur dioxide:

> Air pollution is a local, regional and international problem caused by the emission of pollutants, which either directly or through chemical reactions in the atmosphere lead to negative impacts on human health and ecosystems. There are many sources of air pollution, including power stations, traffic, household heating, agriculture and industrial processes.[1] (Defra, 2013, p 2)

In developed nations air quality standards have generally been improving over the very decades when carbon emissions have been increasing. According to Defra's (2013) statistics for 1987–2012, 'urban background' and roadside particulate pollution have shown long-term improvement, although they remained stable after 2008. From 1990 to 2010, emissions of sulphur dioxide fell by 89 per cent and emissions of nitrogen oxides by 62 per cent.[2] (Urban background ozone pollution has shown a long-term increase, however.) Defra attributes such improvements to the move away from coal to gas in electricity generation, and to the introduction of emission standards for vehicles. Nevertheless, the UK still has one of the worst records in Europe, and in 2013 it was reported that air quality laws would be breached in 15 regions until 2020, with Londoners having to wait until 2025 for pollution to enter legal limits.[3]

Climate change and air pollutants *are* linked, as we shall see shortly, but while the former can sound abstruse to many people, air pollution has a more immediate, visceral recognition. From the London smogs of 1952, which killed at least 4,000 people, to cross-national worries about acid rain in the 1980s, those 350-400

---

cubic feet of air speak to our bodies, our fears, our sheer sense of mortality, more than abstracts such as 'climate' or 'atmosphere'.

Not surprisingly, then, it is the health implications that have dominated public debates, and we review this in the first section. Then we move on to the connections between air pollution, climate change and poverty, and to what I call the 'knotted complexities' that any attempt to understand them must grapple with. Due to the relative absence of research into UK water poverty, this section is shorter, but leads us into our final discussion that concerns the extent to which air quality can be an object of rights and of social control.

Pollutants and health

The health implications of air pollution are wide-ranging.[4] For instance, air pollution is correlated with low birth weight, and babies born below 5lb 8oz are more likely to suffer from conditions such as heart disease, strokes and chronic illnesses later in life (Collins, 2013), including cognitive impairment (Gray, 2011). Defra (2010) estimates the annual health costs of air pollution to the UK at roughly £15 billion.

Although the long-term health effects of exposure to it are still not well understood, abundant statistics can be found. Air pollution is thought to reduce the life expectancy of every UK person by an average of 7-8 months (Defra, 2007, p 7), and cutting long-term exposure to particulates by half could increase life expectancy by an average of 1-11 months (Defra, 2002). Air pollution may take two years off the lives of 200,000 people (Gray, 2011). The House of Commons Environmental Audit Committee (2010) estimated that air pollution could contribute to 50,000 deaths in the UK every year; and 29,000 deaths per year may occur due to human-made particulate pollution (Moore, 2012, p 8). London Councils (an organisation representing all London boroughs) states that poor air quality in London is responsible for the premature deaths, by an average of 11 years, of 4,300 people every year.[5] Janke et al (2007) estimate that reductions in particulates and ground-level ozone could save 4,600 lives per year in England alone. Across Europe,

> ... it is currently estimated that around 21,000 hospital admissions a year can be linked to ozone exposure, and admissions linked to particulate matter exposure are almost five times greater. (European Commission, 2010, p 7)

What explains figures such as these?

For those in poor health, pollutants can cause eye irritation, coughing and breathing difficulties (Defra, 2002). Nitrogen dioxide, sulphur dioxide and carbon monoxide irritate airways and increase the symptoms of those suffering from lung diseases. Carbon monoxide can lead to a significant reduction in the supply of oxygen to the heart, particularly in people suffering from heart disease.

Particulates cause inflammation of the lungs and the worsening of lung and heart diseases, with elderly people particularly susceptible. Nitrogen dioxide increases the symptoms and severity of asthma and can even trigger an attack:

> … more than 320,000 children (including more than 180,000 children under the age of 11) attend schools in London within 150m of roads carrying more than 10,000 vehicles per day. This is the level of traffic that has been found to increase risk of developing or exacerbating asthma in children. (Moore, 2012, p 9)

And ground-level ozone affects cardiovascular and respiratory systems. In addition, those who live close to busy roads but also far from green spaces – such as parks – experience a double affliction since green spaces help to disperse pollutants, as well as facilitating exercise (Coombes et al, 2010, p 821).

So far as the future is concerned, although concentrations of most pollutants are estimated to decline by the middle of the century, the concentration of ozone is expected to rise, leading to 1,500 extra deaths and hospital admissions per year (Ross Anderson, 2008).

Climate change

None of this means we can afford to separate policies relating to air quality from those relating to climate change. Air pollution and climate change are distinct phenomena, as acknowledged above. Action to tackle pollutants can have more immediate results. They exist closer to the surface and do not last long in the atmosphere, compared to GHGs that are more active in the upper atmosphere and endure for much longer.

Nevertheless, air pollution and climate change are both essentially created by the burning of fossil fuels, and neither is respectful of national borders (Jacobson, 2012). In addition, air pollution makes climate change worse. Black carbon is thought to be responsible for approximately 15 per cent of the current excessive warming of global temperatures (European Commission, 2010, p 4). And global warming can exacerbate air pollution. Ground-level ozone peaks during the summer months, and if heatwaves (such as the one that hit Europe in 2003) become more frequent and severe, so various parts of Europe, especially southern regions, can expect to experience more of it. Furthermore, '60% of sensitive habitats exceed the critical load for nitrogen' (Moore, 2012, p 20).

When it comes to the solutions here, too, we find similarities. If properly designed, measures to tackle climate change may assist measures to address air pollution, and *vice versa*. One of the world's leading authorities on the links between both has offered an assessment of the main energy alternatives in terms of their likely effects on water supply, land use, wildlife, resource availability and undernutrition, among several other criteria (Jacobson, 2009). Jacobson concludes that the following provide the most benefits:

1. wind
2. concentrated solar power
3. geothermal
4. tidal
5. solar–photovoltaics
6. wave

Wind power is the clear winner. Hydropower, carbon capture and storage, and nuclear power are at the bottom of Jacobson's (2009, p 170) list.

Such recommendations are more sympathetic to renewables than most governments seem willing to accommodate. Nonetheless, the European Commission (2010) advises that reductions in carbon emissions and in air pollution must accompany one another, since doing both is likely to produce greater benefits over the long term than the total gains that would accrue from pursuing each policy independently of the other.

Through improvements in air quality alone, Defra (2010) anticipates savings of £24 billion per year (at current prices) by 2050, created by promoting ultra low carbon vehicles, renewable (and non-combustible) sources of electricity, energy efficiency and reducing the agricultural demand for nitrogen. London Councils' recommendations include:

• more walking and cycling;
• incentives and infrastructure for low emission vehicles;
• traffic reduction programmes;
• greater energy-efficiency schemes and technologies;
• rail electrification.

And the Greater London Authority (GLA) (2010, p 2) cites recent initiatives:

• development of an electric vehicle infrastructure;
• congestion charging and a low emission zone;[6]
• a shift to greener modes of transport;
• car clubs;
• reducing the contribution of particulate matter from road surface wear;
• traffic smoothing;
• a bus emissions programme.

Since much of this echoes what has been said in previous chapters, there are clearly many synergies between the climate change and air pollution agendas (Williams, 2007).

Knotted complexities

However, rather than assuming that those synergies will arise automatically, they must be carefully assembled and constructed as matters of social, economic and public policy.

This is, first, because some pollutants are more dangerous to the climate than others. Ground-level ozone and black carbon store heat and ozone reduces the capacity of vegetation to absorb carbon, reducing crop yields. Yet sulphate aerosols emitted from industrial smokestacks reflect sunlight and so have a *cooling* effect (Mann, 2012, pp 15-16). (This does not imply that we should simply pour industrial sulphates into the atmosphere, although some do recommend a 'sulphate sunshield'; see Eggleton, 2013, pp 207-9.) Second, as we shall see shortly, because the social effects of air pollution manage to be both simple and yet complex, our policy responses must be appropriately fit for purpose.

My basic point is that we should seek synergies between the climate change, air pollution and anti-poverty agendas while being sensitive not just to complexities but also to the knottedness of those complexities. By a 'knotted complexity' I mean any system which:

1. is characterised by multiple strands, which
2. are densely interconnected and interwoven, to the extent that
3. it can be difficult to know which strand is which or even what the knot signifies (for example, danger versus security), so that
4. by contributing to the complexity of the system our interventions may unravel the knot, or tighten it, or do both simultaneously, meaning that the system
5. is pervaded by uncertainty, which might
6. demand a precautionary (safety-first) approach.

The atmosphere is such a dynamic, holistic system. The positive and negative feedbacks operating within it can be modelled to some extent, although the level of interactive complexity is often too knotted and 'chaotic'.[7] For example, the repairs to the hole in the ozone layer may have led to reductions in the moist, bright clouds that have offered some protection for Antarctica from GHG warming (Korhonen et al, 2010; see also Mann, 2012, pp 201, 331, note 31). Similar knotted complexities characterise many of the social-natural interdependencies with which this book has been concerned. Therefore, solutions here will have an impact elsewhere in ways that should be carefully considered and monitored.

This may sound like a mundane point, yet UK governments can still seem a long way from appreciating it. The air quality strategy of the London Mayor contains not one mention of poverty, deprivation or low income (GLA, 2010), while the 2007 strategy of the 1997–2010 Labour government gave it only a brief reference (Defra, 2007, p 41).[8] The official assumption appears to be that because the poorest are most adversely affected by air pollution – and at least this recognition is thankfully widespread – dealing with the latter will create 'hey presto' improvements for the former. Perhaps so. But what is clear from the literature on the social contexts of air pollution is that although the general picture is straightforward, various complications appear once you drill into the details (Diekmann and Meyer, 2010). Take two examples.

The first concerns spatial diversities. According to McLeod et al (2000, pp 83-4),

> ... there appear to be three separate clusters of regions, in order of increasing pollution: (1) Wales, South West, North; (2) East Anglia, South East, North West, East Midlands, West Midlands, Yorkshire, Humberside; and (3) Greater London.

Therefore, if crudely designed and implemented, carbon taxes may have a regressive effect (the poorest pay too) that *increases* the poorest's vulnerabilities (by reducing their income), while preserving environmental inequalities (the relative distance between clusters is maintained). Furthermore, in some cities affluent households are more likely to be found near the centre – perhaps trading exposure to pollution for access to amenities – while the poorest are often pushed to the fringe where pollution levels can be lower. Here, too, a crude reform, for example, traffic restrictions, may benefit the wealthiest by reducing city centre pollution, but be potentially iniquitous for those on the fringes if it reduces their access to the centre.

Thus pulling on one strand by introducing 'blanket', spatially insensitive carbon taxes and traffic restrictions may disadvantage the already disadvantaged and only increase their vulnerability to climate- and pollutant-related hazards. One possible alternative is to prioritise those 'hotspots' where air pollution and social deprivation both peak; McLeod et al recommend contemplating differential carbon taxes for different regions, for example. Therefore, policy-makers must incorporate a rigorous understanding of the complex, intricate and interactive links between air pollution, geographical location and social class into the policy process.[9]

The same applies to a second example, returning us to the subject of health. The variables and causal factors that relate to ill health are often multiple and entangled. Power et al (2011, pp 170-6) show that depression and anxiety are driven by a variety of neighbourhood and family pressures. Some of their interviewees lived near major roads, incinerators or airports, and could cite apparently minor events relating to air pollution – needing to keep windows closed, having to use a nasal spray, constant dusting – that nonetheless compounded the strains they felt and that had an impact on their wellbeing. Health problems are therefore multifaceted, each one embedded in and by many others. We can recommend exercise as a remedy for obesity or depression, but a daily walk near a busy road may increase your exposure to pollutants even as it burns away calories. A better diet may improve your immune system but you will still have to shop in supermarket-dominated cities that require many people to take long, often expensive journeys that increase their exposure to pollutants, in addition to the pollution created by getting the food to the store in the first place (see Chapter Seven earlier).[10]

We can therefore see what knotted complexity regarding air pollution can mean with reference to space and health. What of the more general picture?

Air pollution and poverty

For years, most of the research into social deprivation and air quality was conducted in the US, reflecting that country's particular patterns of poverty and racial segregations. By and large a correlation between social deprivation and air pollution was identified.

For instance, Pastor Jr et al (2006) found that schools located in areas with higher respiratory hazards also tend to have higher proportions of poor and minority ethnic students, 'respiratory risks' helping to explain lower academic performance. Grineski et al (2007) found that poorer neighbourhoods are disproportionately exposed to higher levels of nitrous oxides, carbon monoxide and ozone (see also Grineski and McDonald, 2011, p 385).

What might explain such correlations? Does social deprivation help create air pollution, for example, low-income households owning cars with fuel-inefficient engines? Does air pollution help create social deprivation, for example, affluent households fleeing areas with inadequate air quality, leaving those places to the less well-off? Some are insistent that air pollution in socially deprived areas is a product of continued racial discrimination and class oppression:

> … white privilege has driven urban development since the late 19th century and is reflected in urban settlement patterns, residential and job segregation, social exclusion of minorities, industrial location, and the emplacement of urban infrastructure…. (Grineski et al, 2007, pp 549-50; see also Collins et al, 2011)

However, in his literature review, Walker (2012, pp 107-23) conveys a sense of something both straightforward and yet deeply complex, for reasons we outline shortly:

> Any form of simple generalisation about what the body of analysis says about the relationship between air quality and social difference in the US is … problematic. (Walker, 2012, p 111)

In the UK research did not really commence until the latter part of the 1990s and confirmed the general conclusions of US researchers.[11] According to Friends of the Earth (2001, p 1):

- 66% of carcinogen emissions are in the most deprived 10% of wards;
- 82% of carcinogen emissions are in the most deprived 20% of wards;
- Only 8% of carcinogen emissions are in the *least* deprived 50% of wards.

The Environment Agency stated that people in the tenth most deprived areas in England experience the worst air quality, including concentrations of nitrogen dioxide from transport and industry 41 per cent higher than the average.[12] Wheeler and Ben-Shlomo (2005) found that in urban areas the poorest households live in wards with the worst air quality, adversely affecting respiratory functions (especially for men), although not asthma, probably reflecting cumulative life course disadvantages. They invoke an 'inverse air law': 'people with the worst lung function tend to live in areas with the worst air quality, and the health effects of air pollution seem to be greatest among those (men) in lower social classes' (Wheeler and Ben-Shlomo, 2005, p 953). However, *rural* households demonstrated a reverse gradient, perhaps because rural areas include both wealthier commuter populations *and* deprived populations in more remote, less polluted places.

Much research has focused on particular cities and regions, in order to try to map geographical disparities such as these. The data throws up some surprises. The Environment Agency has said that in Wales the highest concentrations of air pollution are found in the *least* deprived wards.[13] And King and Stedman (2000) found tentative evidence that deprivation was correlated with air pollution in London, Belfast and Birmingham, but *not* in Glasgow.

Often, however, geographical studies confirm the general picture. Fairburn and Smith (2008, pp 82-3) found the poorest two deciles account for 65 per cent of those living in areas with the most pollution (nitrogen dioxide and particulates), while the richest half accounted for just 7 per cent. Of the population experiencing the very worst air quality, approximately 12,000 of them were children. In Birmingham, Brainard et al (2002) found that a disproportionate burden of pollutant exposure was being borne by non-white communities and populations exhibiting higher levels of deprivation. They raise a distinction, similar to the one encountered in Chapter Nine, between (1) air pollution being located near disadvantaged communities, and (2) disadvantaged households being attracted to areas with poor air quality due to its cheap housing. Since both are undoubtedly relevant,

> ... future policies to reduce inequities in exposure to these pollutants should place a particular emphasis on the mechanisms driving changes in land-use patterns, urbanisation, and the development of transportation corridors. (Brainard et al, 2002, pp 713-14)

In his recent review of the UK literature Walker (2012, p 111; Deguen and Zmirou-Navier, 2010, p 33) echoes these earlier research findings, going on to say that, although the poorest communities generally experience the worst air quality, 'this is not always and everywhere the case, or necessarily a simple linear relationship.' For instance, while air quality improves as income improves, some data suggests that it worsens again for the most affluent income deciles, as noted above.

Walker accounts for this by observing that since most UK deprivation is found in urban areas, and since transport and industrial emissions will concentrate in urban locations, taking longer to disperse than is the case in the countryside, those wealthy enough to escape from cities have also been escaping pollution. But in so far as air quality worsens again, for the most affluent this is because some of the richest communities can be found in cities (particularly London). In other words, spatial, social and geographical contexts always matter. And as with his account of fluvial flooding (see Chapter Nine), Walker observes that exposure to a hazard should not be confused with its impact. Many variables matter, including: daily and hourly variations in levels and spatial concentrations of pollution; bodily and mental health; lifestyle; household composition; neighbourhood environments; and socioeconomic circumstances. Air pollution, in short, implies different things for different people.

In general terms, then, there *is* a clear negative externality, one that is also a positional externality if the arguments of the last two chapters are credible. In other words, those who create the most air pollution, in their attempt to stay ahead of the rows behind, suffer the least harm *from* it. As noted in Chapter Nine, deprived households are much less likely to own a car. Is it therefore the case that affluent drivers – driving into city centres from their commuter towns, villages and leafy suburbs in the morning and out again in the evening – leave behind pollutants that have a most severe impact on the poorest? Some argue this depiction is by no means a simplification (Grineski et al, 2007, p 550).

However, because places differ, and because a minority but sizeable proportion of low-income households own cars too, we might hesitate to imagine that things everywhere are so straightforward:

> …in general across Britain the poor contribute a significant proportion of the pollution that they are exposed to (although we do appreciate that drivers who lack the income to move to a cleaner area may also be unable to purchase cleaner vehicles).... The exception, however, is for a minority of the poor who experience high pollution exposure but who contribute little in the way of emissions. (Mitchell and Dorling, 2003, p 926)

Not everyone, even in deprived neighbourhoods, will experience pollution to the same extent or in the same way

We can therefore conclude that poverty and air pollution accompany one another, but establishing how, why, to what extent and therefore which kind of intervention is best is not always a clear-cut exercise. We are facing something that is straightforward in general terms and yet also deeply complex and intricate.

Solutions?

So how should we respond to such problems in our social and public policies? In addition to the above measures (see p 190) there are a range of useful policy recommendations that have been summarised by Moore (2012, Chapter 5), including: reducing perverse incentives for polluting technologies, expanding low emission zones, relating vehicle emissions to parking charges, retrofitting and improving public awareness. Moore, however, does not locate such recommendations within a wider context of justice.

In his discussion of justice, Walker argues that everyone has a right to a minimum of decent clean air. One advantage of this 'minimal decency' approach is that it appeals to established understandings of rights and entitlements. Variations in air quality are permitted, and perhaps inevitable, so long as the minimal threshold is not breached. This might require policies to observe and enforce not just a decent minimum but also a sufficient margin of error (a cordon) so that the basic threshold is properly protected. But Walker emphasises the importance of context, rather than a one-size-fits-all minimum. Since vulnerabilities and resilience vary, we might have to countenance differing minimum thresholds, with some areas subject to more stringent standards than others.

If Walker is correct, this could imply identifying poverty-pollution hotspots for immediate attention, as indicated earlier; other areas (where deprivation is high but air pollution is low, or *vice versa*) would be of secondary priority; and some areas (with low levels of deprivation and pollution) might be safely ignored.

Walker's findings are confirmed by another recent literature review that relates air quality firmly to the kind of critiques explored in previous chapters:

> The housing market biases land use decisions and might explain why some groups of people suffer from both a low socio-economic status and bad air quality at their place of residence. One reason is that the presence of pollution sources depresses the housing market and provides an opportunity for local authorities to construct council housing at low cost. Symmetrically, the presence of council housing in a given urban area tends to depress the price of land over time, encouraging the setting up of activities and facilities that generate pollution. (Deguen and Zmirou-Navier, 2010, p 33)

And although many affluent households reside in city centres, some also possess second homes, thereby reducing their overall exposure to pollution:

> Conversely, subjects in deprived areas live in old dilapidated homes with poor ventilation and insulation, factors which favour the concentration of indoor pollutants. Moreover, they may be more likely to spend time close to or in the traffic, for example, working on the

street rather than inside office buildings, or doing long commuting in public transport. (Deguen and Zmirou-Navier, 2010, p 33)

Deguen and Zmirou-Navier (2010, p 34) support something resembling the 'decentralised concentration' mentioned in Chapter Eight:

> ... 'multipolarity' calls for urban poles that provide a range of amenities (housing, workplaces, commercial, cultural or leisure sites) tending to reduce the need for long distance commuting in polluted environments. Diversity is a complementary principle of multipolarity, where each pole would provide the widest possible variety of activities and, most importantly, of housing profiles, places for the rich being intermingled with council residence. This diversity scheme would prevent the formation of peripheral clusters of poor housing, which is typically associated with lack of access to good education and other cultural amenities....

Wood et al (2007) concur, echoing the broad recommendations of the last chapter, specifically: targeting short journeys by facilitating a modal shift to walking, cycling and public transport; effective public communication; and reducing the need to travel through spatial planning.

The basic lesson would appear to be that the more we treat a host of issues – energy use, food chains, housing development, land use, transport and air pollution – in isolation from one another, the more we make it harder to resolve the problems afflicting each. If a system demonstrates knotted complexity, we must at least attempt a holistic understanding of it. This demands an integrated, cross-sectoral and cross-disciplinary approach, one concerned not only with 'policy', but also with relevant social and environmental conditions.[14] Yet if policy and domain integration is the desired end, what should the means be? We return to this issue shortly.

Water poverty

Before we do this, let's examine our final socionatural resource: water. This section is brief because although water poverty occupies a large role in the social development literature, it is quite new so far as the UK is concerned. Sewerage and water hygiene have long been recognised as issues of concern to public health, but debates about water poverty have several distinct, contemporary elements.

A common definition regards those households that spend 3 per cent or more of their income on water, after housing costs, as experiencing water poverty. On that basis, Fitch and Price (2002) identified a considerable overlap between those in water poverty and those in fuel poverty. More recently, Snell and Bradshaw (2009) estimated 14.6 per cent of the population to be in water poverty, with some significant regional variations (ranging from 20 per cent in Wales to 11 per cent in London), while Benzie et al (2011) found that approximately four million households in Britain are water-poor. According to Bradshaw and Huby (2012), 23.6 per cent of English and Welsh households were in water poverty in 2009-10.

As always, certain groups are particularly vulnerable. Fitch and Price (2002, p 3) found that 'UK households in the lowest three income deciles spend on average 3% of their net income on water bills whereas the average spend for all households is just 1%.' Snell and Bradshaw (2009) state that single pensioners, workless households and those on means-tested benefits are twice as likely to be water-poor. Also:

- 54.9 per cent of those in the lowest income quintile are in water poverty;
- 71.3 per cent of those in water poverty are in the lowest income quintile.

Ofwat's (nd, p 8) calculations for water poverty are shown in Table 10.1, based on data from 2008–09.

Bradshaw and Huby (2012) found that single adults (especially lone parents) and those on benefits are three to four times more likely to experience water poverty. They highlight how rates of water poverty will climb if, as has happened over the last quarter of a century, water prices continue to increase faster than average earnings and inflation.

Ofwat (nd, p 4) also observes that low-income households are likely to use more water, being less able to afford water-efficient appliances and fittings. Furthermore, direct debit discounts are less available to those who lack credit cards, bank accounts or simply need to juggle priorities – perhaps by going into arrears. In their qualitative research for the Consumer Council for Water, Creative Research (2009) found that, out of 14 items of household expenditure, water debt occurred most frequently. People will delay paying water bills because of a perception that the consequences are less drastic than for, say, energy bills (despite many people assuming that water services can be disconnected, something which has not been true since 1999). Creative Research (2009) also found that:

Table 10.1: Percentages of different household types in water poverty (using 3% and 5% of household income as water poverty thresholds)

Household type	After housing costs		Before housing costs	
	>3%	>5%	>3%	>5%
Multi-unit	10	5	7	3
Single without children	36	22	23	11
Couple with children	14	7	7	3
Lone parent	42	18	22	6
Couple without children	13	6	9	4
Pensioner couple	16	5	13	4
Pensioner single	36	14	26	9
Grand total	23	11	15	6

- People with meters feel that behavioural changes seem to make no difference to their bills (possibly because standing charges represent a floor below which bills cannot fall).
- There was a lack of awareness of various support schemes (see below).
- There was a general feeling that water companies should fund such schemes – rather than other customers or the government, that is, taxpayers.
- Small reductions in bills have little impact on vulnerability.
- Companies could do far more to help customers in financial difficulty.

In terms of climate change, the implications for water resources are likely to be highly variable (Archer and Rahmstorf, 2010, pp 181-3). Water supplies in North America are increasingly affected by diminishing snow packs – water levels in lakes and rivers are expected to fall, with consequences for electricity generation. Southern Europe will probably become drier and northern Europe wetter (leading to more flooding). Water stress in the former may increase the risk of wildfires, decrease hydropower generation, reduce crop yields, increase soil erosion and compromise biodiversity. In decades to come changes to the saltiness of the oceans may increase rainfall in the higher latitudes, while their acidification will affect marine life and so a vital element of the food chain (Archer and Rahmstorf, 2010, Chapter 5). Nichols and Kovats (2008) observe that global warming may have various effects on supplies of drinking water, increasing pressure on water treatment processes. The UN's (2012, p 197) view is that:

> While climate change is likely to have positive effects in the short term in Northern Europe, these are expected to be outweighed by negative effects as climate change progresses.

At the very least, since we are almost certain to face more pressure on, and volatility in, water supplies, we need a distribution and use of water that is more efficient and climate-sensitive.

The existing approach relies on monetary incentives, although more for customers than companies. Although it still loses 3.36 billion litres of water every day in leaks (enough to supply 22.4 million people),[15] fines are not always levied on the water industry lest companies simply pass them on to customers through their bills.[16]

For customers, however, the story is increasingly different: water metering is being rolled out nationally (due for completion in 2020). If individuals prefer to maximise their income by spending less money wherever possible, then charging for water usage is presumably advantageous. The assumption is that people will monitor their meters and adjust their habits accordingly in the light of their budgets, either by using less water, for example, taking showers rather than baths, or recycling water whenever possible. This contrasts with the current arrangement – where most people are still charged a flat rate irrespective of usage – which encourages waste. If droughts, heatwaves and 'water stress' increase in frequency and severity, a sustained change in habits could be required.[17]

Yet if households are charged according to usage, might poorer households alter their practices in ways that could compromise their health and quality of life, for example, drinking less water? Indeed, some with health problems may simply be unable to reduce water usage at all:

> This tends to mean that low income groups, single-occupier households, pensioners and large families are more likely to be vulnerable to affordability problems, as are people who need more water for health reasons (eg to support additional clothes washing or bathing). (Benzie et al, 2011, p 6)

Bradshaw and Huby (2012) reveal that those with water meters experience less water poverty than those without, but only further research can reveal whether this is due to greater efficiency or a form of reduced usage in which the already vulnerable are left *more* vulnerable.

As is the case with other public utilities (such as energy and transport), the market-led approach includes schemes designed to assist some of those on low incomes. Benzie et al (2011, p 7) studied several measures introduced by South West Water – block tariffs (see below), bill capping[18] and supporting those in debt – concluding that without adequate support schemes, water metering is likely to be regressive. Furthermore, where households are slightly above the poverty threshold they may be hit twice, disadvantaged by metering without qualifying for support. Yet overall:

> … the current support schemes protect at least some vulnerable people from any adverse effects of differential water charging … the challenge for the future is to improve the coverage of existing support schemes and ensure that pricing and efficiency measures reflect the true value of water yet protect consumers from water poverty.… Water is an essential resource for life; it is imperative to ensure that customers' access is not determined by their ability to pay. (Benzie et al, 2011, pp 7-8)

Bradshaw and Huby (2012, p 13) also advocate the use of tariffs where these are consistent with climate change goals:

> Current tariffs are mainly regressive, with small consumers paying more for each unit of water used.… Under rising block tariffs, the high volumetric rates paid for luxury high use could be used to subsidise very low rates for low levels of essential water use or unavoidably high use by low income households.

This idea therefore resembles the reverse tariffs (where 'essential' use is charged at a low rate, and further consumption is charged at a higher rate) defended in Chapter Six when we discussed energy usage.

But there are also more traditional responses that we should not neglect:

- Rather than discount and support schemes, which target those in difficulty, we could increase the incomes of the poorest households so that they are less likely to encounter difficulties in the first place.
- What about publicly funded reductions in water bills relative to inflation and earnings, backed by rising block tariffs to make usage more climate-sensitive?

Bill reductions would obviously benefit the affluent too, but this can be counterbalanced through progressive taxation. For social democrats, a system that targets the affluent in this way is more consistent with a universalist ethos than one that constantly interferes in the lives and lifestyles of those whom the principle of social justice demands should not be poor in the first place (Barry, 2005, pp 171-85). This ethos and principle may also demand that while we cannot avoid some monetary incentives – if it reduces waste, differential charging makes environmental sense – public goods should largely be run on a not-for-profit basis.

There are clear tensions in the existing market-led system between long-term investment needs, consumers' interests and commercial imperatives. Through their water bills customers make a contribution to maintaining and renewing the distributional infrastructure, yet are they bearing too high a burden given water companies' emphasis on profits and share values? Can UK households trust a public resource to be bought and sold as a marketable commodity – often by non-UK investors and private equity funds – without public values, standards and interests being compromised? Much clearly depends on the extent to which statutory oversight is genuinely robust, but regulatory agencies meant to oversee privatised utilities can be charged with being too soft on the firms they are meant to regulate. Water companies have been accused of prioritising shareholders to the neglect of social and ecological goods, and building up debt rather than reserves for future investment in the belief that the latter will be underwritten by government guarantees and financial assistance (Hutton, 2012).[19] What makes the 'free market' ideology doubly pernicious is the fact that water companies have a monopoly over local supplies, for example, you cannot shop around and decide to buy your water from the Outer Hebrides. Regional variations in water bills are nothing that customers can do anything about.

In conclusion, existing water charges are effectively a local tax paid to private companies making a profit for shareholders for managing a socionatural resource on which we all depend and cannot choose not to use.

The atmospheric commons

Whether you agree with this conclusion or not we are faced with an obvious difficulty. We do not pay for air since nobody collects, purifies, distributes and monitors it in ways equivalent to water.[20] In what way, then, does it make sense to apply debates about ownership and control to air? Does this mean that the argument advanced and question posed at the end of the previous to last section – if policy and domain integration is the desired end what should the means be? – are irrelevant?

Yet recall Walker's insistence that everyone has a right to a minimum of decent clean air. This right is not an abstract one, but something that relates to important, material circumstances. We *do* pay for air, after all. As the statistics presented earlier highlight, we all pay for unhealthy air quality with a proportion of our lives, the poorest usually paying the highest price of all. And this *does* have monetary implications. If air pollutants damage the health of vulnerable people, then this obviously has an impact on their earning capacity, expenditure and future prospects. Since pollution is a product of social and economic activity, the nature of those socioeconomic practices, and the property regime that underpins them, *is* relevant to a discussion of air pollution. Perhaps air is not so very different to energy, food, land and water after all.

It would be impossible here to discuss in any detail the socioeconomic and property regime most appropriate to Walker's 'decent minimum', but we can explore some contrasting ideas. Two basic options seem available.

The first is the deregulated option. Block and Barnett (2005) advocate a *laissez faire* capitalism in which the state is at best a referee, setting up rules and regulations for market exchanges, but not a market 'player'. Environmental problems such as air pollution are due to the absence of private property rights, they argue, especially 'punishment for trespass'. If your pollution invades my air space then that represents a trespass for which you should pay a penalty, enforceable in law. Trespass does *not* apply, however, if you were polluting an unowned space into which I subsequently decide to locate. Since I chose to live in a place I knew (or should have known) was polluted, I have no right of redress. Government's role should be limited to analysing dust particles, determining their source and imposing penalties on perpetrators. And *laissez faire* should extend to every public good. Block and Barnett recommend the privatisation of waste management facilities, natural resources and public transport.

To the objection that the poorest would suffer from these reforms, there is a simple answer:

> The reason people are poor is because: their God-given mental and/ or physical capabilities are low; they are indolent; they are imprudent, and do not invest in their own human capital; and/or, the government short-circuits the market.… It has little or nothing to do with whether they are minority-group members. (Block and Barnett, 2005, p 37)

All forms of discrimination should be permissible – including racism and sexism – because some employers will hire those discriminated against by other employers, raising wages and counteracting the original discrimination (see Friedman, 1962, pp 109-10). Because it is poor people themselves and the resource-hungry state that create poverty, the solution is to abolish minimum wages (which price the unskilled out of labour markets), welfare programmes and social security (which undermine the family). The best safety-net is private charity, since this embodies moral instruction (many charities are religious organisations), highlights the origins of funds (recipients should be required to thank donors personally) and enforces the distinction between the deserving and undeserving poor.

The second, regulated option rejects such market libertarianism.[21] Empirical evidence can be cited, first of all. Since Block and Barnett (2005, p 31) evoke the demise of the former Soviet Union and the failures of the Federal Emergency Management Agency (FEMA) during Hurricane Katrina,[22] we can counter with the events of 2007-09 which consisted of market failures driven by too little regulation, not too much. Or we can revisit the evidence from the last few chapters. If the already advantaged are able to maintain their relative advantages through positional racing and externalities, then poverty is due in part to the monopolisation of resources by the non-poor. There is *less* social mobility in competitive market societies (Wilkinson and Pickett, 2009, Chapter 12),[23] which supplements a general point that socioeconomic status is largely, if not entirely, driven by undeserved luck (particularly inheritances of birth) (Fitzpatrick, 2011c, pp 35-6). That being the case, to say that some air pollution is unproblematic because people choose to be polluted *could* apply to affluent households but not to the socially deprived who suffer the greatest exposure and the highest risks.

But the economic liberal argument fails even on its own terms. Free markets only work if there is perfect information (transparent information available to all parties) and perfect competition (market forces are unrestricted). Block and Barnett thereby advocate the abolition of anti-trust legislation on the grounds that monopolies are a product of freedom of association.[24] But if monopolies are permitted, then market distortions are inevitable as corporations collude with one another to protect their mutually advantageous dominance, for example, through price fixing and alignment, aggressive practices, privileged access to the legal system, advertising, political lobbying, agenda setting and sometimes outright conspiracy (as in the LIBOR scandal). Instead of the state becoming first a referee and then a player, it is powerful corporations that become the *de facto* referees, shaping the conditions that ensure their continuance as the dominant players. It is therefore market outcomes themselves that undermine the very conditions on which free markets depend. We can authorise government to deal with market distortions, but, as the 2007–09 crisis confirmed, this requires that the state be more willing to regulate and be more independent of corporate interests than has been the case throughout the era of economic liberalism.

If a regulated approach is therefore preferable, what might this imply for air pollution? Many advocates of market regulation prefer cap-and-trade policies

(Burtraw and Evans, 2009). There are several versions of a cap-and-trade approach (Fitzpatrick, 2011d, pp 77-9), but the essential idea is for a system of tradable permits in which high polluters have to buy permits unused by low polluters. The latter benefit financially while the former either have to pay for the privilege of polluting *or* pollute less, whichever is most cost-effective. The state intervenes but does not undermine the basic logic of capitalist dynamics. Cap-and-trade became a popular solution to climate change precisely because many saw it as working in the 1990s to reduce air pollutants in the US, addressing the problem of acid rain (Libecap, 2009, p 136).

There are two key problems with tradable permits, however (cf Hansen, 2009, pp 212-22). First, there is the risk of market manipulation where powerful actors shape the scheme to ensure that their interests prevail above social and ecological needs. The European Emissions Trading Scheme is almost universally perceived to have failed because it allocated too many permits at too low a value (*The Economist*, 2013). But second, permits are only as effective as the objectives they are designed to achieve. Even if the state counteracts market manipulation and genuinely tries to internalise those social and environmental costs that are currently externalised, there is the sheer difficulty of estimating the relevant values. If the price of a unit of oil, or anything which creates air pollutants, is to be determined not just by the cost of fossil fuel extraction but by its 'lifetime' impact on the natural environment and society (particularly the lives of the poorest), then there are so many variables that estimates are likely to vary widely.

This, in other words, is a knotted complexity! Scientific methods can take us part of the way, but ultimately it's matter of moral judgement; for example, there is no 'scientifically correct' discount rate. Simms (2013, pp 59-62) argues that markets work best when they serve a precautionary principle. We cannot afford to overshoot the 2°C of warming (above pre-industrial levels) beyond which we may face disaster, and then scale back later, because negative environmental feedbacks are unpredictable and uncontrollable, for example, a catastrophic release of methane as permafrost melts. Simms' argument is about carbon markets, and we acknowledged earlier that air pollution and climate change are distinct phenomena. Nonetheless, given the connections between the two (their similar causes and solutions), there is every reason to also apply its precautionary logic to the latter. In short, as Jacobson proposes, we need a much more urgent push towards renewable sources of energy than governments and businesses have initiated to date.

So, in terms of air pollution, the state can set, monitor and enforce pollution standards, while facilitating R&D (research and development), knowledge transfer and requiring that industrial and consumer practices be orientated towards the long term. Markets can incentivise, for example, those with low or non-polluting engines can sell permits to others in a system of exchange (similar to personalised carbon trading). And communities could be given powers of veto against any project with pollutants above a particular threshold and/or be entitled to appropriate compensation, with such rights weighted towards the least advantaged communities (recall the experience of Sinfin in Chapter Nine). Yet, to repeat, unless the scale of the problem – the job these sectors are designed to perform – is appreciated, all of this is moot.

There is thus a difference between regulated markets in a market-led context and regulated markets that serve well-defined social and ecological goals. Daly (2007, pp 96-9, 109-11) argues that economics has emphasised allocation and distribution of resources to the neglect of scale, that is, the physical size of the economy relative to the natural ecosystem. Quantitative restrictions on markets cannot come through efficiencies due to the rebound effect, he says. Instead, self-imposed limitations (frugality) will create new efficiencies and innovations, and demand that we stop trying to fund social justice from economies that can no longer afford to expand in the old way (that is, GDP growth).[25] The precautionary principle means setting the price of carbon and air pollutants at levels high enough to ensure that the atmospheric commons is not overloaded by either, altering our priorities and practices accordingly – how gradually, to allow citizens, businesses, policy-makers and consumers time to acclimatise, is a matter of debate. 'The point is to stay afloat, not just to make sinking expensive,' says Simms (2013, p 62). Emphasising social and ecological imperatives may or may not help us to make sense of the knot, but it is based on the view that the values, practices, institutions and aspirations that created global warming are unlikely to resolve it without new moralities of scale. Technological solutions, price mechanisms and statutory regulations are vital, but markets and states are not going to do a thing unless we grab the wheel and make them change course.

Therefore answers to the question we started with – what should the means be? – are dependent on getting all sectors to align in pretty much the same direction (Victor, 2008, pp 207-8). *It really is the end that matters above all: the protection of the atmospheric commons.* I elaborate on this point in the Conclusion in relation to what I think the purpose of an ecosocial politics should be in the 21st century.

Conclusion

Table 10.2 offers a schematic summary of this chapter.

We began by reviewing air pollution and health, then established the connections between air pollution and climate change. I proposed that the synergies at work here have to be carefully understood and constructed as matters of policy intervention because systems often exhibit a 'knotted complexity'. This is certainly true of ecosystems (such as the atmosphere) and social systems, and all the more so when we consider their interrelations and interdependencies. Research into deprivation, spatial distribution and air quality reveals a general picture in which those who typically produce the least pollution suffer the greatest consequences. However, the research also draws attention to complexities that warn us against overly simplistic interventions. The section on solutions recommended a holistic, integrated approach that incorporates lessons from across several chapters in this book, including housing markets, land use, urban density and transport policy.

Table 10.2: The ecosocial poverties of air and water

	Air and water poverties		
	Causes	Symptoms	Solutions
Quantity	Industrial development, land use and car dependency	Spatial concentration of pollution and poverty ('hotspots'). Greater risk of ill health, related to pollutants, for low-income individuals. Rising water charges and debt	Green transport and spatial planning. Greater sensitivity in policy processes to the links between pollutants, geography and social deprivation
Mobility	Air pollution being located near disadvantaged communities. Disadvantaged households attracted to areas with poor air quality due to cheap housing	Ill health has an adverse impact on earning capacity, employment and other opportunities	Policy priorities given to hotspots. Integration of policy domains across multiple socionatural resources
Value	People at greatest risk of pollutants generally create fewer of them	Ill health has an adverse impact on quality of life, compounding and compounded by other deprivations	Policy priorities given to hotspots. Reduction in water bills
Control	Inadequate and non-integrated attention given to social and environmental justice in pollution strategies. Water companies stressing profit over social and ecological needs	Injustice regarding exposure to and impact of pollutants. Water company monopolies	Rights to a decent minimum of clean air. Tradable permits in effective ecosocial context. Not-for-profit water system
Sharing	Air and water treated as economic resources without sufficient reference to climate change	Air pollutants as positional externalities. Increasing water stress and volatility in supply	Precautionary principle; protection of atmospheric commons. Regulated approach. Coordination of state, market and civic forms of action. Not-for-profit water system
Caring	Indiscriminate burning of fossil fuels. Separation of air pollutant and climate change strategies	'Polluter pays' principle dominant. Patchy and inadequate support for impoverished water customers	Precautionary principle; protection of atmospheric commons. Greater emphasis on renewables to reduce pollution and not simply pay for it *post facto*

The section on water argued that reducing waste through water metering makes environmental sense, yet the risks to the poorest are real (even with compensatory support schemes) and exacerbated by the profit motive of water companies. The final section argued that we should indeed relate air to discussions of rights, ownership and control, something that demands a regulatory approach so long as this makes markets the servants of well-defined social and ecological objectives. As important as they are, technical, technological and administrative measures will only work if we set them in an appropriate moral and precautionary context.

Recall my claim that the ecologically excessive, careless and destructive use of key socionatural resources is connected to the social deprivations that characterise that usage for millions of those on low incomes. We have long treated air as a costless, self-replenishing resource that is the same resource for all, that is, insensitive to social context. Given the visceral, health-related impacts of air pollutants, this cavalier approach has been altered over the last few decades, although still with limited progress and still with insufficient attention to the needs of the poorest. Much the same is true of water and water poverty. There is an urgent need to establish synergies between the air pollutants and climate change agendas given that solutions to one are appropriate for the other, namely, renewables. This implies types of long-term planning, regulation and investment – and the prioritisation of social and ecological ends – for which our economic liberal assumptions and habits appear particularly ill suited.

Notes

[1] Ground-level ozone does not have a source *per se*. It is formed when sunlight acts on nitrogen dioxide and other atmospheric substances close to the ground, especially due to petrol fumes.

[2] See www.politics.co.uk/reference/air-pollution

[3] See http://populationmatters.org/2013/newswatch/uk-court-air-pollution

[4] Although note that it is the world's most impoverished who are at greatest risk from air pollution, due especially to the indoor burning of wood in solid fuel stoves.

[5] See www.londoncouncils.gov.uk/policylobbying/environment/climatechange/heathairquality.htm

[6] Owners of vehicles that do not meet emissions standards must pay a daily charge if they wish to enter the zone.

[7] Chaos, in the sense understood by mathematicians and scientists, means that systems are highly sensitive to relatively small variations, making the knock-on effects of those variations difficult to model.

[8] Defra (2006) produced a report on social deprivation, but this is only mentioned once in the 2007 publication. Furthermore, the 2006 report neglected to analyse pollution-poverty hotspots (see below) and examined environmental *inequalities*, claiming that terms such as

'equity' or 'injustice' 'are subjective ... and therefore requiring value judgements' (Defra, 2006, p 3). The technocratic avoidance of value judgements (except when designed to appease the prejudices of conservative newspapers) was unfortunately endemic to the New Labour project.

[9] To be fair, New Labour's emphasis on 'accessibility planning' nodded in this direction, although with inconsistent results at local authority level (Lucas, 2011, pp 213-15).

[10] Now add another strand, deriving from the same source as air pollution: noise pollution. In Birmingham, Brainard et al (2004, p 2594) found that 'some inequalities may exist, but not strong ones.' Some affluent populations live close to airports and busy roads, perhaps prepared – as in the case of air pollution – to accept noise disturbances in return for access to good transport links. And some deprived neighbourhoods can be very quiet. Yet recall the distinction between exposure and vulnerability (resistance and resilience). Cheaper housing may also be less well insulated from outside noise, including loud neighbours, and much depends on personal tolerance and social circumstances. Those who are housebound due to age, disability or chronic ill health could be exposed to higher levels of noise that, in turn, might increase their vulnerabilities since constant, excessive noise affects sleep, induces stress and engenders feelings of disempowerment (see www.euro.who.int/en/what-we-do/health-topics/environment-and-health/noise/facts-and-figures).

[11] Townsend (1979, Chapter 14) referred to air that is 'dirty, smoky or foul-smelling', but contemporary pollutants are not always as visible or malodorous as this.

[12] See www.environment-agency.gov.uk/research/library/position/41189.aspx

[13] See note 12.

[14] New Labour believed in what they called 'joined-up policy' but seemed less attracted to the idea of joined-up social conditions.

[15] See www.bbc.co.uk/news/uk-17622837

[16] 'Water companies being let off leak targets "to spare customers higher bills"', *The Telegraph*, 9 May 2012, www.telegraph.co.uk

[17] But as Creative Research highlights, realities do not always mirror such cost-benefit assumptions about behaviour change.

[18] England's WaterSure scheme caps water bills at the amount of the average household water bill for their water company. There is a similar scheme in Wales.

[19] As those of us around at the time can testify, these are the very kind of state handouts that the architects of the mass privatisations of the 1980s and 1990s claimed would no longer be needed.

[20] It is also distinguishable from land and food for the same reason. Air and energy are the more immaterial of our socionatural resources, but energy resembles water in that getting it to your home requires human intervention.

[21] This is the point to acknowledge the simplicities of this distinction. Obviously, there are many types of regulation and deregulation and many frameworks to which they can apply, but exploring a more comprehensive spectrum is not something we have space for here.

[22] When FEMA was overseen by a *laissez faire* government – not that Block and Barnett allow this fact to break their stride.

[23] See the 2012 paper 'The rise and consequences of inequality in the United States' by Alan Krueger, Chair of the Whitehouse's Council of Economic Advisers at www. whitehouse.gov/sites/.../krueger_cap_speech_final_remarks.pdf

[24] In other words, they echo Hayek. The trouble with Hayek's (1976, Chapter 11) argument that we should never impose ends on 'voluntary' actions is that ends are always imposed on actions by those with the power to do so. Unfortunately, in their obsession with political power, economic liberals ignore economic power, waving private monopolies and corporate dominance away as unintended and as entities that the market will correct, given time.

[25] This 'post-productivism' obviously requires international agreement, otherwise countries try to out-compete one another through forms of productivity growth that ignore and so exacerbate the problem of scale (Daly, 2007, p 30).

Conclusion

The first four chapters are summarised in Chapter Five, and so there is no need to repeat what was said there.

The remaining chapters, Six to Ten, have demonstrated that an ecosocial framework can:

- summarise, catalogue and classify key literatures, relevant evidence and recent developments relating to those resources that are socially and naturally interdependent;
- enable us to critique diverse research fields so that we can understand the causes, symptoms and possible solutions to the poverty and deprivations which pertain to those resources;
- allow us to read across those fields, which often remain isolated from one another, suggesting a more integrated agenda that can shape future thinking, research, collaboration, campaigning, lobbying and organising.

The specific task set in Chapter Five was to fill the empty cells in Table 5.2. Are we now in a position to do this? Chapters Six to Ten have been summarised in the tables at or towards the end of each chapter. Imagine that we stack these tables on top of one another vertically. Now let's read down the columns, one by one.

Table C.1 summarises the 'causes' column, and we might extrapolate the main points accordingly:

> *Quantity:* widening gaps between income/assets and prices of the relevant services or goods.
> *Mobility:* rising costs and so restricted choice.
> *Value:* disadvantages neglected or pathologised, leading to policy agendas and priorities which further disadvantage.
> *Control:* exclusion from resources and relevant political processes.
> *Sharing:* short-term, anthropocentric selfishness.
> *Caring:* ecological bases of social wealth taken for granted and consequently depleted through excessive demand.

The 'symptoms' column is summarised in Table C.2:

> *Quantity:* unmet needs, limited access and increased vulnerabilities.
> *Mobility:* various traps impair opportunities for social participation.
> *Value:* residual assistance; burdens of poverty falling disproportionately on poor people themselves.
> *Control:* dominance of consumerist values emphasising market choice at expense of users' voices.

Table C.1: Summary of ecosocial causes and explanations

Deprivation categories	Socionatural resources: causes and explanations				
	Energy	*Food*	*Land 1*	*Land 2*	*Air/water*
Quantity	Energy inefficiency; low incomes; high energy prices	High food prices, especially relative to the lowest incomes	Property booms. Emphasis shifted away from bricks and mortar; inadequate Income Support	Emphasis shifted to profit-based services, with subsidies for particular groups. Inadequate flood defences and waste recycling	Industrial development, land use and car dependency
Mobility	Proportionately high energy expenditure reduces capacity to save	Prevalence of supermarkets; restricted choice and diversity. Food deserts	Demand exceeding supply. Rising cost of housing and development land	Expensive fares and costs. High premiums. Impoverished locations	Air pollution being located near disadvantaged communities. Disadvantaged households attracted to areas with poor air quality due to cheap housing
Value	Fuel-poor given insufficient priority within energy markets and government policies	Individualisation of social problems; assumption of consumer freedom and market sovereignty	Sociostructural and political factors (effects of economic liberalism) effaced	Deregulation and profit-based services rather than social needs	People at greatest risk of pollutants generally create fewer of them
Control	Fuel-poor lack social and political power	Alienation and exclusion from the food production process. Emphasis on consumers' responsibilities	Dominance of market values. Empowerment of homeowners and developers at expense of non-owners	Dominance of market values. Emphasis on private control and choice regarding transport and insurance	Inadequate and non-integrated attention given to social and environmental justice in pollution strategies. Water companies stressing profit over social and ecological needs
Sharing	Lack of integration of fuel poverty and climate change objectives	Domination by food corporations; consumer passivity. Over-consumption of meat and dairy	Sprawl and exclusivity	Sprawl and exclusivity	Air and water treated as economic resources without sufficient reference to climate change
Caring	Lack of integration of fuel poverty and climate change objectives	Energy imbalance due to reliance on fossil fuels. Separation of social and ecological imperatives	Individualised rent-seeking behaviour	Individualised rent-seeking behaviour	Indiscriminate burning of fossil fuels. Separation of air pollutant and climate change strategies

Table C.2: Summary of ecosocial symptoms

Deprivation categories	Socionatural resources: symptoms				
	Energy	Food	Land 1	Land 2	Air/water
Quantity	Household spaces inadequately warmed	Malnourishment; poor nutrition; debt and heat-or-eat trade-offs; greater risk of ill health	Millions locked out of the housing market; high rents. Residualisation of social housing	Residualisation of publicly funded public transport. Lack of time, resources and resilience	Spatial concentration of pollution and poverty ('hotspots'). Greater risk of ill health, related to pollutants, for low-income individuals. Rising water charges and debt
Mobility	Fuel poverty trap – reduced capacity to escape vicious cycle of inefficiency, income and prices	Food insecurity. Limited availability of and access to good quality food. Impoverished social interaction	Inability to save; rising housing costs as proportion of income	Lack of accessibility and mobility. Inconvenience regarding shops, workplaces and services. Behavioural changes in response to higher fares	Ill health has an adverse impact on earning capacity, employment and other opportunities
Value	Fuel poverty trap. Inadequate assistance in the form of social tariffs	Psychosocial risks and anxieties; reliance on processed foods. Cultural disrespect. Reliance on charity	Moral panics about benefit costs, sink estates, etc. Housing-related poverty treated as a sign of personal, moral failure	Disparagement of public values and social needs. Health vulnerabilities from flooding and waste facilities	Ill health has an adverse impact on quality of life, compounding and compounded by other deprivations
Control	Continued devaluation of fuel-poor households' needs and interests	Poor households judged as 'failed agents and consumers'	Spatial and social distancing. Displacement and gentrification	Reduced local government control and oversight of key services. Collective action problems	Injustice regarding exposure to and impact of pollutants. Water company monopolies
Sharing	Dual injustice: fuel poverty and high carbon emissions. Rebound effect	Negative externalities, eg loss of soil and water capacity, and biodiversity. Avoidable waste contributing to carbon emissions, eg landfill	Housing densities at lower than sustainable levels	Lack of participative inclusion in key social activities. Detachment between spatially distant places	Air pollutants as positional externalities. Increasing water stress and volatility in supply
Caring	Continued dual injustice. Unsustainable energy consumption. Rebound effect	Negative externalities, eg loss of soil and water capacity, and biodiversity. Avoidable waste contributing to carbon emissions, eg landfill	Low densities affecting energy use, eg transport and domestic heating	High carbon emissions. Negative externalities pushed towards vulnerable groups and future generations	'Polluter pays' principle dominant. Patchy and inadequate support for impoverished water customers

Sharing: negative externalities passed on to others.

Caring: persistent social degradation and depreciation of ecological resources.

Finally we come to the 'solutions' column in Table C.3:

Quantity: new forms of revenue raising and expenditure; needs of the poorest prioritised.

Mobility: renewed emphasis on social needs.

Value: rights and entitlements to key resources.

Control: democratic and communal forms of participative inclusion in generation and distribution of resources.

Sharing: re-socialisation and regulation of collective social and ecological risks.

Caring: recognition of social and natural interdependencies; integration of ecological imperatives into social institutions and economic practices.

This account now permits us to fill in those empty cells (see Table C.4).

Based on these various tables, the arguments made in Chapters One to Four can therefore be reaffirmed. For social democrats, social injustice denotes a lack of fairness in the distribution and control of those resources that are essential to social wellbeing. The ecosocial critique does not, as promised, reinvent the wheel, but it does add an important missing dimension such that *social and environmental injustices denote a lack of fairness in the distribution and control of those socionatural resources which are essential to the wellbeing of all human and non-human lives to whom we owe obligations (a duty to value and a duty of care).*

As such, because they relate to the socioeconomic determinants that shape wellbeing, deprivations connected to socionatural resources should be acknowledged as vital within any general account of poverty.

Therefore, ecosocial poverty

- is caused by forms of economic organisation and growth which are neither fully inclusive spatially (many people are excluded from their benefits) nor sustainable across time. Our market-dominated societies are driven by assumptions and practices that facilitate and require excessive demands on the ecosystem and by political and cultural systems of disrespect and exclusion.
- is manifested as both distributive and procedural forms of injustice in the reduced capacity of disadvantaged individuals to cope with the rising costs of key socionatural resources, control their circumstances and so determine their futures as social agents in conjunction with, and with responsibilities for, other social agents and the natural world they inhabit, depend on and affect. Excessive ecological demand is therefore linked to important social deprivations.
- is something that can only be addressed through new forms of economic organisation and growth which are socially inclusive and egalitarian, deriving from renewable, low carbon sources of energy and dedicated to the restoration of natural environments that have been destroyed or eroded in the modern era.

Table C.3: Summary of ecosocial solutions

Deprivation categories	Socionatural resources: solutions				
	Energy	*Food*	*Land 1*	*Land 2*	*Air/water*
Quantity	Tax-funded retrofitting, targeted at low-income households, and other energy efficiencies, eg appliances	Distributive justice	Revenue from LVT diverted to social ends	Investment in public transport, flood defences, sustainable waste solutions. Improved opportunities for walking and cycling	Green transport and spatial planning. Greater sensitivity in policy processes to the links between pollutants, geography and social deprivation
Mobility	Tax-funded retrofitting, targeted at low-income households, and other energy efficiencies. Green assets	Market regulation. Revitalisation of high streets and other shopping boroughs	New rights and powers regarding housing and land	Higher urban densities. Cheaper fares. Shift away from car dependency and privatised insurance	Policy priorities given to hotspots. Integration of policy domains across multiple socionatural resources
Value	Tax-funded retrofitting, targeted at low-income households, and other energy efficiencies	EPH. Renewed emphasis on social determinants. Upstream/choice-editing	Shift in social, economic and political priorities towards social and environmental needs and new forms of citizenship	Socially inclusive policies regarding transport and social insurance, so risks are shared communally	Policy priorities given to hotspots. Reduction in water bills
Control	Control of budgets; improved market regulation and socialised control of utilities	Food democracy. Upstream/choice-editing	Communal participation in housing reform and new urban redevelopments	Revitalised local and regional democracy; spatial and temporal coordinations. More effective and participative political and legal processes	Rights to a decent minimum of clean air. Tradable permits in effective ecosocial context. Not-for-profit water system
Sharing	Synergies between social and environmental 'policy fields'. Non-regressive carbon taxes	EPH; new producer–consumer relationships. New taxes, eg on waste	Higher density housing	Recentralisation. Higher density housing, private and public services. Integrated housing, land use and transport policies. Socialisation of risks and hazards	Precautionary principle; protection of atmospheric commons. Regulated approach. Coordination of state, market and civic forms of action. Not-for-profit water system
Caring	Reverse tariffs; shift to renewable technologies and zero-carbon energy systems; personal carbon allowances	EPH. Scaling-up sustainable, conservation forms of agriculture and aquaculture. Low carbon food chains – including local sourcing and fewer food miles. New taxes, eg on waste	Revenue from LVT diverted to ecological ends	Cleaner technologies and fuels. Flexible, community-based transport; smart technologies. Enhanced sense of responsibility; development of coordinated, collective solutions	Precautionary principle; protection of atmospheric commons. Greater emphasis on renewables to reduce pollution and not simply pay for it post facto

Table C.4: The ecosocial understanding of poverty summarised

Principles	Deprivation categories	Socionatural resources				
		Energy	*Food*	*Land 1*	*Land 2*	*Air/water*
Minimum entitlements	Quantity	Fuel poverty; energy inefficiencies and inadequate Income Support	Food poverty; high costs; poor nutrition; trade-offs with other basic needs	Market bubbles; residualisation of social support	Profits prioritised; emphasis on subsidies	Hotspots; burdens of social and economic development devolved to least well-off
	Mobility	High expenditure and traps, having impact on capacity to save	Restricted choice and diversity; increased insecurities	Rising costs locking people out of market; inability of social housing to compensate	Rising costs in low-density context. Negative impact of accessibility of amenities	Exposure to poor air quality; risk of ill health with effects on wage-earning, etc
Property rights	Value	Lack of sustained attention by policy-makers	Limited access to quality food	Erasure of social determinants	Deregulation and emphasis on individual choice rather than social needs	'Inverse air law'; reduced quality of life
	Control	Lack of power and voice	Dominance of consumerism within food chains	Dominance of market values benefiting rent-seeking of owners	Dominance of market values benefiting rent-seeking of owners	Policies and practices insensitive to vulnerabilities of poor
Voice and democracy	Sharing	Upward pressure on carbon emissions	Over-consumption; food as marketable asset	Low, unsustainable urban densities and sprawl	Lack of participative inclusion; social dislocation	Marketisation; neglect of resource scarcities; positional externalities
Obligations to value	Caring	Unsustainable energy consumption	Avoidable and excessive waste	Low densities producing waste	Neglect of social and ecological costs	Neglect of atmospheric commons; affects of air pollutants worst on poorest

The header "Social and natural interdependencies" spans the Socionatural resources columns.

This definition reflects and consolidates that given in the final row of Table 5.1. It incorporates recognition of social-natural interdependency into the social democratic account of poverty.

At the end of the Introduction I stated my main thesis: the ecologically excessive, careless and destructive use of key socionatural resources is connected to the social deprivations that characterise that usage for millions of those on low incomes. The conclusions of Chapters Six to Ten have reiterated this claim for each resource, and so I trust that enough has now been said to justify this association. The overuse of a resource (excessive demand) in conjunction with the profit-making practices of those – typically corporations – that control it produces scarcities and price rises for which inadequate wages and forms of welfare assistance struggle to compensate, particularly in the UK, which has come to favour residual, targeted and underfunded forms of assistance. Overuse and misuse go together. The resulting deprivations are so damaging to individuals' wellbeing that people are impelled towards a continuation of the very social practices and habits that generate overuse in the first place. In the chapters on land this was theorised specifically in terms of rent-seeking and positional racing. But the basic point is that since life at the bottom of the social ladder is so impoverished and disrespected, people (poor and non-poor) spend much of their lives trying to scramble up the ladder to avoid the bottom. Excessive ecological demand is therefore linked to important social deprivations. And so the circle goes round. If we wish to dampen the excessive, careless and destructive use of resources, we should devise new, socially just and typically egalitarian institutions and practices in an economic context that takes the principles of sustainability and precaution as central.

In the ecosocial frame, poverty is thus caused by systemic distributive and procedural inequalities in resources. Those inequalities are driven by a desire for security and status in economies dominated by goods that, because their value derives from their exclusivity, can guarantee neither. The oppressive practices experienced by poor individuals are related to those to which the non-human world is subjected because both derive ultimately from irrational practices developed to cope with the concentration of power, wealth and resources in the hands of the relatively few. This squandering of human and non-human life is endemic to our social and economic cultures. We cope with mortality by denying its inevitability and lavishing the few years we have on profligate, destructive, self-indulgent habits. The culture of waste creates poverty – low-income individuals are most vulnerable to air pollutants, for instance – and is created by it, since fear of poverty (fear of joining the ranks of a population judged surplus to requirements) encourages people to try to outdistance others in a scrambled race to join the ranks of the affluent few. Those positional drives occlude what all lives share in common: the need to flourish, to care for and be responsible for those whose lives are affected by our own. Life has a responsibility to life.

As such, poverty implies a lack of sufficient opportunities to flourish in association with others, that is, to realise existing goals and capacities and to develop new ones. The 'others' with whom we should associate, and on which we are dependent, include fellow members of the natural environment, the multitude of ecological communities with whom we share limited planetary space. Poverty therefore represents forms of estrangement within our social environments *and* a detachment from the natural conditions of those social environments. It is contrary to wellbeing where, among other things, wellbeing implies *being well for and with nature*.

But this convergence of social democratic and ecosocial understandings does not constitute a call for a new ideological pigeonhole. Instead, it implies three things.

First, a mobilisation of *all* those opposed to the assumptions and practices of corporate-dominated free markets, that is, economic liberalism. That implies a mobilisation of the majority of humans, believe it or not. Most of us disdain economic liberalism, and it is in fact economic liberal fundamentalists who are in the minority. Yet because those doctrines flatter, support and offer intellectual sustenance to the interests of the economically powerful, that minority represents a very powerful elite. This is not to treat free market capitalism as a *bête noire* whose dissolution will produce a fairy tale ending. As noted in the Introduction, social democrats and others share culpability for the situation we find ourselves in. But having dominated the last two centuries of social and economic development, the social and ecological failings of free market liberalism are all too obvious to growing numbers of us.

Second, we should not be purists about the road ahead. Although we increasingly know what the answer is *not*, we still need to be open-minded and allow for several possible strategies. Although this book has made a robust defence of a centre-left approach, we also need to be open and receptive to other perspectives. There are many ways in which social-natural interdependencies can be articulated and institutionalised. For a patriot it can derive from devotion towards country, its landscape and heritage; for a spiritualist it can derive from a sense of the world as a feeling of love inhabiting the soul of God; for an atheist it can derive from a sense of wonder at what hydrogen atoms can do if you cook and leave them to simmer for 14 billion years. Not everyone needs to sign up to the same set of motivations, even were this a reasonable expectation. This is not an attraction to diversity for diversity's sake. Yet if the end is what is important and urgent – as proposed at the end of the last chapter – then we should not be too precious about the means. Pluralism, in other words, means deploying whatever means will get us to the end we, and those for whom we are responsible, need: limitations on global warming.

Many people would echo the observation of Eleanor Ostrom (in Chapter Eight) to the effect that the ideal property regime implies a combination of state, market and communal practices working together in the greatest possible harmony, with each sector enabling the others but also acting as a constraining hand on their possible excesses. Such a property regime would likely consists of multiple zones within zones, that is, not just the independent cells of Table C.5, but fluctuating groups of cells.

Table C.5: The means: multiple cells and zones

	Local	Sub-national	National	Regional	Supra-regional	Global
Private						
Communal						
Collective						

There is no single cross-national model that can encompass all of the relevant zonal intersections since these will often be subject to reconfigurations as we respond to new evidence, reflecting on and making readjustments to *all* our social and environmental practices, including the outcomes of previous actions and interventions.

Finally, however, this does not mean we should shrink from promoting those solutions that have, to date, shown results. If it is the case that, with important caveats, the social democracies have come closest to reducing poverty rates while addressing climate change, we would be foolish to ignore their record and the lessons they hold (Fitzpatrick, 2011d, pp 68-73). If we need to recognise the natural sources of our social wealth by treating as common property those resources that stand at the intersection of our social-natural interdependencies, socialised forms of ownership might be recommended. The global community established a moratorium on drilling in the Antarctic and holds a collective interest on *not* extracting a good three-quarters of the fossil fuels still in the ground. Yet to repeat: in a world of political, religious, moral and cultural pluralism, such solutions have to be translated into other idioms and contexts. We cannot simply expect everyone to line up behind one another in a queue labelled 'European social democracy'.

Similarly, although I believe that reductions in carbon emissions are less likely to occur without reductions in poverty levels, and vice versa, there is no iron law that says that if you have one you must have the other (Fitzpatrick, 2003, pp 141-4). A society desperate for survival might adopt authoritarian, justice-insensitive measures. Alternatively, if two billion people in developing countries suddenly decide that they want to escape poverty by emulating western affluence – and that fixing global warming is the responsibility of the west – then while that may not be a sustainable, long-term solution, it's not entirely an unreasonable one either. In short, in Figure C.1 we need to cajole and prod nations as far towards the top right corner as we can, but there may be instances where trade-offs are required: either high, short-term emissions in a dash for growth that reduces poverty, or emissions reductions that temporarily compromise anti-poverty programmes.

All of which is to say that if there is no one model of a green society, there is no fuzzy-less, 'high-definition' version of social and environmental justice. Green societies are likely to be 'low definition', which is why throughout this book I have stressed the need for a reflexive, dynamic approach to the forms of organisation that might be adopted. The ecosocial approach must always be a work in progress. Policy programmes and agendas have to lay the ground of their

Figure C.1: Strong (but non-necessary) correlations between sustainability and social justice

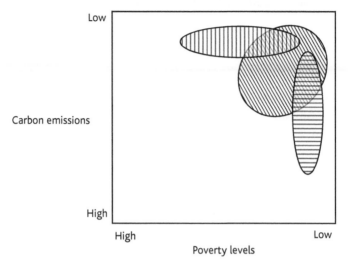

own future development. This is equivalent to throwing a series of balls into the air at such a trajectory that they can be caught effectively by our future selves and by future generations.

In one sense, those participating in the Peasants' Revolt, the Diggers' occupation of St George's Hill or the Swing Riots did not prevail. History passed them by. Yet the very attempt to make social changes is itself a form of victory that can inspire progress further down the road. Without their example, think how different our history might have been. And historical events are always pregnant with other possibilities, with lost histories which might have developed had chance, fate, or whatever you want to call it, been slightly different. Progressives are adept at self-flagellation, at obsessing on conflicts they lost. Yet progressives have also won many conflicts, and appreciating this is important if those victories are to inspire the conflicts to come, indeed the conflicts we are waging *already*. We make the history that future generations will look back on as somehow inevitable, as examples of 'common sense'. And if we don't make it in a just, sustainable one, then others will make it correspond to principles that the poorest and the planet can no longer afford.

References

Adam, B. (1990) *Time and social theory*, Cambridge: Polity.

Adam, B. (1998) *Timescapes of modernity: the environment and invisible hazards*, London: Routledge.

Adam, B. (2004) *Time: key concepts*, Cambridge: Polity.

Adebowale, M. (2008) 'Understanding environmental justice', in G. Craig, T. Burchardt and D. Gordon (eds) *Social justice and public policy*, Bristol: Policy Press.

Adger, W.N., Brown, K. and Waters, J. (2011) 'Resilience', in J. Dryzek, R. Norgaard and D. Schlosberg (eds) *Oxford handbook of climate change and society*, Oxford: Oxford University Press.

Agyeman, J. (2013) *Just sustainabilities: policy, planning and practice*, London: Zed Books.

Alcock, P. (2006) *Understanding poverty* (3rd edn), Basingstoke: Palgrave Macmillan.

Aldred, R. (ed) (2011) *Social justice, social policy and the environment*, Special Issue of *Critical Social Policy*, vol 31.

Anderson, E. (2010) 'Justifying the capabilities approach to freedom', in H. Brighouse and I. Robeyns (eds) *Measuring justice: primary goods and capabilities*, Cambridge: Cambridge University Press.

Anderson, W., White, V. and Finney, A. (2012) 'Coping with low incomes and cold homes', *Energy Policy*, vol 49, pp 40-52.

Archer, D. and Rahmstorf, S. (2010) *The climate crisis: an introductory guide to climate change*, Cambridge: Cambridge University Press.

Aurand, A. (2010) 'Density, housing types and mixed land use: smart tools for affordable housing?', *Urban Studies*, vol 47, pp 1015-36.

Baker, W. (2006) *Social tariffs – a solution to fuel poverty?*, Bristol: Centre for Sustainable Energy.

Ballingall, J. and Winchester, N. (2010) 'Food miles: starving the poor?', *The World Economy*, vol 33, no 10, pp 1201-17.

Barker, T., Ekins, P. and Foxon, T. (2007) 'The macro-economic rebound effect and the UK economy', *Energy Policy*, vol 35, pp 4935-46.

Barling, D., Lang, T. and Caraher, M. (2002) 'Joined-up food policy? The trials of governance, public policy and the food system', *Social Policy & Administration*, vol 36, no 6, pp 556-74.

Barry, B. (1999) 'Sustainability and intergenerational justice', in A. Dobson (ed) *Fairness and futurity: essays on environmental sustainability and social justice*, Oxford: Oxford University Press.

Barry, B. (2005) *Why social justice matters*, Cambridge: Polity.

Bateman, M. (2010) *Why doesn't microfinance work? The destructive rise of local neoliberalism*, London: Zed Books.

Bauman, Z. (1998) *Globalisation: the human consequences*, Cambridge: Polity.

Bauman, Z. (2000) 'Time and space reunited', *Time & Society*, vol 9, nos 2-3, pp 171-86.

Bauman, Z. (2005) *Work, consumerism and the new poor* (2nd edn), Maidenhead: Open University Press.

Beaumont, J. (2006) 'London: deprivation, social isolation and regeneration', in S. Musterd, A. Murie and C. Kesteloot (eds) *Neighbourhoods of poverty*, Basingstoke: Palgrave Macmillan.

Beck, U. (1999) *World risk society*, Cambridge: Polity.

Beck, U. (2002) 'The cosmopolitan society and its enemies', *Theory, Culture & Society*, vol 19, nos 1-2, pp 17-44.

Beder, S. (2000) *Selling the work ethic: from puritan pulpit to corporate PR*, London: Zed Books.

Bednar-Friedl, B., Koland, O. and Steininger, K. (2011) 'Urban sprawl and policy responses: a general equilibrium analysis of residential choice', *Journal of Environmental Planning and Management*, vol 54, no 1, pp 145-68.

Bell, D. (2004) 'Environmental justice and Rawls' difference principle', *Environmental Ethics*, vol 26, pp 287-306.

Bell, K. (2014) 'Degrowth for sustainability, equality and poverty reduction: some lessons from Cuba', in T. Fitzpatrick (ed) *The international handbook of social policy and the environment*, Cheltenham: Edward Elgar.

Bell, M., Wingfield, J., Miles-Shenton, D. and Seavers, J. (2010) *Low carbon housing: lessons from Elm Tree Mews*, York: Joseph Rowntree Foundation.

Belsky, E. and Retsinas, N. (eds) (2005) *Building assets, building credit: creating wealth in low-income communities*, Washington, DC: Brookings Institute Press.

Bennett, R. (2013) 'Middle class children most likely to be obese, says school study', *The Times*, 13 February.

Benton, T. (ed) (1996) *The greening of Marxism*, New York: Guilford Press.

Benzie, M., Harvey, A., Burningham, K., Hodgson, N. and Siddiqi, A. (2011) *Vulnerability to heatwaves and drought*, York: Joseph Rowntree Foundation.

Berners-Lee, M. and Clark, D. (2013) *The burning question: we can't burn half the world's oil, coal and gas. So how do we quit?*, London: Profile.

Bernstein, J. (2005) 'Critical questions in asset-based policy', in M. Sherraden (ed) *Inclusion in the American dream*, New York: Oxford University Press.

Bichard, E. and Kazmierczak, A. (2012) 'Are homeowners willing to adapt to and mitigate the effects of climate change?', *Climatic Change*, vol 112, pp 633-54.

Blackburn, R. (2002) *Banking on death or, investing in life: the history and future of pensions*, London: Verso.

Block, W. and Barnett, W. (2005) 'A positive programme for laissez-fair capitalism', *The Journal of Corporate Citizenship*, vol 19, pp 31-42.

Bloomberg New Energy Finance (2012) *UK Big 6 utility investment trends: a report for Greenpeace UK on the generation investments of the Big 6 utilities*, Bloomberg New Energy Finance.

Boardman, B. (2010a) *Fixing fuel poverty: challenges and solutions*, London: Earthscan.

Boardman, B. (2010b) Memorandum submitted to the Energy and Climate Change Committee on Fuel Poverty, *Fifth report of session 2009-10: Volume II*, London: House of Commons.

Boardman, B. (2012a) *Achieving zero: delivering future-friendly buildings*, Oxford: Environmental Change Institute, University of Oxford.

Boardman, B. (2012b) 'Fuel poverty synthesis: lessons learnt, actions needed', *Energy Policy*, vol 49, pp 143-8.

Boardman, B. with Bullock, S. and McLaren, D. (1999) *Equity and the environment*, London: Catalyst and Friends of the Earth.

Boardman, B., Darby, S., Killip, G., Hinnells, M., Jardine, C., Palmer, J. and Sinden, G. (2005) *40% house*, Oxford: Institute of Climate Change.

Bourguignon, F. (2005) 'From income to endowments: the difficult task of expanding the income poverty paradigm', in D. Grusky (ed) *Poverty and inequality*, Palo Alto, CA: Stanford University Press.

Bradshaw, J. (2011) 'Poverty', in A. Walker, A. Sinfield and C. Walker (eds) *Fighting poverty, inequality and injustice*, Bristol: Policy Press.

Bradshaw, J. and Huby, M. (2012) 'Water poverty in England and Wales', Family Resources Survey User Meeting, Royal Statistical Society, London, 22 June.

Brainard, J.S., Jones, A., Bateman, I. and Lovett, A. (2004) 'Exposure to environmental urban noise pollution in Birmingham, UK', *Urban Studies*, vol 41, no 13, pp 2581-600.

Brainard, J.S., Jones, A., Bateman, I., Lovett, A. and Fallon, P. (2002) 'Modelling environmental equity: access to air quality in Birmingham, England', *Environment and Planning A*, vol 34, pp 695-716.

Bramley, G. (2012) 'Affordability, poverty and housing need: triangulating measures and standards', *Journal of Housing and the Built Environment*, vol 27, pp 133-51.

Bramley, G. and Karley, N.K. (2007) 'Home ownership, poverty and educational achievement: school effects as neighbourhood effects', *Housing Studies*, vol 22, no 5, pp 693-721.

Brand, C. and Boardman, B. (2008) 'Taming of the few: the unequal distribution of greenhouse gas emissions from personal travel in the UK', *Energy Policy*, vol 36, pp 224-38.

Brand, C., Tran, M. and Anable, J. (2012) 'The UK transport carbon model: an integrated lifecycle approach to explore low carbon futures', *Energy Policy*, vol 41, pp 107-24.

Bretherton, J. and Pleace, N. (2011) 'A difficult mix: issues in achieving socioeconomic diversity in deprived UK neighbourhoods', *Urban Studies*, vol 48, no 16, pp 3433-47.

Bridge, G. and Le Billion, P. (2013) *Oil*, Cambridge: Polity.

Briggs, A. (1990) *Victorian cities: Manchester, Leeds, Birmingham, Middlesbrough, Melbourne, London*, London: Penguin.

Briggs, D., Abellan, J.J. and Fecht, D. (2008) 'Environmental inequity in England: small area associations between socio-economic status and environmental pollution', *Social Science & Medicine*, vol 67, pp 1612-29.

Brighouse, H. and Robeyns, I. (eds) (2010) *Measuring justice: primary goods and capabilities*, Cambridge: Cambridge University Press.

Brisley, R., Welstead, J., Hindle, R. and Paavola, J. (2012) *Socially just adaptation to climate change*, York: Joseph Rowntree Foundation.

Brittan, S. (2012) 'It is time to tax England's green and pleasant land', *The Financial Times*, 24 February.

Brueckner, J.K. and Helsley, R.W. (2011) 'Sprawl and blight', *Journal of Urban Economics*, vol 69, pp 205-13.

Brunner, K.-M., Spitzer, M. and Christanell, A. (2012) 'Experiencing fuel poverty: coping strategies of low-income households in Vienna/Austria', *Energy Policy*, vol 49, pp 53-9.

Bryson, V. (2007) *Gender and the politics of time*, Bristol: Policy Press.

Bulkeley, H. (2013) *Cities and climate change: urban sustainability and global environmental governance*, London: Routledge.

Bulkeley, H. and Betsill, M. (2003) *Cities and climate change*, London: Routledge.

Bulkeley, H. and Fuller, S. (2012) *Low carbon communities and social justice*, York: Joseph Rowntree Foundation.

Bulkeley, H. and Mol, A.P. (2003) 'Participation and environmental governance: consensus, ambivalence and debate', *Environmental Values*, vol 12, pp 143-54.

Bunting, M. (2004) *Willing slaves: how the overwork culture is ruining our lives*, London: HarperCollins.

Burchardt, T. (2004) 'Capabilities and disability: the capabilities framework and the social model of disability', *Disability & Society*, vol 19, no 7, pp 735-51.

Burchardt, T. (2008) 'Monitoring inequality: putting the capability approach to work', in G. Craig, T. Burchardt and D. Gordon (eds) *Social justice and public policy*, Bristol: Policy Press.

Burningham, K., Fielding, J. and Thrush, D. (2008) '"It'll never happen to me": understanding public awareness of local flood risk', *Disasters*, vol 32, no 2, pp 216-38.

Burtraw, D. and Evans, D. (2009) 'Tradable rights to emit air pollution', *The Australian Journal of Agricultural and Resource Economics*, vol 53, pp 59-84.

Butler, P. (2013a) 'Food banks feeding thousands more as welfare curbs kick in', *The Guardian*, 11 July.

Butler, P. (2013b) 'Food poverty "puts UK's international human rights obligations in danger"', *The Guardian*, 18 February.

Cahill, K. (2002) *Who owns Britain? The hidden facts behind land ownership in the UK and Ireland*, Edinburgh: Canongate.

Cahill, K. (2006) *Who owns the world? The hidden facts behind land ownership*, Edinburgh: Mainstream Publishing.

Cahill, K. (2010) 'Who really owns Britain?', *Country Life Magazine*, 16 November.

Cahill, M. (2010) *Transport, environment and society*, Maidenhead: Open University Press.

Campaign for Better Transport (2008) *Transport costs and carbon emissions*, London: Campaign for Better Transport.

Campaign for Better Transport (2012) *Car dependency scorecard 2012: the top UK cities for sustainable transport*, London: Campaign for Better Transport.

Campbell, D. (2013) 'Processed meat eaters run higher cancer risk', *The Guardian*, 7 March.

Caraher, M., Lloyd, S., Lawton, J., Singh, G., Horsley, K. and Mussa, F. (2010) 'A tale of two cities: a study of access to food, lessons for public health practice', *Health Education Journal*, vol 69, pp 200-10.

Carrington, D. and Salvidge, R. (2013) 'Flooding threatens £250bn worth of homes as cutbacks weaken defences', *The Guardian*, 18 May.

Carson, R. (2000) *Silent spring*, Harmondsworth: Penguin.

Carter, A. (2004) 'Projectivism and the last person argument', *American Philosophical Quarterly*, vol 41, no 1, pp 51-62.

Carter, A. (2011) 'Environmental ethics', in T. Fitzpatrick (ed) *Understanding the environment and social policy*, Bristol: Policy Press.

Casey, L. (2012) *Listening to troubled families*, London: Department for Communities and Local Government.

Castells, M. (1999) 'Grassrooting the space of flows', *Urban Geography*, vol 20, no 4, pp 294-302.

Cheng, V. (2010) 'Understanding density and high density', in E. Ng (ed) *Designing high-density cities*, London: Earthscan.

Christoff, P. (1996) 'Ecological modernisation, ecological modernities', *Environmental Politics*, vol 5, no 3, pp 476-500.

Clarke, A. and Monk, S. (2011) 'Residualisation of the social rented sector: some new evidence', *International Journal of Housing Markets and Analysis*, vol 4, no 4, pp 418-37.

Clement, M.T. (2010) '"Let them build sea walls": ecological crisis, economic crisis and the political economic opportunity structure', *Critical Sociology*, vol 37, no 4, pp 447-63.

Clifton, K. and Lucas, K. (2004) 'Examining the empirical evidence of transport inequality in the US and UK', in K. Lucas (ed) *Running on empty: transport, social exclusion and environmental justice*, Bristol: Policy Press.

Coates, R. and Silburn, R. (1970) *Poverty: the forgotten Englishmen*, Harmondsworth: Penguin.

Cole, I. and Goodchild, B. (2001) 'Social mix and the "balance community" in British housing policy – a tale of two epochs', *Geojournal*, vol 51, pp 351-60.

Collins, N. (2013) 'Air pollution during pregnancy linked to low birth weight', *The Telegraph*, 6 February.

Collins, T., Grineski, S., Chakraborty, J. and McDonald, Y. (2011) 'Understanding environmental health inequalities through comparative intracategorical analysis: racial/ethnic disparities in cancer risks from air toxics in El Paso County, Texas', *Health & Place*, vol 17, pp 335-44.

Committee on Climate Change (2010) *The fourth carbon budget: reducing emissions through the 2020s*, London: Committee on Climate Change.

Connelly, S., Markey, S. and Roseland, M. (2011) 'Bridging sustainability and the social economy: achieving community transformation through local food initiatives', *Critical Social Policy*, vol 31, no 2, pp 308-24.

Consumer Focus (2009) *Raising the SAP: tackling fuel poverty by investing in energy efficiency*, London: Consumer Focus.

Coolen, H. and Meesters, J. (2012) 'Private and public green spaces: meaningful but different settings', *Journal of Housing and the Built Environment*, vol 27, pp 49-67.

Coombes, E., Jones, A. and Hillsdon, M. (2010) 'The relationship of physical activity and overweight to objectively measured green space accessibility and use', *Social Science & Medicine*, vol 70, pp 816-22.

Cowell, R., Bristow, G. and Munday, M. (2011) *Wind energy and justice for disadvantaged communities*, York: Joseph Rowntree Foundation.

Craig, G. and Dowler, E. (1997) 'Let them eat cake! Poverty, hunger and the UK state', in G. Riches (ed) *First world hunger: food security and welfare politics*, Basingstoke: Macmillan.

Creative Research (2009) *Living with water poverty*, Report for the Consumer Council for Water, Birmingham.

CSDH (Commission on Social Determinants of Health) (2008) *Closing the gap in a generation. Health equity through action on the social determinants of health, Final report of the Commission on Social Determinants of Health*, Geneva: World Health Organization.

Cutter, S. and Solecki, W. (2006) 'Setting environmental justice in space and place: acute and chronic airbourne toxic releases in the Southeastern United States', in S. Cutter (ed) *Hazards, vulnerability and environmental justice*, London: Earthscan.

Daly, H. (2007) *Ecological economics and sustainable development*, Aldershot: Edward Elgar.

Daniels, N. (2010) 'Capabilities, opportunity, and health', in H. Brighouse and I. Robeyns (eds) *Measuring justice: primary goods and capabilities*, Cambridge: Cambridge University Press.

Darcy, M. (2010) 'De-concentration of disadvantage and mixed income housing: a critical discourse approach', *Housing, Theory and Society*, vol 27, no 1, pp 1-22.

Darwin, C. (1887) *The life and letters of Charles Darwin*, vol 1, London: John Murray.

Davis, M. (1990) *City of quartz: excavating the future in Los Angeles*, London: Verso.

Davis, M. (1998) *Ecology of fear: Los Angeles and the imagination of disaster*, New York: Metropolitan Books.

Davy, B. (2009) 'The poor and the land: poverty, property, planning', *Town Planning Review*, vol 80, no 3, pp 227-65.

Dean, H. (2009) 'Critiquing capabilities: the distraction of a beguiling concept', *Critical Social Policy*, vol 29, no 2, pp 261-78.

Dean, H. (2010) *Understanding human need*, Bristol: Policy Press.

Dean, H. (2014) 'Social rights and natural resources', in T. Fitzpatrick (ed) *The international handbook of social policy and the environment*, Cheltenham: Edward Elgar.

DECC (Department of Energy and Climate Change) (2009) *Annual report on fuel poverty statistics*, London: DECC.

DECC (2011) *Digest of UK energy statistics 2010*, London: DECC.

DECC (2012) *Annual report on fuel poverty statistics 2012*, London: DECC.

DECC (2013a) *Fuel poverty: a framework for future action*, London: DECC.

DECC (2013b) *Annual report on fuel poverty statistics 2013*, London: DECC.

DECC (2013c) *2012 UK greenhouse gas emissions, provisional figures and 2011 UK greenhouse gas emissions, final figures by fuel type and end-user*, Statistical Release, London: DECC.

Defra (Department for Environment, Food and Rural Affairs) (2002) *Air pollution*, London: Defra.

Defra (2006) *Air quality and social deprivation in the UK: an environmental inequalities analysis*, London: Defra.

Defra (2007) *The air quality strategy for England, Scotland, Wales and Northern Ireland (Volume 1)*, London: Defra.

Defra (2010) *Air pollution: action in a changing climate*, London: Defra.

Defra (2011) *Flooding and insurance: a roadmap to 2013 and beyond*, London: Defra.

Defra (2012a) *Family food 2011*, London: Defra.

Defra (2012b) *Food statistics pocketbook 2012*, London: Defra.

Defra (2013) *National statistics release: air quality statistics in the UK, 1987 to 2012*, London: Defra.

Deguen, S. and Zmirou-Navier, D. (2010) 'Social inequalities resulting from health risks related to ambient air quality – a European review', *European Journal of Public Health*, vol 20, no 1, pp 27-35.

Derby City Council (2011) *Childcare sufficiency assessment March 2011: demographic and socioeconomic profile*, Derby: Derby City Council.

DfT (Department for Transport) (2009) *Low carbon transport: a greener future*, Cm 7682, London: DfT.

DfT (2011) *Factsheets: UK transport greenhouse gas emissions*, London: DfT.

Diekmann, A. and Meyer, R. (2010) 'Democratic smog? An empirical study on the correlation between social class and environmental pollution', *Kölner Zeitschrift für Soziologie und Sozialpsychologie*, vol 62, pp 437-57.

Diesendorf, M. (2011) 'Redesigning energy systems', in J. Dryzek, R. Norgaard and D. Schlosberg (eds) *Oxford handbook of climate change and society*, Oxford: Oxford University Press.

Dimitropoulos, J. (2007) 'Energy productivity improvements and the rebound effect: an overview of the state of knowledge', *Energy Policy*, vol 35, pp 6354-63.

Dobson, A. (1998) *Justice and the environment: conceptions of environmental sustainability and theories of distributive justice*, Oxford: Oxford University Press.

Dobson, A. (ed) (1999) *Fairness and futurity: essays on environmental sustainability and social justice*, Oxford: Oxford University Press.

Docherty, I. and Shaw, J. (2012) 'Transport in a sustainable urban future', in J. Flint and M. Raco (eds) *The future of sustainable cities*, Bristol: Policy Press.

Docherty, I., Giuliano, G. and Houston, D. (2008) 'Connected cities', in R. Knowles, J. Shaw and I. Docherty (eds) *Transport geographies: mobilities, flows and spaces*, Oxford: Blackwell.

Dolphin, T. (2013) *New priorities for British economic policy*, London: Institute for Public Policy Research.

Dominelli, L. (2012) *Green social work*, Cambridge: Polity.

Dorling, D. (2010) *Injustice: why social inequality persists*, Bristol: Policy Press.

Dorling, D. (2011) *So you think you know about Britain?*, London: Constable.

Dorling, D. (2012) *Fair play: a Daniel Dorling reader on social justice*, Bristol: Policy Press.

Dorling, D. and Ballas, D. (2008) 'Spatial divisions of poverty and wealth', in T. Ridge and S. Wright (eds) *Understanding inequality, poverty and wealth*, Bristol: Policy Press.

Dorling, D. and Thomas, B. (2011) *Bankrupt Britain: an atlas of social change*, Bristol: Policy Press.

Dorling, D., Rigby, J., Wheeler, B., Ballas, D., Thomas, B., Fahmy, E., Gordon, D. and Lupton, R. (2007) *Poverty, wealth and place in Britain, 1968 to 2005*, York and Bristol: Joseph Rowntree Foundation and Policy Press.

Dowler, E. (2002) 'Food and poverty in Britain: rights and responsibilities', *Social Policy & Administration*, vol 36, no 6, pp 698-717.

Dowler, E. (2008) 'Food and health inequalities: the challenge for sustaining just consumption', *Local Environment*, vol 13, no 8, pp 759-72.

Dowler, E. and O'Connor, D. (2012) 'Rights-based approaches to addressing food poverty and food insecurity in Ireland and UK', *Social Science & Medicine*, vol 74, pp 44-51.

Dowler, E. and Tansey, G. (2003) 'Food and poverty: current global challenges?', in P. Mosley and E. Dowler (eds) *Poverty and social exclusion in North and South*, London: Routledge.

Dowler, E. and Turner, S. with Dobson, B. (2001) *Poverty bites: food health and poor families*, London: Child Poverty Action Group.

Dowler, E., Caraher, M. and Lincoln, P. (2007) 'Inequalities in food and nutrition: challenging "lifestyles"', in E. Dowler and N. Spencer (eds) *Challenging health inequalities*, Bristol: Policy Press.

Druckman, A., Chitnis, M., Sorrell, S. and Jackson, T. (2011) 'Missing carbon reductions? Exploring rebound and backfire effects in UK households', *Energy Policy*, vol 39, pp 3572-81.

Dunlap, R. and Catton, W. (2002) 'Which functions of the environment do we study? A comparison of environmental and natural resource sociology', *Society and Natural Resources*, vol 15, pp 239-49.

Dunn, A. (2002) *The great rising of 1381: the peasants' revolt and England's failed revolution*, Stroud: Tempus.

Eckersley, R. (2004) *The green state: rethinking democracy and sovereignty*, Cambridge, MA: The MIT Press.

Economist, The (2013) 'ETS, RIP?' 20 April.

EEA (European Environment Agency) (2006) *Urban sprawl in Europe: the ignored challenge*, EEA Report No 10/2006, Luxembourg: Office for Official Publications of the European Communities.

Eggleton, T. (2013) *A short introduction to climate change*, Cambridge: Cambridge University Press.

Ehrenreich, B. (2001) *Nickel and dimed: undercover in low-wage USA*, London: Granta Books.

Ekins, P. and Lockwood, M. (2011) *Tackling fuel poverty during the transition to a low-carbon economy*, York: Joseph Rowntree Foundation.

Ekins, P., Skea, J. and Minskel, M. (2011) 'UK energy policy and institutions', in J. Skea, P. Ekins and M. Winskel (eds) *Energy 2050*, London: Earthscan.

European Commission (2010) 'Air pollution and climate change', Special Issue of *Science for Environment Policy*, vol 24, pp 1-12.

Evans, A. and Unsworth, R. (2012) 'Housing densities and consumer choice', *Urban Studies*, vol 49, no 6, pp 1163-77.

Fagan, B. (2000) *The little ice age*, New York: Basic Books.

Fagan, C., Lyonette, C., Smith, M. and Saldaña-Tejeda, A. (2012) *The influence of working time arrangements on work–life integration or 'balance': a review of the international evidence*, Geneva: International Labour Office.

Fairburn, J. and Smith, G. (2008) *Environmental justice in South Yorkshire*, Leeds: Environment Agency.

Fairburn, J., Walker, G., Smith, G. and Mitchell, G. (2005) *Investigating environmental justice in Scotland: links between measures of environmental quality and social deprivation*, Edinburgh: Sniffer.

Feldman, S. and Gellert, P. (2006) 'The seductive quality of central human capabilities: sociological insights into Nussbaum and Sen's disagreement', *Economy and Society*, vol 35, no 3, pp 423-52.

Few, R. (2007) 'Health and climatic hazards: framing social research on vulnerability, response and adaptation', *Global Environmental Change*, vol 17, pp 281-95.

Fielding, J. (2007) 'Environmental injustice or just the lie of the land: an investigation of the socio-economic class of those at risk from flooding in England and Wales', *Sociological Research Online*, vol 12, no 4.

Fitch, M. and Price, H. (2002) *Water poverty in England and Wales*, Public Utilities Access Forum.

Fitzpatrick, T. (1999) *Freedom and security: an introduction to the basic income debate*, Basingstoke: Macmillan.

Fitzpatrick, T. (2001) 'New agendas for criminology and social policy: globalisation and the post-social security state', *Social Policy & Administration*, vol 35, no 2, pp 212-29.

Fitzpatrick, T. (2002) 'The two paradoxes of welfare democracy', *International Journal of Social Welfare*, vol 11, no 2, pp 159-69.

Fitzpatrick, T. (2003) *After the new social democracy*, Manchester: Manchester University Press.

Fitzpatrick, T. (2004a) 'Time and social policy', *Time & Society*, vol 13, nos 2/3, pp 197-219.

Fitzpatrick, T. (2004b) 'Time, social justice and UK social policies', *Economy and Society*, vol 33, no 3, pp 335-58.

Fitzpatrick, T. (2005a) 'The fourth attempt to construct a politics of welfare obligations', *Policy & Politics*, vol 33, no 1, pp 3-21.

Fitzpatrick, T. (2005b) *New theories of welfare*, Basingstoke: Palgrave Macmillan.

Fitzpatrick, T. (2007) 'Streams, grants and pools: stakeholding, asset-based welfare and convertibility', *Basic Income Studies*, vol 2, no 1.

Fitzpatrick, T. (2008a) *Applied ethics and social problems*, Bristol: Policy Press.

Fitzpatrick, T. (2008b) 'From contracts to capabilities and back again', *Res Publica*, vol 14, no 2, pp 83-100.

Fitzpatrick, T. (2009) 'Deliberative democracy, critical rationality and social memory: theoretical resources of an "education for discourse"', *Studies in Philosophy and Education*, vol 28, no 4, pp 313-27.

Fitzpatrick, T. (2010) 'Basic income, post-productivism and liberalism', *Basic Income Studies*, vol 4, no 2, pp 1-11.

Fitzpatrick, T. (2011a) 'Social paternalism and basic income', *Policy & Politics*, vol 39, no 1, pp 81-98.

Fitzpatrick, T. (ed) (2011b) *Understanding the environment and social policy*, Bristol: Policy Press.

Fitzpatrick, T. (2011c) *Welfare theory* (2nd edn), Basingstoke: Palgrave Macmillan.

Fitzpatrick, T. (2011d) 'The challenge for social policy', in T. Fitzpatrick (ed) *Understanding the environment and social policy*, Bristol: Policy Press.

Fitzpatrick, T. (2012) 'Cash transfers', in J. Baldock, L. Mitton, N. Manning and S. Vickerstaff (eds) *Social policy* (4th edn), Oxford: Oxford University Press.

Fitzpatrick, T. (2014) 'The nature of nature. Aristotle vs Epicurus: the battle at the heart of social and environmental ethics', in T. Fitzpatrick (ed) *The international handbook of social policy and the environment*, Cheltenham: Edward Elgar.

Flaherty, J., Veit-Wilson, J. and Dornan, P. (2004) *Poverty: the facts* (5th edn), London: Child Poverty Action Group.

Flyvbjerg, B. (2001) *Making social science matter*, Cambridge: Cambridge University Press.

Foot, M. (1975) *Aneurin Bevan, 1897-1945*, St Albans: Granada.

Forsyth, A., Nicholls, G. and Raye, B. (2010) 'Higher density and affordable housing: lessons from the Corridor Housing Initiative', *Journal of Urban Design*, vol 15, no 2, pp 269-84.

Foster, J. (1999) 'Marx's theory of metabolic rift: classical foundations for an environmental sociology', *American Journal of Sociology*, vol 105, pp 366-405.

Foster, J., Clark, B. and York, R. (2010) *The ecological rift*, New York: Monthly Review Press.

Frank, R. (1999) *Luxury fever: money and happiness in an era of excess*, Princeton, NJ and Oxford: Princeton University Press.

Frank, R. (2006) 'Taking libertarian concerns seriously: reply to Kashdan and Klein', *Econ Journal Watch*, vol 3, no 3, pp 435-51.

Frank, R. (2011) *The Darwin economy: liberty, compensation and the common good*, Princeton, NJ and Oxford: Princeton University Press.

Franklin, A. (2002) *Nature and social theory*, London: Sage.

Fraser, N. (2008) *Scales of justice*, Cambridge: Polity.

Fraser, N. and Honneth, A. (2003) *Redistribution or recognition?*, London: Verso.

Friedman, M. (1962) *Capitalism and freedom*, Chicago, IL: University of Chicago Press.

Friends of the Earth (2001) *Pollution and poverty – breaking the link*, London: Friends of the Earth.

Gardiner, S. (2011) 'Climate justice', in J. Dryzek, R. Norgaard and D. Schlosberg (eds) *Oxford handbook of climate change and society*, Oxford: Oxford University Press.

Gershuny, J. and Sullivan, O. (2003) 'Time use, gender and public policy regimes', *Social Politics*, vol 10, pp 205-28.

Gibbons, D. and Singler, R. (2008) *Cold comfort: a review of coping strategies employed by households in fuel poverty*, London: Centre for Economic and Social Inclusion.

Giddens, T. (1984) *The constitution of society: outline of the theory of structuration*, Cambridge: Polity.

Giddens, A. (1991) *Modernity and self-identity: self and society in the late modern age*, Cambridge: Polity.

Ginn, J. (2006) 'Gender inequalities: sidelined in British pension policy', in H. Pemberton, P. Thane and N. Whiteside (eds) *Britain's pensions crisis: history and policy*, Oxford: Oxford University Press.

GLA (Greater London Authority) (2010) *Clearing the air: the mayor's air quality strategy*, London: GLA.

Gollier, C. (2012) *Pricing the planet's future: the economics of discounting in an uncertain world*, Princeton, NJ: Princeton University Press.

Gonner, E.C.K. (1966) *Common land and inclosure* (2nd edn), London: Frank Cass & Co Ltd.

Goodin, R., Rice, J., Parpo, A. and Eriksson, L. (2008) *Discretionary time: a new measure of freedom*, Cambridge: Cambridge University Press.

Goodman, M., Maye, D. and Hollow, L. (2010) 'Guest editorial', *Environment and Planning A*, vol 42, pp 1782-96.

Goodwin, P. and Noland, R. (2003) 'Building new roads really does create extra traffic: a response to Prakash *et al*', *Applied Economics*, vol 35, no 13, pp 1451-57.

Gordon, P. and Cox, W. (2012) 'Cities in Western Europe and the United States: do policy differences matter?', *The Annals of Regional Science*, vol 48, pp 565-94.

Gornick, J. and Meyers, M. (2008) 'Creating gender-egalitarian societies: an agenda for reform', *Politics & Society*, vol 36, no 3, pp 313-49.

Gorz, A. (1989) *Critique of economic reason*, London: Verso.

Gough, I. (2013) 'Carbon mitigation policies, distributional dilemmas and social policies', *Journal of Social Policy*, vol 42, no 2, pp 191-214.

Gough, I. (forthcoming) *Climate change and sustainable welfare: towards a new political economy of eco-welfare states*.

Gough, I. and Meadowcroft, J. (2011) 'Decarbonising the welfare state', in J. Dryzek, R. Norgaard and D. Schlosberg (eds) *Oxford handbook of climate change and society*, Oxford: Oxford University Press.

Gray, J. (2007) *Black mass: apocalyptic religion and the death of utopia*, London: Allen Lane.

Gray, R. (2011) 'Air pollution from traffic impairs brain', *The Telegraph*, 9 October.

Greenhalgh, C. (2005) 'Why does market capitalism fail to deliver a sustainable environment and greater equality of incomes?', *Cambridge Journal of Economics*, vol 29, pp 1091-109.

Grineski, S. and McDonald, Y. (2011) 'Mapping the uninsured using secondary data: an environmental justice application in Dallas', *Population Environment*, vol 32, pp 376-87.

Grineski, S., Bolin, B. and Boone, C. (2007) 'Criteria air pollution and marginalized populations: environmental inequity in metropolitan Phoenix, Arizona', *Social Science Quarterly*, vol 88, no 2, pp 535-54.

Grusky, D. and Kanbur, R. (2005) 'Introduction: the conceptual foundations of poverty and inequality measurement', in D. Grusky (ed) *Poverty and inequality*, Palo Alto, CA: Stanford University Press.

Gunter, V. and Kroll-Smith, S. (2007) *Volatile places: a sociology of communities and environmental controversies*, Thousand Oaks, CA: Pine Forge Press.

Gustafsson, U. (2002) 'School meals policy: the problem with governing children', *Social Policy & Administration*, vol 36, no 6, pp 685-97.

Habermas, J. (2005) *Truth and justification*, Cambridge, MA: The MIT Press.

Haigh, C. and Durham, S. (2012) *Checkouts checked out: how supermarkets and high street stores promote junk food to children and their parents*, London: Children's Food Campaign, Sustain.

Hammond, R. (2009) *Climate change, food, poverty and the price of failure to the UK*, London: Friends of the Earth.

Hanley, L. (2007) *Estates: an intimate history*, London: Granta Books.

Hanley, T. (2009) *Engaging public support for eradicating UK poverty*, York: Joseph Rowntree Foundation.

Hannigan, J. (2006) *Environmental sociology* (2nd edn), London: Routledge.

Hansen, J. (2009) *Storms of my grandchildren: the truth about the coming climate catastrophe and our last chance to save humanity*, London: Bloomsbury.

Harding, J. (2010) 'What we're about to receive', *London Review of Books*, vol 32, no 9, pp 3-8.

Hargreaves, K., Preston, I., White, V. and Thumim, J. (2013) *The distribution of household CO_2 emissions in Great Britain*, Supplementary Project Paper No 1, York: Joseph Rowntree Foundation.

Harvey, D. (1973) *Social justice and the city*, Oxford: Blackwell.

Harvey, D. (1996) *Justice, nature and the geography of distance*, Oxford: Blackwell.

Harvey, D. (2000) *Spaces of hope*, Edinburgh: Edinburgh University Press.

Harvey, F. (2013) 'Green deal "unlikely to deliver promises", say experts', *The Guardian*, 28 January.

Haveman, R. and Wolff, E. (2005) 'Who are the asset poor? Levels, trends, and composition, 1983-98', in M. Sherraden (ed) *Inclusion in the American dream*, New York: Oxford University Press.

Hawkes, A., Bergman, N., Jardine, C., Stafell, I., Brett, D. and Brandon, N. (2011) 'A change of scale? Prospects for distributed energy resources', in J. Skea, P. Ekins and M. Winskel (eds) *Energy 2050*, London: Earthscan.

Hayek, F. (1976) *Law, legislation and liberty, Volume 2: The mirage of social justice*, London: Routledge & Kegan Paul.

Heinberg, R. (2011) *The end of growth: adapting to our new economic reality*, Forest Row: Clairview Books.

Heng, C.K. and Malone-Lee, L.C. (2010) 'Density and urban sustainability: an exploration of critical issues', in E. Ng (ed) *Designing high-density cities*, London: Earthscan.

Hewett, C. and Rayment, M. (2000) 'Sustainable development: at the heart of government or at the margins?', *New Economy*, vol 7, no 1, pp 29-34.

Hick, R. (2012) 'The capability approach: insights for a new poverty focus', *Journal of Social Policy*, vol 41, no 2, pp 291-308.

Hickman, M. (2010) 'Nudge or fudge? Public health fears as Lansley retreats from regulation', *The Independent*, 4 December.

Hill, C. (1991) *The world turned upside down*, Harmondsworth: Penguin.

Hills, J. (2007) *Ends and means: the future roles of social housing*, CASEReport 34, London: London School of Economics and Political Science.

Hine, T. (2008) 'Transport and social justice', in R. Knowles, J. Shaw and I. Docherty (eds) *Transport geographies: mobilities, flows and spaces*, Oxford: Blackwell.

Hirsch, F. (1977) *The social limits to growth*, London: Routledge.

Hitchman, C., Christie, I., Harrison, M. and Lang, T. (2002) *Inconvenience food: the struggle to eat well on a low income*, London: Demos.

HM Government (2011) *The natural choice: securing the value of nature*, Cm 8082, London: HMSO.

Hobsbawm, E. and Rudé, G. (1969) *Captain Swing*, London: Phoenix Press.

Holden, E. (2004) 'Ecological footprints and sustainable urban form', *Journal of Housing and the Built Environment*, vol 19, pp 91-109.

Holland, B. (2008) 'Justice and the environment in Nussbaum's "capabilities approach": why sustainable ecological capability is a "meta-capability"', *Political Research Quarterly*, vol 61, no 2, pp 319-32.

Honneth, A. (2007) *Disrespect: the normative foundations of critical theory*, Cambridge: Polity.

Hoskins, W.G. (2013) *The making of the English landscape*, Dorchester: Little Toller Books.

House of Commons Environmental Audit Committee (2010) *Air quality: fifth report of session 2009-10*, London: The Stationery Office.

Houston, D., Werritty, A., Bassett, D., Geddes, A., Hoolachan, A. and McMillan, M. (2011) *Pluvial (pain-related) flooding in urban areas: the invisible hazard*, York: Joseph Rowntree Foundation.

Howard, E. (1985) [1902] *Garden cities of to-morrow*, Powys: Attic Books.

Huan, Q. (ed) (2010) *Eco-socialism as politics*, London: Springer.

Hutton, W. (2012) 'Thames Water – a private equity plaything that takes us for fools', *The Observer*, 11 November.

Illich, I. (1974) *Energy and equity*, London: Calder & Boyars.

Inwood, S. (2002) *The man who knew too much: the inventive life of Robert Hooke*, Basingstoke: Macmillan.

Irwin, A. (2001) *Sociology and the environment*, Cambridge: Polity.

Iversen, V. (2003) 'Intra-household inequality: a challenge for the capability approach?', *Feminist Economics*, vol 9, no 2, pp 93-115.

Jackson, T. (2002) 'Quality of life, sustainability and economic growth', in T. Fitzpatrick and M. Cahill (eds) *Environment and welfare: towards a green social policy*, Basingstoke: Macmillan.

Jackson, T. (2009) *Prosperity without growth: economics for a finite planet*, Abingdon: Earthscan.

Jacobson, M. (2009) 'Review of solutions to global warming, air pollution, and energy security', *Energy & Environmental Science*, vol 2, pp 148-73.

Jacobson, M. (2012) *Air pollution and global warming* (2nd edn), Cambridge: Cambridge University Press.

Janke, K., Propper, C. and Henderson, J. (2007) *Are current levels of air pollution in England too high? The impact of pollution on population mortality*, CASE/128, London: London School of Economics and Political Science.

Jarup, L., Briggs, D., de Hoogh, C., Morris, S., Hurt, C., Lewin, A., Maitland, I., Richardson, S., Wakefield, J. and Elliott, P. (2002) 'Cancer risks in populations living near landfill sites in Great Britain', *British Journal of Cancer*, vol 86, no 11, pp 1732-6.

Jenkins, D.P. (2010) 'The value of retrofitting carbon-saving measures into fuel poor social housing', *Energy Policy*, vol 38, pp 832-9.

Jenkins, S. (2011) *Changing fortunes*, Oxford: Oxford University Press.

Johnson, V., Simms, A. and Cochrane, C. (2008) *Tackling climate change, reducing poverty: the first report of the roundtable on climate change and poverty in the UK*, London: New Economics Foundation.

Jones, O. (2011) *Chavs: the demonization of the working class*, London: Verso.

Joseph, K. and Sumption, K. (1979) *Equality*, London: John Murray.

Joseph Rowntree Foundation (2012) *Temple Avenue Project: energy-efficient refurbished homes for the 21st century*, York: Joseph Rowntree Foundation.

Juniper, T. (2013) *What has nature ever done for us? How money really does grow on trees*, London: Profile Books.

Kahneman, D. (2011) *Thinking, fast and slow*, Harmondsworth: Penguin.

Kahneman, D., Diener, D. and Schwarz, N. (1999) *Well-being: the foundations of hedonic psychology*, New York: Russell Sage.

Kan, M.Y. and Gershuny, J. (2009) 'Gender segregation and bargaining in domestic labour: evidence from longitudinal time-use data', in J. Scott, R. Crompton and C. Lyonette (eds) *Gender inequalities in the 21st century*, Cheltenham: Edward Elgar.

Kant, I. (1991) *Groundwork of the metaphysics of morals*, London: Routledge.

Kaplan, D. (2012) 'Introduction: the philosophy of food', in D. Kaplan (ed) *The philosophy of food*, Berkeley, CA: University of California Press.

Kashdan, A. and Klein, D.B. (2006) 'Assume the positional: comment on Robert Frank', *Econ Journal Watch*, vol 3, no 3, pp 412-34.

Kaufman, F. (2012) *Bet the farm: how food stopped being food*, Hoboken, NJ: John Wiley & Sons.

Kelly, E. (2010) 'Equal opportunity, unequal capability', in H. Brighouse and I. Robeyns (eds) *Measuring justice: primary goods and capabilities*, Cambridge: Cambridge University Press.

Kennedy, L.G. (2004) 'Transportation and environmental justice', in K. Lucas (ed) *Running on empty: transport, social exclusion and environmental justice*, Bristol: Policy Press.

Kielstra, P. (2009) 'Healthcare strategies for an ageing society', *The Economist*, 17 December, London: Economist Intelligence Unit.

King, K. and Stedman, J. (2000) *Analysis of air pollution and social deprivation*, A report produced for Department of the Environment, Transport and the Regions, Scottish Executive, National Assembly for Wales and Department of Environment for Northern Ireland, Didcot: AEA Technology.

Kneafsey, M., Cox, R., Holloway, L., Dowler, E., Venn, L. and Tuomainen, H. (2008) *Reconnecting consumers, producers and food*, Oxford: Berg.

Kober, C. and Paxton, W. (eds) (2002) *Asset-based welfare and poverty: exploring the case for and against asset-based welfare policies*, London: National Children's Bureau Enterprises.

Kohn, M. (2010) *Turned out nice: how the British Isles will changes as the Earth heats up*, London: Faber & Faber.

Korhonen, H., Carslaw, K., Forster, P., Mikkonen, S., Gordon, N. and Kokkola, H. (2010) 'Aerosol climate feedback due to decadal increases in southern hemisphere wind speeds', *Geophysical Research Letters*, vol 37, no 2.

Kropotkin, P. (2007) *The conquest of bread*, Edinburgh: AK Press.

Kuchler, B. and Goebel, J. (2003) *Smoothed income poverty in European counties*, Discussion Paper 352, Berlin: DIW Berlin, German Institute for Economic Research.

Kuhnle, S. and Sander, A. (2010) 'The emergence of the western welfare state', in F. Castles, S. Leibfried, H. Obinger and C. Pierson (eds) *The Oxford handbook of the welfare state*, Oxford: Oxford University Press.

Kumhof, M., Lebarz, C., Rancière, R., Richter, A. and Throckmorton, N. (2012) *Income inequality and current account imbalances*, IMF Working Paper, WP/12/08, International Monetary Fund.

Lambie-Mumford, H. (2013) '"Every town should have one": emergency food banking in the UK', *Journal of Social Policy*, vol 42, no 1, pp 73-89.

Lang, T. (2010) 'From "value-for-money" to "values-for-money"? Ethical food and policy in Europe', *Environment and Planning A*, vol 42, pp 1814-32.

Lang, T., Barling, D. and Caraher, M. (2002) 'Food, social policy and the environment: towards a new model', in M. Cahill and T. Fitzpatrick (eds) *Environmental issues and social welfare*, Oxford: Blackwell.

Lang, T., Barling, D. and Caraher, M. (2009) *Food policy: integrating health, environment and society*, Oxford: Oxford University Press.

Lansley, S. (2012) *The cost of inequality*, London: Gibson Square.

Lawrence, F. (2004) *Not on the label: what really goes into the food on your plate*, Harmondsworth: Penguin.

Lawson, B. (2010) 'The social and psychological issues of high-density city space', in E. Ng (ed) *Designing high-density cities*, London: Earthscan.

Leahy, T. (2004) 'Food, society and the environment', in J. Germov and L. Williams (eds) *A sociology of food and nutrition* (2nd edn), Oxford: Oxford University Press.

Leather, S. (1996) *The making of modern malnutrition. An overview of food poverty in the UK*, St Austell: The Caroline Walker Trust.

Lee, P. (1994) 'Housing and spatial deprivation: relocating the underclass and the new urban poor', *Urban Studies*, vol 31, no 7, pp 1191-210.

Lee, P., Murie, A. and Oosthuizen, R (2006) 'Birmingham: narratives of neighbourhood transition', in S. Musterd, A. Murie and C. Kesteloot (eds) *Neighbourhoods of poverty*, Basingstoke: Palgrave Macmillan.

Leech, D. and Campos, E. (2003) 'Is comprehensive education really free?', *Journal of the Royal Statistical Society: Series A*, vol 166, no 1, pp 135-54.

Leisering, L. and Leibfried, S. (1999) *Time and poverty in western welfare states*, Cambridge: Cambridge University Press.

Lerman, M. and McKernan, S.-M. (2008) 'Benefits and consequences of holding assets', in S.-M. McKernan and M. Sherraden (eds) *Asset building and low-income families*, Washington, DC: The Urban Institute Press.

Levine, D. (2004) 'Poverty, capability and freedom', *Review of Political Economy*, vol 16, no 1, pp 101-15.

Levine, D. and Rizvi, S. (2005) *Poverty, work, and freedom*, Cambridge: Cambridge University Press.

Libecap, G. (2009) 'The tragedy of the commons: property rights and markets as solutions to resource and environmental problems', *The Australian Journal of Agricultural and Resource Economics*, vol 53, pp 129-44.

Liddell, C. and Morris, C. (2010) 'Fuel poverty and human health: a review of recent evidence', *Energy Policy*, vol 38, pp 2987-97.

Lindley, S., O'Neill, J., Kandeh, J., Lawson, N., Christian, R. and O'Neill, M. (2011) *Climate change, justice and vulnerability*, York: Joseph Rowntree Foundation.

Lister, R. (2004) *Poverty*, Cambridge: Polity.

Lister, R. (2008) 'Recognition and voice: the challenge for social justice', in G. Craig, T. Burchardt and D. Gordon (eds) *Social justice and public policy*, Bristol: Policy Press.

Lister, R. (2013) 'Affirming human dignity: poverty and human rights', Paper presented to the School of Sociology and Social Policy, University of Nottingham, 20 February.

Little, A. (2008) 'It's your own fault if you're fat, say Tories', *Daily Express*, 27 August.

Livy, T. (1960) *The early history of Rome*, Harmondsworth: Penguin.

Lockyer, J. (2010) 'Intentional community carbon reduction and climate change action: from eco-villages to transition towns', in M. Peters, S. Fudge and T. Jackson (eds) *Low carbon communities*, Aldershot: Edward Elgar.

Lu, F. (2010) 'On consumerism and the "logic of capital"', in Q. Huan (ed) (2010) *Eco-socialism as politics*, London: Springer.

Lucas, K. (2004) 'Towards a "social welfare" approach to transport', in K. Lucas (ed) *Running on empty: transport, social exclusion and environmental justice*, Bristol: Policy Press.

Lucas, K. (2011) 'Transport and social exclusion: where are we now?', in M. Grieco and J. Urry (eds) *Mobilities: new perspectives on transport and society*, Farnham: Ashgate.

Lucas, K. and Currie, G. (2012) 'Developing socially inclusive transportation policy: transferring the United Kingdom policy approach to the State of Victoria?', *Transportation*, vol 39, pp 151-73.

Luhde-Thompson, N. and Ellis, H. (2008) 'Planning and climate change', in C. Sinn and J. Perry (eds) *Housing, the environment and our changing climate*, Coventry: Chartered Institute of Housing.

Lupton, R., Tunstall, R., Sigle-Rushton, W., Obolenskaya, P., Sabates, R., Meschi, E., Kneale, D. and Salter, E. (2009) *Growing up in social housing in Britain: a profile of four generations, 1946 to the present day*, London: Tenant Services Authority.

Macintyre, S., Macdonald, L. and Ellaway, A. (2008) 'Do poorer people have poorer access to local resources and facilities? The distribution of local resources by area deprivation in Glasgow, Scotland', *Social Science & Medicine*, vol 67, pp 900-14.

Macmillan Cancer Support (2010) Memorandum submitted to the Energy and Climate Change Committee on Fuel Poverty, *Fifth report of session 2009-10: Volume II*, London: House of Commons.

McGranahan, G., Balk, D. and Anderson, B. (2007) 'The rising tide: assessing the risks of climate change and human settlements in low elevation coastal zones', *Environment and Urbanization*, vol 19, pp 17-37.

McKenzie, L. (2009) 'Finding value on a council estate: complex lives, motherhood, and exclusion', Doctoral thesis, Nottingham: University of Nottingham.

McKernan, S.-M. and Sherraden, M. (eds) (2008) *Asset building and low-income families*, Washington, DC: The Urban Institute Press.

McLeod, H., Langford, I.H., Jones, A.P., Stedman, J.R., Day, R.J., Lorenzoni, I. and Bateman, I.J. (2000) 'The relationship between socio-economic indicators and air pollution in England and Wales: implications for environmental justice', *Regional Environmental Change*, vol 1, no 2, pp 78-85.

McMahon, W. and Marsh, T. (1999) *Filling the gap: free school meals, nutrition and poverty*, London: Child Poverty Action Group.

Mahajan, V. (2007) 'Beyond microfinance', in C. Moser (ed) *Reducing global poverty: the case for asset accumulation*, Washington, DC: Brookings Institution Press.

Malthus, T. (2004) *An essay on the principle of population* (2nd edn), New York and London: W.W. Norton & Co.

Mann, M. (2012) *The hockey stick and the climate wars: dispatches from the front lines*, New York: Columbia University Press.

Manuel-Navarrete, D. and Redclift, M. (2010) 'The role of place in the margins of space', in M. Redclift and G. Woodgate (eds) *The international handbook of environmental sociology* (2nd edn), Cheltenham: Edward Elgar.

Marmot Review, The (2010) *Fair society, healthy lives: a strategic review of health inequalities in England post-2010* (www.instituteofhealthequity.org).

Marmot, M. and Wilkinson, R. (2005) *Social determinants of health*, Oxford: Oxford University Press.

Martuzzi, M., Mitis, F. and Forastiere, F. (2010) 'Inequalities, inequities, environmental justice in waste management and health', *European Journal of Public Health*, vol 20, no 1, pp 21-6.

Marx, K. (1976) *Capital, Volume 1*, London: Pelican Books.

Marx, K. (1977) *Selected writings*, edited by David McLellan, Oxford: Oxford University Press.

Massey, D. (2005) 'Race, class and markets: social policy in the twenty-first century', in D. Grusky (ed) *Poverty and inequality*, Palo Alto, CA: Stanford University Press.

Massey, D. and Denton, N. (1993) *American apartheid: segregation and the making of the underclass*, Cambridge, MA: Harvard University Press.

Mathews, P. (2010) 'Mind the gap? The persistence of pathological discourses in urban regeneration policy', *Housing, Theory and Society*, vol 27, no 3, pp 221-40.

Mauss, M. (2002) *The gift: forms and functions of exchange in archaic societies*, London: Routledge.

May, J. and Thrift, N. (2001) *Timespace: geographies of temporality*, London: Routledge.

Mead, L. (ed) (1997) *The new paternalism: supervisory approaches to poverty*, Washington, DC: Brookings Institution Press.

Mészáros, I. (2008) *The challenge and burden of historical time*, New York: Monthly Review Press.

Miller, D. (2005) 'What is social justice?', in N. Pearce and W. Paxton (eds) *Social justice*, London: Politico's.

Mirrlees, J., Adam, S., Besley, T., Blundell, R., Bond, S., Chote, R., Gammie, M., Johnson, P., Myles, G. and Poterba, J. (2011) *Tax by design: the Mirrlees review*, Oxford: Oxford University Press.

Mitchell, G. and Dorling, D. (2003) 'An environmental justice analysis of British air quality', *Environment and Planning A*, vol 35, pp 909-29.

Mitrany, M. (2005) 'High density neighborhoods: who enjoys them?', *Geojournal*, vol 64, pp 131-40.

Mol, A., Sonnenfeld, D. and Spaargaren, G. (eds) (2009) *The ecological modernisation reader*, London: Routledge.

Monk, S., Crook, T., Lister, D., Lovatt, R., Luanaigh, A., Rowley, S. and Whitehead, C. (2006) *Delivering affordable housing through Section 106: outputs and outcomes*, York: Joseph Rowntree Foundation.

Moore, S. (2012) *Something in the air: the forgotten crisis of Britain's poor air quality*, London: Policy Exchange.

Moser, C. (2007) 'Asset accumulation policy and poverty reduction', in C. Moser (ed) *Reducing global poverty: the case for asset accumulation*, Washington, DC: Brookings Institution Press.

Mulheirn, I. (2011) 'Stop the housing Ponzi scheme', *New Statesman*, 22 November.

Mullainathan, S. and Shafir, E. (2013) *Scarcity: why having too little means so much*, London: Allen Lane.

Mumford, L. (1963) *Technics and civilisation*, New York and Burlingame, CA: Harbinger.

National Equality Panel (2010) *An anatomy of economic inequality in the UK*, London: Centre for Analysis of Social Exclusion, London School of Economics and Political Science.

Negri, A. (2005) *Time for revolution*, London and New York: Continuum.

Newman, P., Beatley, T. and Boyer, H. (2009) *Resilient cities: responding to peak oil and climate change*, Washington, DC: Island Press.

Nichols, G. and Kovats, S. (2008) 'Water and disease and climate change', in S. Kovats (ed) *Health effects of climate change in the UK 2008: an update of the Department of Health report 2001/2002*, Harwell: Health Protection Agency.

Niemietz, K. (2011) *A new understanding of poverty*, London: Institute for Economic Affairs.

Nussbaum, M. (2003) 'Capabilities as fundamental entitlements: Sen and social justice', *Feminist Economics*, vol 9, nos 2-3, pp 33-59.

Nussbaum, M. (2006) *Frontiers of justice*, Cambridge, MA: The Balknap Press.

Nussbaum, M. (2011) *Creating capabilities: the human development approach*, Cambridge, MA: The Balknap Press.

O'Neill, J. (1993) *Ecology, policy and politics: human well-being and the natural world*, London: Routledge.

O'Neill, J. and O'Neill, M. (2012) *Social justice and the future of flood insurance*, York: Joseph Rowntree Foundation.

Oakes, J.M., Anderton, D. and Anderson, A. (1996) 'A longitudinal analysis of environmental equity in communities with hazardous waste facilities', *Social Science Research*, vol 25, pp 125-48.

OECD (Organisation for Economic Co-operation and Development) (2010) *Economic policy reforms: going for growth*, Paris: OECD.

Offer, A. (2006) *The challenge of affluence*, Oxford: Oxford University Press.

OFT (Office of Fair Trading) (2010) *Markets and households on low incomes*, London: OFT.

Ofwat (nd) 'Ofwat's response to the Hills fuel poverty review call for evidence', Birmingham: Ofwat.

O'Leary, J. (2013) 'Is the rising cost of public transport leaving us out of pocket?', 27 March (fullfact.org).

Oliver, M. and Shapiro, T. (1990) 'Wealth of a nation: a reassessment of asset inequality in America shows at least one third of households are asset-poor', *American Journal of Economics and Sociology*, vol 49, pp 29-151.

Olson, K. (ed) (2008) *Adding insult to injury: Nancy Fraser debates her critics*, London: Verso.

ONS (Office for National Statistics) (2011) *Life expectancy at birth and at age 65 by local areas in the United Kingdom, 2004-06 to 2008-10*, London: ONS.

Oreskes, N. and Conway, E. (2011) *Merchants of doubt*, London: Bloomsbury.

Osbahr, H. (2007) 'Building resilience: adaptation mechanisms and mainstreaming for the poor', Occasional Paper for the *Human Development Report 2007/08*, New York: Human Development Report Office.

Ostrom, E. (1990) *Governing the commons*, Cambridge: Cambridge University Press.

Ostrom, E. (2012) *The future of the commons: beyond market failure and government regulation*, London: Institute for Economic Affairs.

Owen, D. (2009) *Green metropolis: why living smaller, living closer, and driving less are the keys to sustainability*, New York: Riverhead Books.

Oxfam (2012) *Extreme weather, extreme prices: the costs of feeding a warming world*, Oxfam Issue Briefing, September.

Page, E. (2006) *Climate change, justice and future generations*, Cheltenham: Edward Elgar.

Pastor Jr, M., Morello-Frosch, R. and Sadd, J. (2006) 'Breathless: schools, air toxics, and environmental justice in California', *The Policy Studies Journal*, vol 34, no 3, pp 337-62.

Patel, R. (2007) *Stuffed and starved: from farm to fork*, London: Portobello Books.

Paxton, A. (1994) *The food miles report: the dangers of long-distance food transport*, Sustainable Agriculture, Food and Environment Alliance.

Paxton, W. (2003) 'Introduction', in W. Paxton (ed) *Equal shares? Building a progressive and coherent asset-based welfare policy*, London: Institute for Public Policy Research.

Paxton, W. and White, S. (2006) *The citizen's stake*, Bristol: Policy Press.

Pearce, J. and Kingham, S. (2008) 'Environmental inequalities in New Zealand: a national study of air pollution and environmental justice', *Geoforum*, vol 39, no 2, pp 980-93.

Pearce, W. (2012) 'The meanings of climate change policy: implementing carbon reduction in the East Midlands', Doctoral thesis submitted to the University of Nottingham.

Pepper, D. (1993) *Eco-socialism*, London: Routledge.

Pepper, D. (2010) 'On contemporary eco-socialism', in Q. Huan (ed) *Eco-socialism as politics*, London: Springer.

Pett, J. (2008) *Fuel poverty carbon footprint*, Eaga Charitable Trust, Bristol.

Pett, J. (2009) 'Carbon footprints of low income households; does addressing fuel poverty conflict with carbon saving?', Act! Innovate! Deliver! Reducing Energy Demand Sustainably, ECEEE 2009 Summer Study, pp 1675-86, Stockholm: European Council for an Energy Efficient Economy.

Pinker, S. (2011) *The better angels of our nature: why violence has declined*, Harmondsworth: Penguin.

Pogge, T. (2010) 'A critique of the capability approach', in H. Brighouse and I. Robeyns (eds) *Measuring justice: primary goods and capabilities*, Cambridge: Cambridge University Press.

Polanyi, K. (1957) *The great transformation*, Boston, MA: Beacon Press.

Poppendieck, J. (1998) *Sweet charity? Emergency food and the end of entitlement*, New York: Viking Penguin.

Potter, S. and Bailey, I. (2008) 'Transport and the environment', in R. Knowles, J. Shaw and I. Docherty (eds) *Transport geographies: mobilities, flows and spaces*, Oxford: Blackwell.

Powell, M. and Boyne, G. (2001) 'The spatial strategy of equality and the spatial division of welfare', *Social Policy & Administration*, vol 35, no 2, pp 181-94.

Powell, M., Boyne, G. and Ashworth, R. (2001) 'Towards a geography of people poverty and place poverty', *Policy & Politics*, vol 29, no 3, pp 243-58.

Power, A. (2008) 'Does demolition or refurbishment of old and inefficient homes help to increase our environmental, social and economic viability?', *Energy Policy*, vol 36, pp 4487-501.

Power, A. and Houghton, J. (2007) *Jigsaw cities: big places, small spaces*, Bristol: Policy Press.

Power, A., Willmot, H. and Davidson, R. (2011) *Family futures: childhood and poverty in urban neighbourhoods*, Bristol: Policy Press.

Prabhakar, R. (2008) *The assets agenda: principles and policy*, Basingstoke: Palgrave Macmillan.

Preston, I., Moore, R. and Guertler, P. (2008) *How much? The cost of alleviating fuel poverty*, Report to Eaga Charitable Trust, Bristol.

Preston, I., White, V., Thumim, J., Bridgeman, T. and Brand, C. (2013) *Distribution of carbon emissions in the UK: implications for domestic energy policy*, York: Joseph Rowntree Foundation.

Proudhon, P.-J. (1994) *What is property?*, Cambridge: Cambridge University Press.

Purdy, J. (2008) *Climate change and the limits of the possible*, Duke Law School Public Law and Legal Theory Paper No 217, Durham, NC: School of Law, Duke University.

Quastel, N., Moos, M. and Lynch, N. (2012) 'Sustainability-as-density and the return of the social: the case of Vancouver, British Columbia', *Urban Geography*, vol 33, no 7, pp 1055-84.

Quinn, B. (2013) '"Abundance of bad food" makes poorest obese, says minister', *The Guardian*, 23 January.

Rachel Lombardi, D., Porter, L., Barber, A. and Rogers, C. (2011) 'Conceptualising sustainability in UK urban regeneration: a discursive formation', *Urban Studies*, vol 48, no 2, pp 273-96.

Ramesh, R. (2012) 'The families feeling the big squeeze', *The Guardian*, 13 July.

Rawls, J. (1999) *The law of peoples*, Cambridge, MA: Harvard University Press.

Raworth, K. (2012) *A safe and just space for humanity: can we live within the doughnut?*, Oxfam Discussion Paper, Oxford: Oxfam GB.

Rayner, G. and Lang, T. (2012) *Ecological public health: the 21st century's big idea?*, London: Routledge.

Reay, D. (2006) 'The zombie stalking English schools: social class and educational inequality', *British Journal of Educational Studies*, vol 54, no 3, pp 288-307.

Reed, H. and Himmelweit, J. (2012) *Where have all the wages gone? Lost pay and profits outside financial services*, London: Trades Union Congress.

Resource Recovery Solutions Limited and Derby City Council (2009) *Sinfin Lane Derby: statement of common ground*, Application reference der/0509/00571, Appeal reference app/c1055/a/10/2124772/nwf.

Richardson, E., Shortt, N.K. and Mitchell, R. (2010) 'The mechanism behind environmental inequality in Scotland: which came first, the deprivation or the landfill?', *Environment and Planning A*, vol 42, pp 223-40.

Richardson, E., Pearce, J., Mitchell, R. and Shortt, N.K. (2013) 'A regional measure of neighborhood multiple environmental deprivation: relationships with health and health inequalities', *The Professional Geographer*, vol 65, no 1, pp 153-70.

Riches, G. (1997) 'Hunger, welfare and food security: emerging strategies', in G. Riches (ed) *First world hunger: food security and welfare politics*, Basingstoke: Macmillan.

Riches, G. (2002) 'Food banks and food security: welfare reform, human rights and social policy. Lessons from Canada?', *Social Policy & Administration*, vol 36, no 6, pp 648-63.

Roberts, S. (2008) 'Energy, equity and the future of the fuel poor?', *Energy Policy*, vol 36, pp 4471-4.

Room, G. (ed) (1995) *Beyond the threshold: the measurement and analysis of social exclusion*, Bristol: Policy Press.

Rosnick, D. (2013) *Reduced work hours as a means of slowing climate change*, Washington, DC: Center for Economic and Policy Research.

Ross Anderson, H., Derwent, D., Stedman, J. and Hayman, G. (2008) 'The health impact of climate change due to changes in air pollution', in S. Kovats (ed) *Health effects of climate change in the UK 2008: an update of the Department of Health report 2001/2002*, Harwell: Health Protection Agency.

Rowlingson, K. and McKay, S. (2012) *Wealth and the wealthy*, Bristol: Policy Press.

Sandel, M. (2012) *What money can't buy: the moral limits of markets*, London: Allen Lane.

Sarkar, S. (1999) *Eco-socialism or eco-capitalism? A critical analysis of humanity's fundamental choices*, London: Zed Books.

Sarkar, S. (2010) 'Prospects for eco-socialism', in Q. Huan (ed) *Eco-socialism as politics*, London: Springer.

Schaffrin, A. (2014) 'The new social risks and opportunities of climate change', in T. Fitzpatrick (ed) *The international handbook of social policy and the environment*, Cheltenham: Edward Elgar.

Schlosberg, D. (2007) *Defining environmental justice*, Oxford: Oxford University Press.

Schor, J.B. (1992) *The overworked American: the unexpected decline of leisure*, New York: Basic Books.

Schor, J.B. (2010) *Plenitude: the new economics of true wealth*, New York: Penguin Press.

Schor, J.B. (2012) 'Working hours in the debate about growth and sustainability', Paper presented to the *About Time* Colloquium, London: New Economics Foundation/Centre for Analysis of Social Exclusion, London School of Economics and Political Science, 12 January.

Schreiner, M. and Sherraden, M. (2007) *Can the poor save? Saving and asset accumulation in in Individual Development Accounts*, Piscataway, NJ: Transaction Publishers.

Schumacher, E.F. (1973) *Small is beautiful: economics as if people mattered*, London: Abacus.

Schuppert, F. (2012) 'Reconsidering resource rights: the case for a basic right to the benefits of life-sustaining ecosystem services', *Journal of Global Ethics*, vol 8, nos 2-3, pp 215-25.

Scott, J. (2006) *Social theory: central issues in sociology*, London: Sage.

Scott Cato, M. and Bickle, R. (2010) 'A co-operative path to food security in the UK', *Journal of Co-operative Studies*, vol 43, no 2, pp 4-15.

Scott-Smith, L. (2011) *Going Dutch: local government and fuel poverty*, London: New Local Government Network.

Scruton, R. (2013) *Green philosophy*, London: Atlantic Books.

Sen, A. (2006) *Identity and violence*, London: Allen Lane.

Sen, A. (2009) *The idea of justice*, London: Allen Lane.

Sentence, A. (2009) 'Developing transport infrastructure for the low carbon society', *Oxford Review of Economic Policy*, vol 25, no 3, pp 391-410.

Seyfang, G., Lorenzoni, I. and Nye, M. (2009) *Personal carbon trading: a critical examination of proposals for the UK*, Working Paper 136, Norwich: Tyndall Centre for Climate Change Research, School of Environmental Sciences.

Seymour, J. (2000) *Poverty in plenty*, London: Earthscan.

Shapiro, D. (2007) *Is the welfare state justified?*, Cambridge: Cambridge University Press.

Shaw, K. and Robinson, F. (2010) 'UK urban regeneration policies in the early twenty-first century: continuity or change?', *Town Planning Review*, vol 81, no 2, pp 123-49.

Sherraden, M. (1991) *Assets and the poor: a new American welfare policy*, New York: M.E. Sharpe.

Sherraden, M. (2002) 'From a social welfare state to a social investment state', in C. Kober and W. Paxton (eds) *Asset-based welfare and poverty: exploring the case for and against asset-based welfare policies*, London: National Children's Bureau Enterprises.

Sherraden, M. (2003) 'Assets and the social investment state', in W. Paxton (ed) *Equal shares? Building a progressive and coherent asset-based welfare policy*, London: Institute for Public Policy Research.

Sherraden, M., Sanders, C. and Sherraden, M.S. (2004) *Kitchen capitalism: microenterprise in poor households*, Albany, NY: State University of New York Press.

Sibley, D. (1995) *Geographies of exclusion: society and difference in the west*, London and New York: Routledge.

Simms, A. (2009) *Ecological debt: global warming and the wealth of nations* (2nd edn), London: Pluto.

Simms, A. (2013) *Cancel the apocalypse: the new path to prosperity*, London: Little, Brown.

Simms, A., Moran, D. and Chowla, P. (2006) *The UK interdependence report*, London: New Economics Foundation.

Singer, P. and Mason, J. (2006) *Eating: what we eat and why it matters*, London: Arrow Books.

Skea, J., Ekins, P. and Winskel, M. (eds) (2011) *Energy 2050*, London: Earthscan.

Skidelsky, R. and Skidelsky, E. (2012) *How much is enough? The love of money and the case for the good life*, London: Allen Lane.

Sloman, L., Cairns, S., Newson, C., Anable, J., Pridmore, A. and Goodwin, P. (2010) *The effects of smarter choice programmes in the sustainable travel towns: research report*, Report to the Department for Transport, London.

Snell, C. and Bradshaw, J. (2009) *Water affordability in England and Wales*, Report for the Consumer Council for Water, Birmingham.

Snell, C. and Thomson, H. (2013) 'Reconciling fuel poverty and climate change policy under the coalition government: green deal or no deal?', in G. Ramia, K. Farnsworth and Zoë Irving (eds) *Social Policy Review 25*, Bristol: Policy Press.

Snider, L. (1998) 'Crimes against capital: discovering theft of time', *Social Justice*, vol 28, no 3, pp 105-20.

Soper, K. (1995) *What is nature?*, Oxford: Blackwell.

Sorrell, S., Dimitropoulos, J. and Sommerville, M. (2009) 'Empirical estimates of the direct rebound effect: a review', *Energy Policy*, vol 37, pp 1356-71.

Spicker, P. (2007) *The idea of poverty*, Bristol: Policy Press.

Standing, G. (2011) *The precariat: the new dangerous class*, London: Bloomsbury.

Steel, C. (2007) *Hungry city: how food shapes our lives*, London: Chatto & Windus.

Stenner, P., Church, A. and Bhatti, M. (2012) 'Human–landscape relations and the occupation of space: experiencing and expressing domestic gardens', *Environment and Planning A*, vol 44, no 7, pp 1712-27.

Stephens, C., Willis, R. and Walker, G. (2007) *Addressing environmental inequalities: cumulative environmental impacts*, Science report: SC020061/SR4, Bristol: Environment Agency.

Stern, N. (2007) *The economics of climate change*, Cambridge: Cambridge University Press.

Stevenson, J. (1974) 'Food riots in England, 1792-1818', in R. Quinault and J. Stevenson (eds) *Popular protest and public order*, London: George Allen & Unwin.

Stevenson, J. (1979) *Popular disturbances in England, 1700-1870*, London: Longman.

Stewart, K., Sefton, T. and Hills, J. (2009) 'Introduction', in J. Hills, T. Sefton and K. Stewart (eds) *Towards a more equal society? Poverty, inequality and policy since 1997*, Bristol: Policy Press.

Stiglitz, J.E. (2012) *The price of inequality*, London: Allen Lane.

Stiglitz, J.E., Sen, A. and Fitoussi, J.-P. (2010) *Mis-measuring our lives: why GDP doesn't add up*, New York: New Press.

Stratton, A. (2012) 'Open land can solve housing shortage, says minister', BBC News, 28 November (www.bbc.co.uk/news/uk-politics-20510692).

Strelitz, J. and Darton, D. (2003) 'Tackling disadvantage: place', in D. Darton and J. Strelitz (eds) *Tackling UK poverty and disadvantage in the twenty-first century*, York: Joseph Rowntree Foundation.

Stuart, T. (2009) *Waste: uncovering the global food scandal*, Harmondsworth: Penguin.

Sullivan, H., Barnes, M. and Matka, E. (2006) 'Collaborative capacity and strategies in area-based initiatives', *Public Administration*, vol 84, no 2, pp 289-310.

Swyngedouw, E. (2004) *Social power and the urbanization of water*, Oxford: Oxford University Press.

Tawney, R.H. (1964) *The radical tradition*, London: George Allen & Unwin.

Terzi, L. (2010) 'What metric of justice for disabled people? Capability and disability', in H. Brighouse and I. Robeyns (eds) *Measuring justice: primary goods and capabilities*, Cambridge: Cambridge University Press.

Teske, S. (2010) *Energy [r]evolution: towards a fully renewable energy supply in the EU 27*, The Netherlands and Brussels: Greenpeace International, European Renewable Energy Council.

Thomas, B. and Dorling, D. (2007) *Identity in Britain: a cradle-to-grave atlas*, Bristol: Policy Press.

Thompson, E.P. (1991) *Customs in common*, Harmondsworth: Penguin.

Thompson, P. (2012) 'Nature politics and the philosophy of agriculture', in D. Kaplan (ed) *The philosophy of food*, Berkeley, CA: University of California Press.

Tight, M.R. and Givoni, M. (2010) 'The role of walking and cycling in advancing healthy and sustainable urban areas', *Built Environment*, vol 36, no 4, pp 385-90.

Townsend, P. (1979) *Poverty in the United Kingdom*, Harmondsworth: Penguin.

Townsend, P. (1993) *The international analysis of poverty*, Hemel Hempstead: Harvester Wheatsheaf.

Toynbee, P. (2003) *Hard work: life in low-pay Britain*, London: Bloomsbury.

Tunstall, R., Bevan, M., Bradshaw, J., Croucher, K., Duffy, S., Hunter, C., Jones, A., Rugg, J., Wallace, A. and Wilcox, S. (2013) *The links between housing and poverty*, York: Joseph Rowntree Foundation.

UK National Ecosystem Assessment (2011) *The UK National Ecosystem Assessment: understanding nature's value to society*, Cambridge: United Nations Environment Programme (UNEP)-World Conservation Monitoring Centre (WCMC).

UN (United Nations) (2012) *Managing water under uncertainty and risk: the United Nations world water development report 4, Volume 1*, Paris: UNESCO.

UNDP (1995) *Human development report 1995*, Oxford: Oxford University Press.

Unsworth, R. (2007) '"City living" and sustainable development: the experience of a UK regional city', *Town Planning Review*, vol 78, no 6, pp 725-47.

Ürge-Vorsatz, D. and Herrero, S.T. (2012) 'Building synergies between climate change mitigation and energy poverty alleviation', *Energy Policy*, vol 49, pp 83-90.

Urry, J. (2007) *Mobilities*, Cambridge: Polity.

Urry, J. (2011) *Climate change and society*, Cambridge: Polity.

Urry, J. (2013) *Societies beyond oil*, London: Zed Books.

Vale, B. and Vale, R. (2010) 'Is the high-density city the only option?', in N. Ng (ed) *Designing high-density cities*, London: Earthscan.

van Parijs, P. (1995) *Real freedom for all: what (if anything) can justify capitalism?*, Oxford: Oxford University Press.

Vernon, J. (2007) *Hunger: a modern history*, Cambridge, MA and London: The Belknap Press.

Verrinder, G. (2011) 'Health and environment', in T. Fitzpatrick (ed) *Understanding the environment and social policy*, Bristol: Policy Press.

Victor, P. (2008) *Managing without growth*, Aldershot: Edward Elgar.

Wacquant, L. (2009) *Punishing the poor: the neoliberal government of social insecurity*, Durham, NC: Duke University Press.

Walker, G. (2010) 'Beyond distribution and proximity: exploring the multiple spatialities of environmental justice', in R. Holifield, M. Porter and G. Walker (eds) *Spaces of environmental justice*, Oxford: John Wiley & Sons.

Walker, G. (2012) *Environmental justice*, London: Routledge.

Walker, G. and Burningham, K. (2011) 'Flood risk, vulnerability and environmental justice: evidence and evaluation of inequality in a UK context', *Critical Social Policy*, vol 31, no 2, pp 216-40.

Walker, G. and Day, R. (2012) 'Fuel poverty as injustice: integrating distribution, recognition and procedure in the struggles for affordable warmth', *Energy Policy*, vol 49, pp 69-75.

Walker, G., Mitchell, G., Fairburn, J. and Smith, G. (2005) 'Industrial pollution and social deprivation: evidence and complexity in evaluating and responding to environmental inequality', *Local Environment*, vol 10, no 4, pp 361-77.

Webb, K. (2012) *Bricks or benefits? Rebalancing housing investment*, London: Shelter.

Weber, M. (1990) *The protestant ethic and the spirit of capitalism*, London: Unwin Hyman.

Wheeler, B. (2012) 'Should claimants be paid vouchers to stop spending on "vices"?', BBC News, 2 October (bbc.co.uk/news/uk-politics-19792066).

Wheeler, B. and Ben-Shlomo, Y. (2005) 'Environmental equity, air quality, socioeconomic status, and respiratory health: a linkage analysis of routine data from the Health Survey for England', *Journal of Epidemiological Community Health*, vol 59, pp 948-54.

Wheeler, S. (2011) 'Planning and the urban environment', in T. Fitzpatrick (ed) *Understanding the environment and social policy*, Bristol: Policy Press.

Whelan, C., Layte, R. and Maitre, B. (2003) 'Persistent income poverty and deprivation in the European Union: an analysis of the first three waves of the European Community Household Panel', *Journal of Social Policy*, vol 32, no 1, pp 1-18.

Whitehead, A.N. (2004) *The concept of nature*, New York: Prometheus Books.

Whitrow, G. (1988) *Time in history*, Oxford: Oxford University Press.

WHO (World Health Organization) (2004) *Report on road traffic injury prevention*, Geneva: WHO.

Widerquist, K. and Sheahen, A. (2012) 'The United States: the basic income guarantee – past experience, current proposals', in M.C. Murray and C. Pateman (eds) *Basic income worldwide*, Basingstoke: Palgrave Macmillan.

Wilkinson, R. (1996) *Unhealthy societies: the afflictions of inequality*, London: Routledge.

Wilkinson, R. and Pickett, K. (2009) *The spirit level: why equality is better for everyone*, London: Allen Lane.

Williams, M.L. (2007) 'UK air quality in 2050 – synergies with climate change policies', *Environmental Science & Policy*, vol 10, pp 169-75.

Wilson, W.J. (1987) *The truly disadvantaged: the inner city, the underclass, and public policy*, Chicago, IL: Chicago University Press.

Winston, N. (2010) 'Regeneration for sustainable communities? Barriers to implementing sustainable housing in urban areas', *Sustainable Development*, vol 18, pp 319-30.

Wolff, J. and de-Shalit, A. (2007) *Disadvantage*, Oxford: Oxford University Press.

Wood, F.R., Burgan, M., Dorling, S. and Warren, R. (2007) 'Opportunities for air pollutant and greenhouse gas emission reduction through local transport planning', *Local Economy*, vol 22, no 1, pp 40-61.

Woods, M. (2006) 'Redefining the "rural" question: the new "politics of the rural" and social policy', *Social Policy & Administration*, vol 40, no 6, pp 579-95.

Woolf, S.H. and Aron, L. (2013) *US health in international perspective: shorter lives, poorer health*, for the National Research Council and Institute of Medicine, Washington, DC: National Academies Press.

Wrigley, N. (2002) '"Food deserts" in British cities: policy context and research priorities', *Urban Studies*, vol 39, no 11, pp 2029-40.

Wyatt, A. (2008) '"Greening" the housing market – putting the green housing market in context', in C. Sinn and J. Perry (eds) *Housing, the environment and our changing climate*, Coventry: Chartered Institute of Housing.

Yergin, D. (2011) *The quest: energy, security, and the remaking of the modern world*, Harmondsworth: Penguin.

Zerubavel, E. (1981) *Hidden rhythms: schedules and calendars in social life*, Berkeley, CA: University of California Press.

Zsamboky, M., Fernández-Bilbao, A., Smith, D., Knight, J. and Allan, J. (2011) *Impacts of climate change on disadvantaged UK coastal communities*, York: Joseph Rowntree Foundation.

Index

Note: a 't' after a page number indicates a table and 'f' indicates a figure. An 'n' indicates a note, with the note number following.